Lewis Alsamari was born in Iraq and spent a few years of his early childhood in the UK. He is now an actor and recently starred in Paul Greengrass's massively acclaimed film *United 93*, in which he plays an Al Qaeda hijacker. He now lives in London.

D0774498

OUT OF IRAQ

Lewis Alsamari

CORGI BOOKS

TRANSWORLD PUBLISHERS
61-63 Uxbridge Road, London W5 5SA
A Random House Group Company
www.rbooks.co.uk

**OUT OF IRAQ
A CORGI BOOK: 9780552155397**

First published in Great Britain
in 2007 by Bantam Press
a division of Transworld Publishers
Corgi edition published 2008

This book is a work of non-fiction based on the life, experiences and recollections of
the author. In some cases names of people or the details of events have been changed
to protect the privacy of others. The author has stated to the publishers that, except
in such minor respects not affecting the substantial accuracy of the work, the
contents of this book are true.

Picture Acknowledgements: Background images: p.1 © Robin
Meredith/Shutterstock; pp.4–5 © Dainis Derics/Shutterstock; pp.6–7 © Yazid
Masa/Shutterstock. Photograph on page 8 from *United 93* © Jonathan
Olley/Universal Pictures. All other photographs courtesy Lewis Alsamari.

A CIP catalogue record for this book
is available from the British Library.

Addresses for Random House Group Ltd companies outside the UK
can be found at: www.randomhouse.co.uk
The Random House Group Ltd Reg. No. 954009

The Random House Group Limited supports The Forest Stewardship Council (FSC),
the leading international forest certification organisation. All our titles that are
printed on Greenpeace approved FSC certified paper carry the FSC logo.
Our paper procurement policy can be found at www.rbooks.co.uk/environment

Typeset in 11.25/16pt Granjon by
Falcon Oast Graphic Art Ltd.

Printed in the UK by CPI Cox & Wyman, Reading, RG1 8EX.

2 4 6 8 10 9 7 5 3 1

Mixed Sources
Product group from well-managed
forests and other controlled sources
www.fsc.org   Cert no. TT-COC-2139
© 1996 Forest Stewardship Council
FSC

For my family

'We set forth these parables to men that they may reflect.'

The Koran, 59:21

Contents

Author's Note

Throughout my life many people have helped me enormously, and an almost equal number have hindered me. Some of these people operated within the law, others didn't. As a result, I have changed certain names to protect both the innocent and the guilty.

When I arrived in England, I took the name Lewis. My Arabic name is Sarmed, which is how I refer to myself throughout much of the book.

Prologue

August 1994. The Iraqi desert, somewhere near the Jordanian border, several hours before daybreak

I stood perfectly still and tried to accustom myself to the solitude and the silence.

It took me some minutes to compose myself, but eventually I started to make my way towards the road. Now that I was alone my senses became heightened as I strained my eyes and ears to judge if any unknown danger was close by. Occasionally I would look back and think I had caught a glimpse of the patrol cars' headlights; but if I did, they were distant – they would not be able to see me from so far away. I could just make out the road from where I was, and there were no patrols ahead; I would be very unlucky to meet anybody now – unless I was forced to fire the Beretta, and as all seemed reasonably silent around me I decided not to do that.

I soon realized, however, that in the desert sounds could be deceptive. More than once I stopped still because I thought I heard a noise alarmingly close, but I told myself over and over again that it was a faraway sound carried to me by the fickle night breeze. I kept the pace as fast as my wounded leg would allow, with my eyes fixed on the occasional light from the road ahead, and I realized that it was not only sounds that could be deceiving, but distances also. Although I had no conception of time, the road did not appear to be getting any closer, and the longer I hurried through that dark expanse, the more unnerving my solitude became. As I walked, I could feel the swab around my bullet wound become wet – clearly the stitches had opened slightly from the movement.

Then, out of the darkness, I heard a sound that immediately stopped me dead. It was not new to my ears – it was unmistakably the same howling that I had heard earlier that evening – but it was shockingly close. I stood still for some moments, aware only of the trembling whisper of my own heavy breath, before hearing another howl that made the blood stop in my veins. It was as loud as the first and no less desperate, but it was not its closeness that filled me with a sickening sense of horror: it was the direction from which it came. The first wolf had been somewhere to my right, the second to my left.

I have never known fear like it. A cold wave of dread crashed over me; I felt nauseous and all the strength seemed to drain from my body. I know I should have fired my gun in the air, but in that minute some other impulse took over, an impulse that forced any faculty of reason from my head and replaced it with blind panic. Foolishly, I ran.

I could never have outrun them. They were lean, desperate with hunger; this was their territory. I was limping and terrified. The more noise I made, the more I attracted their attention. I became aware of more wolves around me – I don't know how many, but it was clear they were hunting as a pack and I was their quarry. Blinded by my tears, I stumbled, and their baying became more frenzied.

Then, as if by some prearranged signal, the pack fell silent . . .

PART ONE

THE ESCAPE

1

The Interrogation

Baghdad, nine months earlier

Baghdad military training centre lay by a main road on the outskirts of the city. It was large and utilitarian, and I felt dwarfed by it as I approached the main entrance. The sun was burning, and the cars in the busy street had all their windows wound down, their drivers crumpled and oppressed by the midday heat. I wiped a trickle of sweat from my forehead and looked up at the high walls of the building: a huge picture of Saddam Hussein returned my gaze. It was a familiar sight, one that had been common-place in my life for as long as I could remember. The gates of Al-Zahawi primary school, which I had attended as a child, were colourful, painted with a huge yellow bumble bee to welcome the children; but on the walls on either side of the bumble bee were paintings of Saddam. His Excellency smiled down benevolently upon us, and around his head flew birds painted in the colours of the national flag. Inside, high up on the walls, were more pictures of Saddam and the slogans of the Ba'ath party – 'One Arab nation with an everlasting message', 'Unity, Freedom and Communism' – as well as one of Saddam's favourite sayings: 'Always look your enemy in the eye'.

Today, however, the images seemed more threatening than ever – the very embodiment of everything from which I had been trying to break free.

'I don't want to be in the army,' I had told my uncle Saad petulantly when it had become apparent that no other option was open to me.

'You haven't got any choice. You've been called up, and if you don't go they will consider you to be an absconder. When they catch up with you – which they will if you are still in the country . . .' He made a deft flicking sign by his right ear to indicate its removal, the standard punishment for anyone who went AWOL. 'I've seen people selling these ears on the black market so that absconders can have them sewn back on. Trust me, they are not a pretty sight.'

For a moment I thought he was joking, but one glance at his face told me that he wasn't. 'Will you keep looking for someone to help us?'

Nervously Saad checked that no passer-by – no matter how innocent they seemed – could overhear our conversation. Idle talk tended to find its way back to the intelligence services, and the consequences could be severe. 'I don't know, Sarmed. The stakes are higher now. Not attending university is one thing, but running away from the army is quite another. If any of my colleagues were caught absconding twice during the Iran–Iraq war, they were shot in front of their relatives. They were told it was their fault their sons were being executed, because they had allowed their children to grow up into opponents of the regime.'

'I know,' I insisted quietly. 'That's why I want to leave. I don't want to be part of it. Please, keep looking for me.'

I stepped down from the truck with my fellow cadets and approached the entrance to the centre.

Inside, everything was painted an austere military green. Huge metal structures around the edge of the main parade ground housed the various quarters, and nowhere was there any decoration – apart, of course, from the ubiquitous pictures of Saddam in military uniform. In some pictures his military medals were on display; others showed him firing an RPG or an AK-47. I was handed my military ID, given my uniform, boots, beret and belt and shown to my quarters. I was in a huge dormitory with metal beds neatly arranged along its length, and a thin strip of window along the top of the wall let in only a small amount of light. Once I had stowed my few belongings under my bed, I was taken off to have my hair shaved. There was no time after that to get settled in: my training began that very day.

The first month at the centre was an extension of the national education programme I had undergone at school. We were taught all about the army: how it was split into divisions and what the responsibilities of each division were. We were told about the facilities of the compound, and it was explained that we would be expected to undergo a very tough regime of physical and military training to ensure that we were fit enough in three months to join our unit – wherever that might be. We were taught how to salute superior officers, how we should store and look after our weapons once they were issued – all the little nuggets of knowledge that would start to make this mismatched bunch of citizens look a bit more like soldiers.

But the officers were not much fussed about prolonging our mental education; it was our physical education that mattered to them. We were rudely woken one morning at first light – about six o'clock – and taken to a canteen area where we were given a glass of milk and two hard biscuits. We were then led to the parade ground, where an officer shouted, '*Darwim bil-tadreeb!* Start your training!' We were instructed to form an orderly line by a bed of evil-looking barbed wire. Two *arifs* – not officers exactly, more like NCOs, who were in charge of our training – stood stony-faced, AK-47s at the ready. We stood silently as they examined each and every one of us, checking our nails and our hair, and making sure our uniforms were spotless. Then the training began. 'You each have sixty seconds to crawl under the barbed wire and come out unscathed at the other end,' one of them barked. I looked at the barbed wire more carefully. It was spindly and knotted and raised little more than a foot from the ground. To crawl underneath it without being horribly scratched, you would need to take it slowly. 'You,' the *arif* shouted at the first recruit in line. 'Go!'

The recruit crouched down on all fours, then flattened himself on his belly. As he crawled gingerly under the barbed wire, the two *arifs* started firing their Kalashnikovs into the ground. The guns were clearly shooting blanks, but the poor recruit was not to know this. As the first shot was fired, he jumped almost out of his skin; a piece of barbed wire tore into his trousers, and the rough cloth was briefly soaked red. He scurried faster and sustained a few more wounds; but he made it out the other side in the allotted time, and was packed off to tend to his injuries.

I was next. Reluctantly I crouched down in front of the barbed wire with my gun in my hand and, trying to ignore the explosions of the nearby AK-47s, I gently wove my way to the other side, managing to emerge unscathed. As I stood up, the first *arif* looked at his watch. 'Sixty-eight seconds,' he announced with menace in his voice. 'Come with me.'

He grabbed me by the shoulder, pushed me in front of him and kicked me hard from behind. I fell to my knees. 'Over there,' bellowed the second *arif*.

About twenty metres from the barbed wire was a muddy pit, perhaps four metres in diameter and a couple of metres deep. The two *arifs* pushed me towards it while my comrades looked on. Once we were beside it, one of them struck me a blow in the pit of my stomach with the butt of his Kalashnikov. Winded, I collapsed to the floor once more. Gasping, I felt a heavy boot kick into my ribcage as the two proceeded to beat me with their hands and feet until my body was bruised and bloodied. At no point did they touch my face, however; I later found out that this was because I had to look presentable when I was on display, and bruises or cuts to the face were not acceptable. But any parts of my body that could be covered by a uniform were fair game.

The beating felt like it lasted an hour – in fact it probably lasted only a minute – and when they had finished making an example of me, I was pushed over the side of the pit. I fell into a pool of cool mud at the bottom, and felt it seeping through the coarse material of my uniform. 'Stand up!' one of the *arifs* shouted at me. Painfully I pushed myself up off the ground. 'Now,' he shouted, 'climb out of there, and next time I tell you to do something in sixty seconds, do it in sixty seconds. Understood?'

It had been my first encounter with the pit, but it was not to be my last. Whenever one of us failed to fulfil a task — maybe we had not climbed over a wall as quickly as we had been instructed to, or not let ourselves remain suspended at the top of an obstacle course for long enough — we were beaten and thrown into the pit. The beatings varied in their intensity, according either to the gravity of our misdemeanour or to the whim of the *arif* in charge, but they were always brutal enough to persuade us to pay very close attention to what we were told to do, and carry it out to the letter. We soon learned to make every attempt to land on our feet when we were thrown over the side of the pit: if our uniforms became too muddy, we would often be forcefully hosed down and left to complete our exercises in sopping wet clothes. The soaked material chafed unpleasantly against our torn skin, and if the hosing-down happened to take place in the heat of the day, the wet uniform would turn boiling hot and scorch our skin before the water evaporated and dried.

Nobody was spared these beatings, even those who performed well. The *arif* wanted everybody to know exactly what sort of brutality they could expect if they stepped out of line. Gradually, however, as our skill at the various tasks increased, they became less frequent — although when they did occur they were inflicted with much greater vigour, and with a larger dose of humiliation, as the *arifs* knew it would reflect poorly on them if they delivered sub-standard recruits to the unit bases at the end of the three-month training period. Instead, we would see the more recent recruits at the other end of the parade ground receiving the same treatment that had been meted out to us only weeks earlier. Some of our group would laugh when they saw this – it was only natural, I suppose, that having been treated like animals, some of them would turn into animals themselves; the rest of us just looked on grimly as we did our best to get on with the job in hand.

Once a week, a graduation ceremony would be held at the training compound, where those recruits who had completed their training period would be assigned to the unit that would be their home for the next three years. The ceremony would be held on the parade ground: we would salute the flag and the name of each departing soldier would be read out, along with his destination. I awoke on the morning of my ceremony with a dreadful feeling of foreboding. I had only endured the hardships of the training compound in the vague hope that I would be able to get out of Iraq, away from the brutality and the torment, before being assigned to my unit, and comforted by the knowledge that my family were only a few miles away. How would I cope if I were sent to one of the further reaches of the country, where my family and my hopes of freedom would seem even more remote?

We lined up in front of the whole population of recruits

and saluted the flag. Then, one by one, our names were called out. When I heard mine, I stepped forward to be told my fate. 'The brave and courageous soldier Sarmed Al-Samarrai will be leaving to join our glorious regiment in Al-Amarah!'

My heart sank. Al-Amarah was a good 400 kilometres from Baghdad, more than halfway to the southern city of Basra and close to the Iranian border. I was to join the Third Brigade in this region. The road there was slow, and getting back to see my family on leave would be difficult. But I did not let these thoughts appear on my face as I received my honour. I stood back in line – the camp officers were eyeing us all carefully, and a look of disappointment would have been insubordination if they were of a mind to make it so. The news had bruised me enough as it was; I felt no desire to add physical pain to my mental turmoil.

I couldn't believe it. I had never been to the south before, and now I was being packed off to a military unit miles from anywhere for three years. I called my uncle to see if there was anything he could do, any favours he could call in or bribes he could pay to keep me at least in Baghdad. But there was nothing to be done, and when the day came I prepared to be transported to my unit.

We piled into the green-painted Russian-built *eva* truck covered with thick green canvas that was waiting outside the compound. There were perhaps twenty other recruits who were going to Al-Amarah with me, but we would be dropping off other soldiers at various units along the way. The front seats were already taken up by the *arif* and some of the more thuggish recruits – as the rest of their contemporaries walked on, they eyed us threateningly, as if daring us to complain about the seating arrangements.

We left Baghdad behind us, and as we did so I felt as though I was leaving civilization. The roads became rougher, and the villages we passed seemed more ragged the further south we went. Villagers would stop and stare at the convoy of *eva* trucks as they passed through, making me feel like a curiosity. I had become used to acting around soldiers with a care born of suspicion; now, I suddenly realized, I would be treated with suspicion by others. At each checkpoint we were stopped and thoroughly searched by Al-Indibaat – the military police or Red Berets – but as we headed further south our numbers dwindled as the soldiers were dropped off at their respective units. By the time I alighted at Al-Amarah, only the few poor souls who were to be stationed at Basra remained.

The unit building was practically identical to the military training compound, both inside and out. Observation posts covered with scrambled barbed wire stood at each corner, and a heavy military presence was on display guarding the entrance. On the front wall was yet another massive picture of Saddam in military uniform. One of the *arifs* from the training camp lined us up inside the barracks and barked at us to stand quietly as we waited for the head of the unit to come and take charge of us. After perhaps half an hour he came out of his office and looked us up and down, disdainfully. 'I hope you have all come prepared,' he called out in a teacherly tone of voice. 'If any of you feel you have *not* come prepared, tell me now and I will arrange for you to be sent back to the training camp.'

Not one of us moved a muscle. We didn't want to make any gesture that could be interpreted as a desire to go back to that godforsaken place.

'Good,' continued the officer. 'You are now under my command. Any action that brings shame upon this regiment or upon our beloved leader, may God protect him and bless him, will be dealt with swiftly and severely. If you are called upon to fight for the great and glorious Iraqi army, it will be an honour. You will therefore keep yourselves in a state of utmost readiness. You will continue to train in the art and techniques of warfare, and I advise you to pay close attention at all times – you never know when our leader, may God protect him and bless him, will call upon you to make use of them to serve and protect our glorious country from our cowardly enemies.'

He gave us a look of barely concealed contempt as the *arif* shouted, 'Attention!' We saluted; he saluted back before turning on his heel and retreating to the comforts of his office.

We were taken to our quarters. I had been allocated a

bed in a large dormitory that housed about sixty people; one white sheet had been supplied, and the rest of the bedding was a dirty army green. I stowed away my few personal belongings – a pen and some paper for writing home, and a small portable cassette player with a few Western tapes. Western music, unlike the music of Israel or Iran, was allowed in Iraq, with a few exceptions. 'By The Rivers Of Babylon' by Boney M was one of those exceptions, though I remember that Saad and I would blast it out in his car when I was young – a small gesture of defiance. But in the army, Western music was banned, so those of us who wanted to bring it in were forced to use subterfuge. On one of my short periods of leave from the training camp, I had placed tapes of the music I liked to listen to – Michael Jackson, Bon Jovi, Wet Wet Wet, A-Ha – in cassette boxes on which I had written the names of Middle Eastern singers so that they would not be confiscated.

I took a shower before changing into more comfortable clothes. A number of people tried to phone home from one of the communal telephones. A stern-faced *arif* sat next to the telephone, listening intently to everyone's conversations and making a note of how long each person spent on the phone so that they could be charged appropriately. The queues for the telephone were long, however, and I was not in the mood to hear the playful laughs of my brother and sister in the background. I decided to rest before the rigours of the next day.

The following morning we were each assigned a weapon – an Iraqi-made AK-47 – plus three magazines. Each gun had a number scrawled on it in white paint so that the quartermasters could keep track of who had been issued with which weapon. I soon found out that, although our training period was at an end, there was much that we were still expected to learn. At the training compound, we had been taught how to handle weapons on the most basic level; now our skills were to become honed and specialized. A special unit came in, for example, to teach us how to plant landmines. We were each given a box containing several heavy, defused landmines; as I slowly took one of the weapons from its packaging, I was very aware that this was the instrument that had almost killed my uncle during the Iran–Iraq war.

Stationed on the front line, on Iranian territory near Basra, he had been instructed to lead his men into a mine-field. Saad was one of the lucky few to escape with his life – debris from a nearby explosion detonated a cluster of mines and he was blown unconscious. He awoke to discover that he had been blown one way, his leg the other. His remaining leg had been cut deeply enough to expose the bone of his knee joint, and his whole body was splintered with sharp, angry pieces of hot shrapnel. How he survived is a mystery even to him. The day I went with my family to visit Saad in the hospital is one of the most vivid memories of my childhood. We all packed into his tiny hospital room, and had I not known it was Saad I wouldn't have recognized him. His face and body were bandaged up – the outer layer of his skin had been burned and peeled away by the force of the blast; what remained was red and sore. His leg had been severed below the knee, but the remainder of the limb was so riddled with shrapnel that it had to be amputated several inches above. The other leg was little more than a patchwork of skin grafted from different areas of his body. You could place a magnet on certain parts of him and it would stick because of all the shrapnel embedded beneath his skin. He was unconscious when we saw him, and my mother and grandmother wailed tearfully at the sight of their beloved Saad in such a state. I remember my father standing emotionless in a corner of the room. 'I told you this was what would happen if you ran off to war,' the look on his face seemed to say. For a six-year-old it was a stark introduction to the realities of battle.

Now I was learning how to plant the same weapon so that it could mutilate some foreign soldier, or maybe an unsuspecting civilian. A circle of grey metal perhaps two inches thick, it had a second, smaller circle protruding from the top. The mine was to be placed in the earth, or underwater in the mud, so that it was not visible, and then a small pin removed to arm it. Even the slightest movement above the mine would detonate it, and the results would be devastating. We were not taught how to defuse them – that knowledge, we were told, was not for regular soldiers.

We were taught how to arm and fire heavy BKC machine guns that could hit targets over two kilometres distant. It required two soldiers to operate them, one to fire the weapon, the other to feed the long chain of ammunition into it. On the grounds of the unit was the shell of a Russian-style tank. We were not taught to drive the machines – that was a specialized job not suited to such low-ranking soldiers as ourselves. Instead we were taught how to fire the machine gun at the top. In a battle we would be on full display – cannon-fodder for enemy troops who could pick us off with ease.

I remembered the maxim I was taught at school, a favourite saying of Saddam's and one that we were forced to commit to memory: 'He who does not sweat to build his country will not bleed defending it.' We had been trained since childhood to see weaponry as part of everyday life. Guns were commonplace, of course, but even when I was young I had come into contact with weapons of far greater destructive power. As a boy I lived with my father for a few years in the northern city of Mosul, in the semi-rural surroundings of the College of Forestry and Agriculture. One day my friends and I decided to go hunting for the foxes that had been terrorizing my beloved chickens that I kept in the yard, so we set off along the road that led into the forest.

After walking for an hour or so, we came across an area enclosed by barbed wire. We had all been into the forest before, but none of us had stumbled across this enclosure. Not far inside, we saw a huge mound covered with army camouflage material. Peeping out from under the camouflage were large metal objects with pointed tips; they were clearly either Scud missiles or some other form of rocket-propelled weapon. A family of foxes were playing among the missiles, or nestling peacefully under their tips. We stood in silence for a few moments, staring at our discovery, when suddenly we heard the sound of an engine. A red Chevrolet approached slowly; not wanting to be caught in such a place by a member of the security forces, we ran away as quickly as we could, vowing to return the next day.

Every time we went back to spy on the missiles, the red Chevrolet was always nearby. We never got close enough to find out who was in it, nor did we want to, for fear of being seen. Gradually, though, we began to work out the times that it disappeared – presumably so that the driver could get something to eat or hand over to somebody else – and so we formulated a plan. We took an old wheelbarrow to a part of the wall surrounding the compound that had either crumbled naturally or been destroyed by villagers trying to get in, and filled it with small pieces of rubble. We then took it to the weapons dump, waited for the Chevrolet to disappear, and rolled it close to the barbed wire. If we could throw the rubble at the missiles, we naively thought, and explode one of them, we could launch our first strike in the battle against the foxes. They would be painlessly dispatched, and we would be far enough away to avoid hurt.

Of course, the missiles were too deep inside the barbed-wire area for us to score many direct hits, and our aims were not that true. Occasionally a small stone would rebound off the metal with a satisfying clunk, but after about forty-five minutes we saw the red Chevrolet approach, so we scampered away. The foxes lived to scavenge for chickens another day.

The next time I spoke to Saad on the phone, I casually told him about our exploits. He listened attentively and then spoke very quietly but with the full weight of his authority. 'Listen to me carefully, Sarmed,' he told me. 'You must *never* do that again. The chances of exploding one of those missiles with a piece of rubble are minuscule, but if you did manage it, you wouldn't just be wiping out your foxes – you'd be wiping out your home and probably the surrounding villages too.'

I fell silent as the implications of our stupidity were spelled out to me.

'Promise me you'll never go back there, Sarmed,' Saad continued, 'even just to look. It's not the sort of place you want to be caught snooping around.'

'I promise,' I replied quietly.

Back at my unit, we learned how to use different types of grenade; special honour was reserved for those soldiers who threw them the furthest, and the day after a training session our arms would be bruised from the effort of several hours of hurling these heavy weapons into the desert surrounding the camp. We practised disassembling and assembling AK-47s – as a child I had learned to use these weapons on the wasteland outskirts of Baghdad with my uncle so I required no instruction, but none of my superiors questioned my ability with the guns. My sharp-shooting skills went from good to excellent.

There were, however, plenty of instances when I elected not to use my skills with a gun, and I was not the only one. Our unit was close to the Iranian border, and although the Iran–Iraq war was long finished, there were still skirmishes. From time to time we would come under attack from the forces of Al-Badr Brigade, an army made up of Shiite Iraqis who had fled Iraq because they had been persecuted by Saddam. They would cross the Iranian border and approach the area where our unit was stationed under cover of the tall reeds in the marshlands that separated us, before opening fire on us – sometimes with AK-47s, sometimes with RPGs, sometimes with mortar fire when they had it. Their goal was simple: to kill as many of us as they could. They were often success-ful: when Al-Badr attacked, soldiers would die.

The attacks of Al-Badr did, however, vary in their

severity. If it was a major attack, we would have no option but to defend ourselves by shooting to kill. If it was more of a skirmish, an exercise for Al-Badr rather than an all-out attempt to capture the unit, we would be more sympathetic. We would be ordered to shoot them, of course, on pain of being sent to a military tribunal. But despite the fact that these men were trying to kill us, there was a sympathy for them. They were Iraqis, after all, who had fled for reasons most of us understood only too well. We might have been on opposite sides of the battleground, but we were joined in our hatred for the regime. We would aim our guns to fire just above the attacking soldiers, rather than directly at them.

We were taught basic martial arts movements for use in hand-to-hand combat, and we learned how to fight with the dagger from the end of our Kalashnikovs. After only a few weeks' training I had learned how to break a man's kneecap with one solid kick, and I had mastered several different methods of rendering an opponent helpless so that I could plunge my Kalashnikov dagger deep into his throat. I learned how to approach someone from behind and kill them in one swift, simple move. Gradually, and despite my reluctance to be there, I was being proficiently instructed in the mechanics of killing. There was an unspoken acknowledgement that, as simple soldiers, we were the pawns in Saddam's bombastic shows of military bravado. Iraq was never far away from war, and everybody knew somebody who had been killed or horribly injured in one of the leader's campaigns: should we find ourselves on the front line, our ability to kill the other man would be the only thing that might save us from a similar fate.

A couple of months into my time at the unit, I looked at the noticeboard that listed everybody's duties and training sessions for a particular day. '*Al'Tadreeb ala Al-Istijwab*', announced one of the sheets, 'Interrogation Training'. My name was one of four on the list.

Certain units – especially those in Shiite areas like the one I was in – would have visits from a high-ranking Ba'athist civilian. This individual would be part of Al-Tawjee Al-Siyasi Lil-Widah – the Unit for Political Guidance. He would come every couple of weeks to give us interrogation training.

At the appointed time, I made my way to the prison cells. At the training centre, misdemeanours were punished by the pit; here they simply hurled you into prison if you refused to toe the line. Next to the cells were small, bare interrogation rooms. The room in which my interrogation training was to take place had nothing but a dull lamp, a metal table and three metal chairs. The Ba'athist and an *arif* sat at the table with clipboards and pencils; the third chair had been placed in the middle of the room, directly under a fan that did not so much provide ventilation as simply recycle the stale air. I stood to attention against one of the walls and waited for my colleagues to arrive.

Once we were all assembled, the Ba'athist addressed us. 'You,' he pointed at the burliest of our number, 'sit down.' He was from the south. Until now I had avoided him, as did most of the camp; I had noticed in the dining room that he had a habit of spitting copiously into the *qastah* – our main meal – to put people off eating it. He fraternized only with those members of his own community who also found themselves at this unit – all of them large and thick-set, with an arrogance bordering on contempt for anybody who was not part of their clique. Despite his overpowering self-confidence, however, he could not hide his nervousness as he took the third seat. His hands were bound tightly with rope behind the back of the chair. 'You have been captured,' the Ba'athist continued. 'Your regiment is moving north, and this is the information that your captors are trying to force you to reveal. They will use any means to get it, but you must reveal nothing.' He turned to the three of us still standing against the wall. 'Do what you must to extract this information,' he told us, 'with two exceptions: you are not to cut his face, and you are not to break his bones. He needs to be presentable for lineout. Anything else is acceptable.'

The three of us remained silent; the only noises in the room were the regular whirr of the ceiling fan and the heavy breathing of the soldier tied to the chair. We looked at each other apprehensively, unwilling to attack our colleague but uncertain how to avoid it. 'You!' The Ba'athist pointed at me. 'You start.'

I stared into the eyes of the prisoner; he looked defiantly back at me. Slowly I approached him and then, with a brief look back at the Ba'athist, struck him a blow in the stomach. It was as gentle as I dared make it, although it was enough to make him cough sharply and catch his breath. As he did so, the Ba'athist raised his voice. 'Harder!' he shouted.

I looked apologetically into the eyes of my victim, and punched him more forcefully. His eyes bulged as he struggled to breathe. 'Harder!' the Ba'athist shouted again. He took hold of a thick cane and hit me hard across the back of my legs.

I found myself shaking as I prepared to deliver another blow; my breath trembled in my lungs. Suddenly I heard scuffling behind me. I turned round to see one of my colleagues hurl himself at the chair, knocking the victim sideways on to the ground. His head cracked as it hit the floor and he cried out; almost simultaneously my associate started to kick him violently in the stomach and the genitals, screaming as though he himself were being attacked. Each time the victim tried to say anything, he received another sharp blow that knocked the speech out of him. After a minute and a half of severe kicks, however, his attacker stopped for breath himself. His victim took the brief window of opportunity to whimper, 'North. My regiment is headed north.'

Suddenly the *arif* and the Ba'athist were on their feet. Still carrying their clipboards they placed themselves in front of the chair. 'You,' the Ba'athist pointed at the attacker, who stood shaking with suppressed rage, 'good.' He looked round at the victim: he was still on his side, his hands still bound; tears of pain and humiliation fell directly to the floor and the chair clattered against the ground as his body convulsed. 'The rest of you *niswan*, women, un-impressive. I hope you will act in a manner more befitting your uniform at our next session.' He looked directly at me. 'Untie him.'

I bent down and fumbled at the knot, managing finally to loosen it and free the battered body of my fellow soldier. Slowly he stood up; as he did so he gave me a look of absolute venom, and without waiting to be dismissed by the *arif* he stumbled from the room.

I had been totally shocked by what had just happened: not so much by the fact that we were expected to do this to our fellow soldiers – once random brutality becomes the norm, you start to accept it almost without thinking – but rather by the effect the situation had had on my colleague who had gone on the attack with fire in his eyes. When I saw him around the base over the next few days, he walked with his head held high and an arrogant bear-ing that seemed to suggest his actions had bolstered his own opinion of himself. I saw our victim too, although I tried to avoid him. He refused to speak to me, but every time we met his eyes seemed to say, 'Just wait.'

My time was to come quicker than I thought. Only a couple of weeks later, the four of us were called to the interrogation room once more. On this second occasion, the Ba'athist directed me to the chair. The rough rope dug into my skin as he tied my hands tightly; if I tried to move my wrists I felt them burn even more. 'This prisoner has recently been caught. He was wearing a white T-shirt under his coat with a picture of Saddam Hussein. He claims to be a civilian, but we know that he is a member of military intelligence. You need to make him admit this.'

Sometimes the threat of violence is more terrifying than the violence itself. The air was tense with what was to come; even the Ba'athist sensed it. 'When you undergo interrogation or torture at the hands of the enemy,' he told me quietly, 'you must think of your family and your country. Remember, the pain will be transitory, but Iraq and her glorious armies will live for ever. They will soon come and rescue you in repayment for your loyalty and your silence.'

There was an eagerness in the eyes of both the soldier who had performed the terrible kicking during our last session – he had clearly developed a taste for this part of our education – and the victim I had been forced to attack. He even smirked vaguely as he stood before me, waiting for the Ba'athist's permission to start the questioning. My body went weak with dread. Involuntarily I shook my head as I looked up at my two inquisitors, and those few moments seemed to last an age.

There were no shouts this time, neither from me nor from my attackers: they went about their business with a ruthless silence. Having already witnessed one of these beatings, I was vaguely prepared for what was in store, so when my chair was pushed over on to its side I had the foresight to tilt my head so that it did not slap against the ground. Nevertheless, my right arm was crushed between the back of the metal chair and the concrete floor. I tried to shuffle the weight away from my bruised arm, but before I could move I felt the first kick to my ribs. The force of the blow seemed to thud through my whole body, and I barely had time to let out an involuntary grunt before a second kick to my genitals sent a shriek of pain down my legs. Who did what in the melee that followed, I have no idea. I vaguely remember trying to shout out the information that they wanted, but the blows were incessant and utterly debilitating. After a while I even stopped feeling the pain – my body became numb as the kicks and punches merged into one brutal cocktail.

The last thing I remember seeing was the face of the Ba'athist, looking on approvingly. Then I blacked out.

2

The Shadow of a Tyrant

It was in December 1982 – when I was six years old – that I was taken to England. My father had a government scholarship to study in England for a PhD, so my mother, my brother and sister and I went with him. He attended the University of Manchester, so we lived in the Manchester area – Poynton Fallowfield and Moss Side – where my father became deeply involved in the Middle Eastern community centred around the local mosque. My mother, however, pined for Baghdad and the family that she had left behind. Her reluctance to embrace the increasingly religion-orientated world my father was making for himself led to terrible tensions between them, and our little family unit, so far from home, became volatile. Eventually my parents' marriage failed and my mother, along with my brother and sister, returned to Iraq. My relationship with my father, even as a young boy, was not good; but I loved England, where I would spend five of my formative years, so I was pleased to remain.

By 1987, the Iran–Iraq war was coming to an end. It had been devastating for both countries. It cost more than US$250 billion in total damages and, thanks to the fact that both armies had launched massive air strikes against each other's oil infrastructures, the economies of these two once-wealthy nations were battered almost beyond recognition. But the human cost of the war was more shocking than any economic effects. More than 1.5 million people lost their lives, victims of forms of warfare that horrified the civilized world. Chemical and biological weapons killed and mutilated soldiers and civilians on both sides; almost every family had someone involved, so no one remained untouched by the horrors of that conflict.

Saddam was faced with an unforeseen social and economic quandary: so many men had lost their lives in the war that Iraq suddenly found itself with a surfeit of widows. Their lives destroyed, and with most having no means of supporting themselves, they became an intolerable burden on the already shattered economy, and the government had to decide what to do with them.

Saddam's answer was novel: he decided to bribe men to marry them. Iraqi men were offered a payment of 10,000 Iraqi dinars – at the time about US$33,000 – if they would marry a war widow, and so shoulder the economic burden that they presented to the government.

Word of this tempting offer reached my father's ears in England via his brother. Unbeknown to me, a widow was found for my father, and he travelled back to Iraq to meet her, with me in tow. Ostensibly it was for a holiday; I had no idea that I was returning to Baghdad for good. I formed no part of my father's plans for life with his new wife back in England; without warning I was left with my mother and her family in the middle of Baghdad. I was twelve years old, and the culture shock was massive.

My young friends in the West were cajoled into good behaviour by threats of an imaginary bogeyman. In Iraq, there was no need for invented horrors.

I was not yet a teenager and had been back in Iraq only a couple of months when, in 1988, I saw a cavalcade of black Mercedes with blacked-out windows sweep up the length of Al-Mansour Street. They had no number plates. Iraqis from all walks of life turned to stare, but not too hard: nobody wanted to draw attention to themselves, especially when they did not know who these official cars were carrying. My friend Hakim and I, perhaps emboldened by our youth, stared more intently than the other pedestrians as the sleek, expensive vehicles pulled up, not outside one of the fashionable shops that lined this desirable road in Baghdad, but in front of a fast-food restaurant, Al-Multaqa. Its insignia – a familiar golden M

– gave an impression of the West, even if it was not quite the same thing.

After school that day Hakim and I had met at the beginning of 14th Ramadan Street, by Souk Al-Ghazi. Shopkeepers stood guard as passers-by examined their goods: watermelons, *baklava*, material for *dishdash* – the same wares that could be found at any number of similar places across the Middle East, and items that were of no interest to my twelve-year-old mind. The few coins in the pocket of my prized black jeans would be spent on something far more precious: Coca-Cola.

Chatting happily, we turned into 14th Ramadan Street and visited a run-down kebab shop. Its rusting, corrugated-iron roof protected the owner from the fierce rays of the afternoon sun, but the large shop windows – plastered in garish Arabic letters – along with the grills that burned all day long and the crush of people constantly congregated there meant that it was at least as hot inside as out. I caught the eye of the shopkeeper and he smiled. 'Sarmed, my young friend,' he called. 'Falafel?'

'And a bottle of Coca-Cola,' I nodded. 'Put it on my tab,' I added nonchalantly.

The owner raised his hand dramatically as we continued the little play that we performed several times every week. 'Are you trying to put me out of business?' he shouted in mock indignation. 'The falafel I'll put on your tab – but you pay me next week, otherwise I shall be having words with my friends at Abu Ghraib.' He winked at me. 'The Coca-Cola you pay for now.'

I handed him a coin and watched him fill a piece of flat bread with a generous helping of falafel and the fiery sauce of which I was fond. Then he turned to the fridge behind the counter and removed an icy bottle with the famous logo written in red Arabic letters along its length. He turned to Hakim. 'And for you, sir?'

Laden with our treats, we started to walk the length of 14th Ramadan Street, holding our bottles like status symbols, smiling at any girls who passed, and talking animatedly. As we walked, the shops became gradually more sophisticated, catering to the expensive tastes of the rich families who lived in the vicinity of Princess Street. Computer shops, clothes shops, antiques shops: it would be another couple of years before the sanctions against Iraq made these small but expensive luxuries a thing of the past. Then the Coca-Cola that was one of the few remaining links I had with the West would disappear for good, to be replaced by a poor approximation made of dates. When that happened, though, the lack of Coca-Cola was the least of our worries. When the water tanks were bombed during the first Gulf War, water itself became scarce. Families had to concentrate on what they needed to survive; luxuries such as hair-washing became a thing of the past. After a few months, however, children began to develop head lice. Petrol was considerably cheaper than water – you could fill up your car for the equivalent of a few American cents – so this was used to wash the hair of young Iraqi children. Scrupulous mothers would then apply rough washing powder to remove the petrol. You could always tell who had had this treatment – the strange cocktail put ruddy orange flecks in their hair when they went out in the sun.

For now, though, I could pretend: pretend that I lived a life that bore at least some resemblance to that which I had enjoyed in England; pretend that hanging around the stalls where unscrupulous merchants made a living out of pirating cassettes of Western music to order was a good alternative to being able to turn on the radio at will and listen to Michael Jackson; pretend that I was not living in a world where, at every turn, I was being told by a domineering regime what to do, what to say and what to think.

We did not intend that afternoon to be different to any other. Perhaps we would wander down Al-Mansour Street and I would visit the animals in the pet shops I loved so much, only to be chased out by the shopkeepers when they saw me: they knew that I seldom had any money to buy anything. Perhaps we would loiter near one of the pirate cassette shops, hoping to hear some Western music. Occasionally I would have enough money to buy a cassette myself; but not today.

If we found ourselves in a residential area, we would

watch men cajoling their roosters to fight each other in front of the houses. Perhaps we would see a young woman being followed by a potential suitor. It would be most unseemly for a young man to approach a woman in the street – such was not the Arab way – but if his intentions were to be encouraged, the girl would nonchalantly drop to the ground a scrap of paper on which her phone number had been scrawled. If the relationship thrived across the telephone wires, perhaps they might be permitted to meet in person. And if the sun was setting, young Iraqi women would sprinkle water on the front driveways – to cool down the house, certainly, but also to be on show, ready to attract the attention of any young men who were passing.

On this particular day we happened to be outside Al-Multaqa – The Meeting, Baghdad's answer to McDonald's – when the three black Mercedes stopped. The traffic slowed as the cars took up an entire lane. Their rear doors opened and four men from each car, dressed in the distinctive uniform of the special Republican Guard and carrying AK-47s, swiftly alighted and surrounded the front car. A fifth guard entered the fast-food restaurant and quickly came back carrying a milkshake. As the front passenger door of the first car opened, Hakim tugged on my sleeve. 'S . . . Sarmed,' he said with his characteristic stutter, 'it's U . . . U . . . Uday.'

I looked closely. The man in the front seat, perhaps in

his late twenties, was tall with a close-cropped beard. His short hair shone and appeared expensively groomed. He wore a black suit with an open collar and sat, or rather sprawled, with one leg inside the car and the other on the pavement. In his right hand he held a large cigar, in his left the milkshake that he had just been given, and he surveyed the street with an arrogant look on his face, clearly aware that people shuffling by were avoiding his gaze. Hakim was right: it was Uday Hussein, Saddam's son.

Uday's reputation was fearsome. He was known throughout Baghdad for his almost psychopathic contempt for ordinary Iraqis, and stories about his terrible deeds abounded. As a fifteen-year-old he had personally taken part in a massacre of cabinet ministers who opposed his father, but this was just the start. It was rumoured that he sometimes killed the girls who were brought to the presidential palace to entertain him. On one occasion he had shot a civilian in the street, with no provocation and in full view of many witnesses. Nobody intervened or complained – it would have given Saddam's henchmen carte blanche to execute them on the spot – but word of the shootings soon spread and Saddam was forced to take action. It was announced that a punishment would be imposed upon Uday: he was to be exiled from his beloved Iraq for a period of two months. Nobody was fooled, however: this was in the days when the Hussein family could travel freely in the West, and Uday's 'punishment' was little more than a vacation in the casinos of Geneva.

Back in Iraq, Uday took charge of the Iraqi football team, and under his supervision players were routinely beaten and tortured if they played poorly. But his diversions were becoming more extreme. He kept lions as pets; zoological experts would later observe that it seemed probable these lions were fed human meat, and sometimes even live bodies. Saddam's son was breeding man-eaters for his own amusement.

Several metres away, Hakim and I stood staring for some moments, caught between apprehension and the excitement of seeing a famous – if notorious – face. Suddenly Uday's eyes met mine and, unsmiling, he held my gaze. Whether it was through fear or not I can't say, but as I stood so close to one of the most dangerous men in Baghdad, my Coca-Cola bottle slipped from my fingers and spilt on the pavement. I looked down to see the black liquid foaming over my shoes; when I looked up again, Uday had raised his hand and was gesturing at me and Hakim to approach him.

Slowly we walked up to the Mercedes. The pungent smell of the cigar was not strong enough to mask the sickly sweet aroma of the strawberry milkshake. A solid-silver Colt handgun with a glass handle rested on his lap. He had a satisfied air, but who knows what twisted desires he had recently sated. 'Why did you throw that bottle?'

Uday asked. The quietness of his voice failed to conceal its menace. He had a lisp, but Hakim and I were in no mood to mock.

'I didn't,' I replied honestly. 'I dropped it.'

Uday dragged on his cigar, shrouding himself in smoke. The hubbub of the busy street seemed to disappear into the background as he eyed me, cobra-like. 'Where do you live?'

'At the bottom of Princess Street,' I told him.

'Really?' He looked unconvinced, and with good reason. I did not have the bearing of a well-to-do Iraqi, but I was ashamed to admit that although we lived in a relatively affluent area, we were a poor family. Quite why I felt I could mislead this man, I cannot say – it was probably the recklessness, or stupidity, of youth. 'What is your name?' he continued.

'Sarmed.'

'Sarmed what?' he intoned wearily.

'Sarmed Al-Samarrai.'

'Al-Samarrai?' His interest had been caught. The Al-Samarrai tribe had a long-standing feud with the Hussein tribe, which dated back years before Saddam's coming to power. It was over something fairly insignificant – the ownership of a stretch of the Tigris River that divided their two villages – but old enmities run deep, and Uday was the sort of person for whom any pretext would spark his particular brand of unpleasantness. 'From Samarra?'

I nodded. 'Yes.'

'But you live in Baghdad?'

'With my grandparents. They are from Baghdad.'

He stretched out in his seat, making himself more comfortable. He was clearly enjoying himself. 'And what is your father's name?'

'Saadoon Al-Samarrai.'

'Where is he?'

'In London.'

'What is he doing there?'

'Studying for a PhD.'

Uday nodded his head slowly. 'And is he there thanks to the government?'

'Yes,' I nodded.

'Good.' Suddenly he looked over my shoulder. I turned and saw that he was staring at a passer-by who had dared to take an interest in our conversation. Knowing what was good for him, the passer-by hurried on under the threatening heat of Uday's glare. Then he turned his attention back to me. 'How old are you?' he asked.

'Nearly thirteen.'

'Right.' For the first time he smiled, but there was no warmth in his face. He exuded the confidence of a cat playing with a mouse. Leaving his cigar in his mouth, he leaned forward, took my chin between his thumb and forefinger and lifted my head. 'So we can have you married soon.'

I didn't know what he meant, but as Uday surveyed my face through a cloud of smoke he must have seen the fear in my eyes, and it amused him. He chuckled to himself, and as he did so he resembled his father so closely that I was momentarily taken aback. I stood there awkwardly, not knowing what to say. Uday turned his attention to Hakim. 'What about you? What is your name?'

Hakim opened his mouth to speak, but tension accentuated his stutter. He attempted to say his name, but found himself unable to do so. Uday had no time for this. 'Shut up,' he spat waspishly. 'Go away.' Hakim looked nervously at me, unsure what to do. Uday raised his voice and touched his Colt with his cigar hand. 'I said go away!'

Hakim scurried off, leaving me there. Uday said nothing; he just sat looking at me with his dead eyes, taking deep drags on his cigar. I shifted my weight uncomfortably from one foot to the other. Finally he spoke. 'You may go,' he told me. For a brief moment I stood there, not comprehending that I had been dismissed. Then I became aware of two of the guards moving towards me, their hands gripping their weapons. I turned and hurried away.

As the cars drove off – all other vehicles in the street had been diverted to allow their passage – Hakim and I were left with only our sense of fear. As that fear subsided, our encounter with Uday turned into a great adventure, and we recounted our exploits to our contemporaries with increasing elaboration. But as I grew older, and became aware of the reality of life around me, such events would take on a more sinister meaning – less a cause for bravado, more a cause for despair. Many Iraqis were unwilling to go into detail about the horrors they experienced, but plenty of rumours reached my ears. That was how the regime worked. There would be no point to the continuing brutality if ordinary Iraqis did not get to hear of it: how else would Saddam maintain his grip of fear?

Rumours were spread by word of mouth. Some of them were exaggerated in the telling, no doubt, but even the most grisly were not, I am sure, so very far from the truth. AIDS, we were told, was a Western disease, an epidemic confined to the relative promiscuity of the non-Arab world. I was walking down 14th Ramadan Street with Hakim one day, however, when we noticed a poster in a shop window. The names of four women were printed in large letters, and below we were urged to tell the authorities if we knew who these women were. They were HIV+, the poster informed us, and were part of a wicked Zionist plot to spread the disease around our great nation.

Hakim and I did not know these women, of course, so we thought little more of it, although the posters continued to appear in shop windows across Baghdad. A few weeks later, word spread that they had been apprehended. The authorities had made no effort to arrest them formally, and they were certainly not given any opportunity to defend themselves through any legal process. Instead, they were taken to Abu Ghraib prison.

Twenty miles west of Baghdad, Abu Ghraib was notorious enough to chill the fervour of even the most revolutionary citizens. It was said that thousands of men and women were crammed into tiny cells, and that abuse, torture and executions were daily occurrences. The regime tested chemical and biological weapons on the inmates, and some prisoners were given nothing but scraps of shredded plastic to eat. Chunks of flesh would be torn from the bodies of some prisoners and then force-fed to others. Gruesome tortures involving power tools and hungry dogs were routine, and thousands of people had entered the doors of that place never to be heard of again. It was known that mass graves existed in various locations, and it was known in general terms where they were situated; but of course nobody dared to hunt out the final resting place of those corpses who had fallen victim to the enthusiastic guards at Abu Ghraib, for fear of becoming one of their number.

These poor AIDS-stricken women, however, were dealt with in a fashion brutal even by the standards of the prison. Stripped of their clothes, they were placed, alive and screaming, in an incinerator, where they and their vile disease could be utterly destroyed. And thus Saddam delivered our country from the horrific infections of the West, and the iniquities of the evil Zionist state. I kept quiet about my maternal grandmother's Jewish heritage. She lived on Al-Mushajer street off Al-Sadoon street in the Jewish area of Al-Bettaween and was one of only a handful of Jews who remained in Iraq during the exodus of 1950. In the wake of the Arab–Israeli war of 1948, the Arab states began to see Zionism as the cause of the conflict in Palestine; many Arab states forbade the emigration of Jews to Israel because it was thought that such emigration would strengthen the Jewish state. In Iraq, however, a law was passed in March 1950 allowing Jews one year in which to emigrate voluntarily, provided they relinquished their Iraqi nationality. The exodus was encouraged by an Israeli initiative called Operation Ezra and Nehemiah, and also by the death of three Jews in a bombing at a café. Before the exodus, there were about 150,000 Jews living in Iraq; subsequently there were fewer than a hundred. My grandmother was one. The few Jews who remained were forced to sign statements of anti-Zionism; it would have done me no favours, however, had anyone suspected that I might look to my heritage and embrace it.

Other atrocities took place more openly. As living conditions became increasingly intolerable, many women were forced into prostitution in order to make enough money to feed themselves and their families. It was an occupation deemed unacceptable by the state, punishable by death. The administration of justice was left to officials of the

Ba'ath Party, who were given orders to seek and behead all those suspected of prostitution. The standard of proof required was low, but the enthusiasm with which these officials carried out their work was high. Accompanied by two 'witnesses' from the local community, they would force their way into the house of the suspect, then drag her out into the street. There, a specialist executioner would be waiting with a sword: he would slice off the head of the screaming woman with one deft, well-practised stroke. The head would hang outside the woman's house for two days, and her front door would be branded with the warning *Hadhihi Al-Qahba*: This Is The Whore.

As a child, I remember a parade being held down one of the main thoroughfares of Baghdad. The road had been closed to traffic, and thousands of people had joined the march, which was intended to celebrate the glory of Saddam. As the day wore on, however, a small group of insurgents became vocal in their criticism of the regime and started to shout out anti-Saddam slogans. There were very few of them – certainly only a small proportion of the crowd – but the Republican Guard was quick to react. A helicopter immediately flew overhead and poured white paint over the entire crowd, insurgents and non-insurgents alike. A troop of heavily armed soldiers were then dispatched with orders to shoot anybody who had white paint on them. The whole operation took less than an hour. A few lucky souls who had paint only on their clothes managed to escape the crowd and change, but any-body with paint on their hair or body, where it was more difficult to remove, fared less well. The military scoured the whole area and shot dead anybody suspected of being part of the 'uprising'.

The town of Balad north of Baghdad had long been a place of neglect and oppression. Compared to Saddam's home town of Tikrit, it suffered unbearable poverty and degradation. The people of Balad extended an official invitation to Saddam to come to the town to discuss matters. As a cultural mark of respect, the wife of one of the leading tribesmen arranged for Saddam's car to be marked with henna – a sign of blessing; secretly, the tribesmen arranged for militia armed with RPGs to be stationed on the rooftops where Saddam's fleet would pass, their instructions to destroy the henna-marked car on sight. But Saddam's head of security became suspicious and arranged for him to be moved to another vehicle.

As arranged, the militia destroyed the marked car, along with nineteen others. They then came down to street level and destroyed the remaining vehicles, with the exception of three, which retreated in great haste. A checkpoint guard who was collaborating with the tribe reported that Saddam was in one of the escaping cars.

The entire population immediately fled to Mosul or Samarra: they knew retribution would be swift and uncompromising. Within hours, armed helicopters arrived and laid waste the town. Then the bulldozers appeared, utterly to destroy whatever was left of the place. In twenty-four hours, a whole town had been turned to rubble; any civilian unlucky enough to have remained in what was left of their home was bulldozed or burned to death.

During my teenage years, I had made no secret to my family of the fact that I wanted to leave all this. As I grew up, more and more of my friends in Baghdad – many of whom were older than me – somehow managed to make it across the border. Some had made the dangerous trip into Iran, others had made it to Kurdistan. I had even heard that some had claimed asylum in Israel. I longed to do the same. 'At least finish your schooling,' my mother would beg me. 'Then at least you will have some sort of grounding.' So I persevered at school, but with a certain reluctance: I saw school as an obstacle to be got out of the way before I could make attempts to leave the country.

But there were other obstacles, too. In 1990, when I was fourteen, my father – who was by now back from England – took me, against my mother's will and my own, to live with him at the College of Forestry and Agriculture near Mosul where he was based. I didn't want to be there but I was a child and my father would not allow me to leave.

From an early age it had been drummed into me that the best career path I could possibly follow would be medicine. Doctors would always be in demand, it was explained, and it would be a noble calling. To gain a place at medical school, however, was not easy. Applications to university were made on the basis of an average mark for your final exams in high school – the baccalaureate. Unfortunately for me, academic merit was not the only consideration when this final mark was calculated. If the father of a student was an active member of the Ba'ath Party, for example, the student would be awarded an extra five points; if he was an officer in the military, it would be worth another five. It was reasonably common for students to finish high school with an average mark of 110 out of 100.

My father had no military or political connections. I was not a bad student, but my final mark of 86 was always going to be insufficient for me to achieve what I wanted. I applied for medical school, but I knew that against people whose marks had been doctored as a result of their parents' connections I was unlikely to make the grade. Sure enough, I was rejected.

I made other applications, too. My father persuaded me to apply to the College of Forestry and Agriculture – he would be able to keep an eye on me, he said, and make sure my grades were good – and I was offered a place. But I had no desire to live with him any longer than I had to, so I did some research into which colleges in Baghdad were likely to accept me, and was offered two other places:

one to study veterinary medicine, the other to study accounting and finance. I made the applications without much enthusiasm, and chose to enrol on the finance course almost at random. I never expected to go there: I had already made other plans.

There would be a period of two months between the end of high school and starting at university. During that time, if the proper applications were made, the government would allow students to spend a brief period travelling outside Iraq. My dream had always been to return to England, but that would not be allowed. However, I reasoned that if I could at least make it to Jordan, where border control was less strict, I could apply for a student visa and make my way to the UK. My plans were hazy, but bolstered by an inexorable desire to leave. Secretly I made contact with a college in England where I was accepted on a foundation medical course. My mother's brother, Faisal, was a doctor in England, and I was sure that my uncle would help me study to become a doctor myself. But first I had to get there.

In order for me to apply for a visitor's visa, certain papers needed to be compiled. During my final few weeks at school, I applied for a certificate of nationality. When that came through, I had the most difficult hurdle to cross. I approached my father with some trepidation. As part of the application, I needed his written permission, and I had no reason to believe that it would be given willingly – I fully expected to have to beg, cajole and finally argue furiously with him in order to get it.

My relationship with my father was an unhappy one, and not only because he had taken me from my mother in Baghdad and forced me to live in a place I hated, in the north: the compound of the College of Forestry and Agriculture, which was next to a village called Hamam Al-Aleel, near Mosul. Hamam Al-Aleel was something of a Sunni stronghold, a bastion of Saddam's supporters. The village was populated by people who had been loyal to the regime, and a significant proportion of the Special Republican Guard had been recruited from that area. The college compound included not only the living quarters for the lecturers and the students, but also a section of forest. Surrounding it all was a high, concrete wall that made it seem almost a prison; but the fortifications were not to keep students in, they were to keep out the vicious inhabitants of Hamam Al-Aleel. In places, though, the wall had crumbled and toppled, so the compound itself could never be completely secure. Sometimes, groups of young men would enter the college and attack anyone they saw wearing good clothes, not because they needed them or wanted them, but simply because they could – nobody was going to argue with these fearsome animals brandishing Kalashnikovs. On other occasions these marauding groups would wander around looking for girls – there were a number of female students at the college – and would break into the female halls of residence. Sometimes, at night, I would lie in bed and hear the yelling. The police and other authorities, often related to the villagers, would turn a blind eye – these people were loyal to Saddam, and an unspoken law gave them carte blanche to act more or less as they wished.

I would occasionally speak on the telephone to my family in Baghdad, but fear of my father kept me rooted in Mosul. Nevertheless, throughout the years I spent in that place I was filled with a desire to leave. So it was that I carefully waited until he was in what passed for a good mood before I brought up the matter. 'If I am to make an application for students' leave, I will need your permission,' I told him.

'Indeed?' he replied with an uncharacteristic note of joviality. 'Well then,' he stretched his arms out in front of him, 'you have my permission!'

I was so astonished I barely knew what to say. I looked hard at my father and could sense that beneath the veil of helpfulness something was not right. Over the past few years he had gone to all sorts of lengths to keep me close to him, ranging from bribery to abduction to physical and mental violence; why was he now surrendering me without a fight? 'I need your permission in writing,' I told him.

'Certainly,' he said, and accompanied me to my school to sign a piece of paper that I hoped would be my ticket out of Iraq: 'I, Saadoon Al-Samarrai, give my permission for my son Sarmed to travel out of the country before returning to attend university.'

I couldn't believe how easily he had granted his permission. I now required permission from my school. It was not simply a matter of gaining a signature from the right person, however; I approached the registrar with gifts of *baklava* and bananas – which were scarce at the time because of the sanctions – and literally begged him to take the relevant document to the dean to be signed.

The next stage was to take the three documents to military headquarters in Samarra, as that was where my paternal family originally came from. 'Sure,' said my father, 'I'll take you to Samarra.'

'When can we go?'

My father shrugged. 'Two weeks, maybe three.'

'But it's already the middle of July,' I told him. 'They would expect me back in the country at the end of August – it won't give them enough time to process the application.'

'Well, I'm sorry, Sarmed. I'm busy here – I can't just drop everything to take you to Samarra. You'll have to be patient.' Suddenly his attitude seemed to be changing, as though he knew I was going to encounter these difficulties but was pleased that I would not be able to pin them precisely on him.

'OK,' I replied, 'I'll take the coach to Baghdad and get Uncle Saad to take me.'

My father turned stony-faced, as he always did when my uncle was mentioned. 'Saad, eh? *Arrooj*. Peg-leg. Very well.'

I had one more favour to ask. 'There will be a fee to pay,' I told him. 'Fifteen thousand dinars.'

His eyes went flat. 'I'm not going to give you that sort of money,' he told me adamantly.

'Please,' I begged him. 'If you don't lend me the money, there's no way I can get out of the country – no way I can study to become a doctor. The only other way I can raise it is to sell all my stuff.'

'What stuff?'

'My computer, my bike . . .'

'They're not yours to sell. They're mine – you only borrow them. Everything in this house belongs to me.' He turned to leave the room. 'If you need money,' he said with a hint of sarcasm in his voice, 'maybe *Arrooj* can give it to you. But somehow I doubt it . . .'

My father left me to simmer on that thought for a while. The following day I called Saad. 'OK,' he said when I had finished telling him about the conversation. 'Get the coach to Baghdad and we'll sort it all out.'

'What about the money?' I asked.

'Don't worry about that – I'll get the money.'

'Where from?'

'I said don't worry about it. Just get here.'

My father seemed uncharacteristically unconcerned when I informed him boldly that I was going to Baghdad. With any luck I would be departing Mosul for the last time before leaving Iraq, but he clearly did not think my chances of success were high. 'I'll see you soon,' he told me before I left. It was almost as though he knew something I did not.

The office in Samarra was deliciously cool, and the immaculately dressed military official who was to authorize my application made a stark contrast to Saad and me, rumpled and sweating from the torturous heat of the car journey from Baghdad. The room itself was bleak – a table, three chairs and an old metal filing cabinet in the corner – but the official nevertheless maintained an imperious bearing. We needed this man's help, so we made every effort to be scrupulously polite. 'What is the boy's name?' he asked as he examined my papers. His voice was thick with the accent of Samarra.

'This is my nephew, Sarmed Al-Samarrai. He wishes to make an application to travel outside the country.'

'I'm sure he does.' He eyed me with suspicion. 'What is his status?'

'He has just finished high school, and will start university in Baghdad in September.'

'Who is his father?'

'Saadoon Al-Samarrai.' A flicker of recognition crossed the officer's face. 'You will see from the documents that he has given his permission for the application to be processed. He has asked me to accompany Sarmed today.'

'Indeed?' questioned the officer sceptically. 'He should be here himself. Why could he not come?'

'He is an important lecturer in Mosul,' Saad replied smoothly. 'A very busy man. I'm sure you understand.'

The officer remained expressionless as he placed my documents in a folder and scribbled something on a piece of paper. 'Here is a telephone number,' he told Saad. 'You can call it to check the status of your application. Good day.'

'But we were under the impression that the application could be approved today.'

'Then I am afraid, my friend, that your impression was incorrect. There are a number of checks I have to make.'

'What sort of checks?'

'Just checks,' he replied evasively. 'Now, if you don't mind, I am extremely busy.'

Saad looked pointedly at the empty desk. 'So I see,' he said, and led me from the room. 'Something's not right,' he told me once we were out of earshot. 'There's no reason why he shouldn't have processed that application immediately. There's something he wasn't telling us.'

We phoned the number every day for the next couple of weeks, but on each occasion the official made himself unavailable. In the end there was nothing for it. 'We'll have to go there again and talk to him face to face,' Saad decided. 'If you're to get out before the end of August, time is short. Someone is leaning on this pen-pusher to delay the application, and I think I know who it is.'

The military official was, if anything, even less welcoming this time. 'Listen,' he told us impatiently, 'I told you that checks need to be made.'

'Well, have you made them?' Saad put him on the spot.

'It's a very busy time of year,' replied the official, avoiding the question. 'The schools have all finished, there's a great deal to do.'

Saad eyeballed him for a few moments before leaning back in his chair and breathing deeply. 'OK,' he said quietly. '*Akhi*, brother, I am very well connected in Baghdad. People high in the military. It is only a matter of one phone call to military headquarters for me to find out what is going on. Now, are you sure you don't want to move a little more quickly?'

The official gazed back impassively. He had no way of knowing if Saad was bluffing – my uncle was not from Samarra, and so no word of this pushy ex-officer from Baghdad with a false leg and a smooth tongue would have reached his ears – but he decided to take the risk. 'You do what you have to do,' he replied. 'I know my job.'

But Saad was not bluffing. As we drove back to Baghdad he seemed quietly confident that he could get things moving. 'I have a favour to call in' was all he would say. Back at home he elaborated. 'I have a contact,' he told me. 'He sometimes comes to visit us here. He is very high up, a deputy minister, and I have his private number. I've never made any requests of him before now, and this will be a small matter for him. I'm sure he will help us.'

That afternoon he made the call. 'This is officer Saad from Al-Zaafaraniya compound. My nephew is having trouble with an official in Samarra who is being slow in processing his application to travel before he goes to university, and time is becoming short. Is there anything you can do to help things along?'

Approval from Samarra came through the very next day.

One final hurdle remained between me and the Jordanian border. The approval from Samarra had to be taken to the central military office in Baghdad for the final document to be stamped before I could apply for a passport. Saad and I went there that day; I was buoyant with excitement at the prospect of being able to leave as soon as the final piece of this interminable jigsaw of bureaucracy was in place. Outside, a crowd of bearded Iraqis in *dishdash* – long robes with long sleeves – sat at small portable tables, parasols protecting them from the sun. These were the statement-makers: anybody with a request to be made had to pay one of these statement-makers to draw up the request as an official document before they took it to one of the clerks inside the office. Some of them had old-style cameras on tripods with black hoods at the back, as all documents required an accompanying photograph. We paid several hundred dinars to one of these men to produce our written request, and he attached my papers to it with a needle before giving it to us to take inside.

A harassed-looking official took my papers and looked at them. After a few moments he shook his head. 'Too late,' he said.

'What do you mean, too late?' Saad asked.

'My friend, we have tens of thousands of applications. It will take at least four weeks to process this – they need to be thoroughly examined. By that time he will only have a week in which to get a new passport to travel – it won't be worth it.'

'I can spend a week travelling!' I butted in.

'It's not up to you, young man,' the official told me. 'If we say it's not worth it, it's not worth it.' He handed the papers back to me.

'But it's only late because we were delayed by the official in Samarra . . .' I started to argue, but he had already moved away to join his colleague.

Crestfallen, I turned to Saad. 'Come on, Sarmed,' he said quietly. 'We're wasting our time here. Let's go home.'

Saad tried to approach his high-ranking contact once more, but that door seemed shut to us. 'This is the second favour,' my uncle was told. 'I have a job to do – I can't keep sorting out your problems.'

Saad looked demoralized as he put the phone down. 'I'm sorry,' he said. 'I feel as though I've let you down.'

I shook my head. 'I've been let down,' I told him, 'but not by you.' We sat in silence for a while. 'It was my father, wasn't it? He tipped off the official in Samarra about my application and asked him to delay it.'

Saad nodded. 'It can't have been anybody else.'

'No wonder he was so relaxed about me leaving. Why does he have to be like this? I thought he *wanted* me to study medicine.'

'He had his reasons.' Saad muttered the platitude, unwilling to speak badly of my father in front of me; but the steel in his eyes told of less forgiving thoughts.

'There must be something I can do,' I almost whispered. 'I can't stay here – this place is sending me mad.'

Saad looked at me closely. 'I'd hoped that you would be able to get out legally,' he said after a while. 'There is another option, but it is very dangerous.'

'What is it?'

'You would be taking a great risk.'

'I'm not a child any more,' I said impatiently. 'What do you have in mind?'

He still seemed reluctant to tell me. 'I have heard that there are Kurds who are willing to smuggle people north into Kurdistan. They would forge a document saying that you are their son. From there they would get professionals to create false papers and take you over the border into Turkey.'

We were silent for some time. Both of us knew the implications of what he was suggesting. If I was caught trying to leave the country without the proper permissions, the chances were that I would be escorted to Abu Ghraib. Once there, I would have to hope that the guards did not become creative in their dealings with me. I did my best to dispel those thoughts. 'Do you know anyone who does this?' I asked Saad.

He shook his head. 'Not directly. And it will take a while to find someone – I can't just approach people in the street and ask them if they are willing to smuggle my nephew to Turkey. It could take some weeks. You'll have to start at university in the meantime.'

I shrugged. 'If it's only for a few weeks . . .'

'You can't take this decision lightly, Sarmed,' my uncle told me almost with impatience. 'It's not a game, and you know what will happen if you get caught. Maybe you should think about staying – get your degree and see how you feel then.' His piercing eyes looked straight at me. 'I understand why you want to leave, but everybody wants you to stay.'

'I know,' I replied, humbled by the affection my uncle

was showing me. 'But please, Uncle Saad, find out what you can.'

'OK, Sarmed. I'm not promising anything, but I'll do my best.'

I enrolled at university to study accounting and finance with a heavy heart, hanging on to the hope that Saad would find someone who could help us, and soon. I did not consider what would happen if I was caught – such thoughts were too unpleasant to dwell upon – and in any case I was single-minded in my determination not to stay in Iraq for a day longer than was necessary.

My attendance at university was poor. As I look back now I realize I should have made the most of it, but thoughts of escape were foremost in my young mind. I was not to know that my actions would precipitate every-thing that followed, but my enthusiasm for the course was non-existent, and in any case I did not expect to be around for long enough to make it worth my while even turning up. Once my non-attendance hit a certain level, I knew that republican law dictated that a letter would be sent to Samarra – probably to the same official with whom I had had dealings before – and I would be tracked down and called in. I would then be given a choice: find another course and attend it properly, or enlist in the army. But by the time that happened, I was convinced I would be well on my way to Turkey. I saw Saad every day. Sometimes we would play chess together; other times we would just sit and chat. Every day I asked him how his enquiries were going; every day he would skirt around the issue. 'I need a few more days,' he would say. 'Be patient, Sarmed, I'm working on it.'

And I knew he was. It was acknowledged without words that Saad was more of a father to me than my father had ever been. He was beginning to look under pressure, however, and although he would not admit it, it was clear to me that he was having trouble finding one of these mysterious Kurdish smugglers. Most of the Kurdish population was centred around Mosul, and Saad had no contacts in that part of the country.

One morning, the inevitable happened: the local Ba'ath Party official knocked on our door and my mother answered. 'Sarmed Al-Samarrai must attend the military headquarters in Samarra.' There was no point asking questions: it was couched as a request but was very much an order, and if I failed to attend then the Red Berets would soon come asking for me. Once more, Saad and I found ourselves on the route to Samarra. 'It's OK,' Saad told me. 'They will offer you another course – you had better attend this one!'

The same military official was dealing with my case. 'It appears your attendance at university has been poor,' he told me with more than a hint of satisfaction in his voice.

I could not deny it. 'I didn't find that I was suited to it,' I lied. 'I would like to find a different course to study.'

'It's too late for that,' the official told me. He handed me a sheaf of documents. 'These are your call-up papers. You are to report immediately to Baghdad military training centre. You will undergo three months' training before being assigned to your unit.' His words fell upon me like body blows as he turned to Saad. 'And there is no point asking your friends to rap my knuckles this time,' he told him. 'If he fails to attend university, he joins the army. Republican law, and there is nothing you can do about it.'

3

The Road to Al-Mansour

Every month we were granted leave from the army. Papers would be issued by an *arif*, stating how long the leave period was and the date on which it ended. Leave periods were dictated by the army; you could request time off under exceptional circumstances such as the death of a close family member – after enquiries had been made and only if the death was not politically connected – but otherwise you could only go home when you were told.

In the absence of genuinely exceptional circumstances, some soldiers went to the most extreme lengths to engineer them. I saw desperate young men deliberately open fire on their feet – often causing the loss of toes and even legs – in order that they might be awarded temporary or permanent leave from service. I saw them breaking their own arms – or cajoling others to do it for them; I saw them firing their AK-47s close to their eardrums so that they became deaf and could be sent home to recuperate.

Whenever anyone was granted leave – for whatever reason – I used to envy them with all my being. The wake-up call would be blown about half an hour after the early-morning call to prayer, which itself was about half an hour before sunrise so that the faithful could complete their prayers before daylight. But anyone who was going home for a few days would be up well before that, preparing their bags and getting ready to leave. I would pretend to sleep through their noise, not wanting to listen to their good-natured gloats about what they would get up to at home. When it was my turn for a break, however, it was a different matter. I too would be up before the sun, hastily collecting my things, and checking more than once that I had my leave papers all in order. They were thin, easily crumpled pieces of parchment, and the stamps were often blurred and unreadable – checkpoint guards relied more on the fact that a colour-rotation system was used than an ability to read the stamps, but it was common for soldiers to be escorted back to their unit simply because their perfectly valid leave papers were illegible.

Once outside the gates, the soldiers who had been granted leave would buy watermelon or bottles of water for the journey. The richer ones would flag down a taxi to take them to the coach station; the rest of us had to go on foot, but the hour-long walk was always completed with a lighter heart than the trip back. The journey to Baghdad would take a good four or five hours, and I would count every kilometre impatiently, desperate to get back to the comforts of home, such as they were. Once there, I would spend a glorious five or six days in the little house my mother shared with my siblings and grandparents, simply relaxing, away from the regimented horrors and brutality of the army. My mother would ask me what I had been up to, but I would answer her vaguely, keen to protect her from the realities of what was going on. Uncle Saad, on the other hand, had no need to ask. He had been through army life and he knew what it was like. I would do my best to speak to him regularly from the unit, but all our calls were monitored so there was no way I could ask him about the one thing that was constantly on my mind: his attempts to smuggle me out. Back home, it would become clear that things were not going well. Smugglers did not advertise their services on street corners, and they would have every reason to be suspicious of this ex-army officer making enquiries about their illegal activities.

The night before I had to return to my unit would always be a time of bitter despair and anguish, but there was nothing I could do to avoid the fact that I had to go back. My farewells to my mother and my brother and sister would be emotional; my grandmother would cry, while my grandfather, who seemed older every time I saw him, would sit quietly in a corner of the room, his head nodding. I knew I could not allow myself to prolong the moment: if I was late back by even an hour, it would mean my wages would be docked and I would be in a whole world of trouble.

The first evening back at the base was always the worst. I would feel lonely and far from home, divorced in every way from the bustle of activity around me. Sometimes I would walk to one of the further corners of the camp, where nothing but a thick wall of barbed wire divided us from the expanse of the desert, and watch the sun set over the horizon; other times I would lie on my bed and play one of my cassettes of Western music, closing my eyes and thinking of happier times. It was on one of these occasions that an *arif* walked through the dormitory. I can't remember what music I was listening to, but rather than reprimand me he paid a sudden interest to it. 'Do you understand what they are singing about?' he asked curiously.

I nodded. 'Yes, sir.'

'You speak English?'

'I spent some time living there when I was younger.'

He nodded attentively, then left me alone to spend the rest of the evening as I saw fit.

The next day I was summoned to see the chief officer of the camp: to his face we called him 'sir', of course, but behind his back we always referred to him by his real name, Taha. I walked into his office and saluted; he continued to scribble on a piece of paper before looking up. 'At ease,' he told me.

I let my arm fall to my side, but my body remained rigid. Summonses to this office normally led to a punishment of some kind. I didn't know what I had done wrong, but I needed to be on my best behaviour. 'How's your English?' the officer asked out of the blue.

I was caught momentarily off guard – it wasn't the question I had expected. 'Good, sir,' I replied hesitantly.

He turned to a radio on his desk and switched it on. An English news programme crackled into life. 'What are they saying?'

I listened briefly, then translated what I heard into Arabic. The officer nodded slowly to himself. 'Good,' he muttered. 'Good. Where in England have you lived?'

'Manchester,' I told him.

'Ah,' he said with a nod, 'Manchester United! You like it in England?' His face was expressionless and I hesitated, unsure if this was a trick question. 'It's OK,' he encouraged me. 'You can answer me honestly.'

'Yes, sir,' I replied quietly. 'I like it in England.'

'I would like to visit there myself. If I were to do that, could you arrange people for me to stay with?'

It was such an unusual request. Although Taha maintained his superior demeanour, this was a conversation that I might have had with a casual acquaintance on the streets of Baghdad. 'Of course,' I replied. 'I have family there. I would have to ask them first, but . . .' My voice trailed off.

'Naturally,' he replied. Then, suddenly: 'You are dismissed.'

I saluted and left.

Over the next few weeks I received more of these curious summonses. Each time, Taha would ask me more about England, sometimes sounding as if he was merely wanting to satisfy his own curiosity, at other times firing questions in quick succession as if to test the truth of what I was saying. 'Who did you live with in England?' he asked me.

'My parents and my brother and sister, to start with,' I replied. 'Then just with my father, when my mother went home.'

'Why did she not stay?'

I stared ahead, impassively. 'Their marriage ran into problems, sir.'

'What sort of problems?'

I had no desire to tell this man the full truth. As I stood there considering his question, I could not help but remember the sorry image of my mother weeping in a corner, distraught by whatever furious words she had exchanged with my father. It had happened so many times that even I did not know the full truth of what had gone on behind closed doors, but these images had remained locked in my head for too long for me to start discussing them now, especially here. 'Just the usual problems couples have,' I said with a shrug. 'It often happens in the West.'

On other occasions, Taha would ask me in more detail about who I knew in England, and about the lifestyle, and he would listen to my answers with what seemed to me to be great interest. I would be asked to interpret songs and news programmes, and I gradually became aware that I was turning into teacher's pet. My interviews did not go unnoticed. My colleagues started to josh me – 'Hey, don't mess with him, he's got special contacts now!' – and even the *arifs* treated me with less disdain, clearly unaware of the contents of our conversations.

Some time after our first meeting, I was summoned to see Taha once more. He was casually flicking through a file. 'I see you live in Al-Mansour,' he commented.

'Yes, sir.'

'How would you like to be based back there?'

I felt a shudder of excitement. 'I would like that very much, sir.'

'Excellent,' replied the officer. 'Then you will be pleased to hear that I have arranged for you to transfer to the intelligence compound. I'm sure they will find your skills to be of great use.'

Al-Mansour intelligence headquarters was a stone's

throw from my grandparents' house. The officer was offering me a ticket out of the unit I hated so much, straight to the arms of my family.

It was very rare for a soldier to be transferred to the intelligence services – normally people were selected from the Ba'ath Party, or if they wanted linguists they would choose graduates with language degrees. To be given this privilege was something almost unheard of for a lowly soldier. I can only think it must have come about because of what Taha mistakenly believed to be my loyalty to the army, the fact that I came from a Sunni family, like Saddam, and would perhaps therefore be more loyal to him, and also because I was young and had lived in the UK. And there was a shortage of good people.

As a member of the intelligence services, I would occasionally be allowed to wear civilian clothes and would start to earn a decent wage. If I worked hard, I could even become rich, driving expensive cars and brandishing exotic weapons just like I had seen important people in Baghdad do. I don't deny that I had sometimes considered that path – in a society where power was everything, everybody dreamed of having a little. The only way you could be sure of a high standard of living for yourself and your family was to become part of the system, a cog in the massive machine of terror that Saddam had constructed to keep himself in a position of omnipotence.

But I knew my success would come at a high price. No

doubt they wanted me for my interpreting skills, so that I could listen in to Western messages intercepted via radar and satellite and translate them for my superiors. But inexorably I would become entangled in a web so complex I might never escape from it. Al-Mansour was a fearsome place, and those who worked there more fearsome still. As a member of the intelligence services, I would automatically be expected to betray my friends, even my family if need be, for the greater good of the country and its glorious leader. I would have to undergo 'Interrogation Training' of the same type that I had experienced at my unit, to make sure that I was strong enough to resist; but I would also be required to mete out such treatment to ordinary civilians on a daily basis. It was a prison sentence in itself, one that would last for the rest of my life. I would turn into the very symbol of everything I wanted to escape.

Indeed, escape would be further from my reach than it had ever been. As things stood, the dangers involved were too terrible to think about; but if a member of the intelligence services was caught betraying his country, the consequences were unimaginable. If I was caught absconding from Al-Mansour, I would be tortured and killed, certainly, but the retribution would not stop there. Whether they apprehended me or not, they would without question go after my family. My parents and grandparents would undergo horrific cruelty – they would perhaps even be murdered – and I could not be sure that my little brother and sister would not be brutalized in some way.

These were not idle fears: they were part and parcel of life in Iraq – accepted facts that touched every family across the land. I remembered talking to my friend Kamall one day. The heat of the summer was beginning to subside, and heavy clouds in the distance threatened one of the tumultuous deluges that sometimes fell upon Baghdad, turning its wide streets into rivers. Out of the blue, I decided to ask Kamall the question that had been nagging at me ever since we had first met. 'Where's your father?'

Kamall was silent for a moment. 'I don't know,' he told me, looking intently down the street at nothing in particular. For a moment he didn't elaborate, and I sensed that it would not be tactful to press him; but gradually he opened up. 'He was a pilot.'

'In the air force?' I asked quietly, thinking that perhaps he had been one of the many casualties of the war.

Kamall shook his head. 'No,' he replied. 'For the state airline.' Al-Khutoot Aljawiya Al-Iraqia – Iraqi Airways.

It transpired that he and another pilot had spoken out against aspects of the airline's safety policy, so they were arrested. The other pilot agreed to retract his objection, but Kamall's father wouldn't. It was only a few days later that they came for him. Kamall remembered two white security vehicles pulling up outside the house. There was a knock on the door; Kamall's father opened it to see three or four men in civilian clothing brandishing handguns. They did not need to say anything – they just looked at Kamall's father and then at Kamall himself, who was no older than ten, and gestured that they should follow them to one of the security vans. Kamall's father held up his hands. 'OK,' he said. 'Take me. I'll come with you now without any struggle. But please, leave my family alone.'

'Our instructions are to take you and your son,' one of the intelligence officers replied.

A horrible silence ensued. 'Please,' Kamall's father begged quietly, 'he's only a little boy.'

Suddenly, Kamall's mother started to scream. 'Don't take my little one!' she shouted. 'Please, don't take my little one!' She held her son tight to her body.

The intelligence officers looked around nervously. They had no wish to be recognized by other members of the general public for what they were, and the screams of Kamall's mother were bound to attract attention. 'All right then,' one of them said to his father, 'just you. But move quickly.'

Kamall's father nodded. He held his wife for a brief moment, then bent down to hug his son, but no words were spoken. And then he walked out of the door with the guards. He was never seen again.

At home that evening, I told Uncle Saad the story as we

sat playing chess. 'Yes,' he said. 'I knew Kamall's father. He was at school with me.'

I wanted to know more about what I had heard. 'Would they really have taken Kamall?'

'Who knows, Sarmed? I suspect not. More likely, I think, that they were saying that to make his father come quietly. The officers would not have wanted a fuss. They wouldn't have wanted neighbours to see their faces.'

'What do you think happened to his father?'

Saad shrugged. 'A bullet in the head, if he was lucky. Something more inventive if he wasn't.'

'Inventive like what?'

Saad slowly moved one of his chess pieces. 'You don't want to know, Sarmed.'

'Maybe they just put him in prison. Maybe he's still there.'

'Maybe,' replied Saad with an indulgent smile. 'But there aren't enough cells in Abu Ghraib to house everyone who has disappeared in the last ten years. Not by a mile. And besides, who's to say that a bullet in the head isn't preferable to what goes on there?'

'Like what?'

'I don't know, Sarmed. It's just rumours. Forget it.' He obviously didn't want to talk about it any more, and so the fate of Kamall's father was left to my imagination, as it had been to Kamall's these past few years.

In a horrible, warped kind of way, Kamall had been

lucky; I had no reason to assume that my family would be so fortunate. 'What if I say no?' I asked Taha.

He was evidently surprised – he thought he was offering me a tempting promotion, perhaps by way of recompense for my agreeing to introduce him to people in England should he ever visit. He was giving me a way out of being a simple soldier, despised by everyone, and the look he gave me was quizzical; but of course, he had no inkling of my escape plans. 'If you say no,' he replied slowly, 'I will inform the authorities that, having been allowed to spend time in England as a result of the government's generosity, you have now declined to serve your country in return.' He held his hands out and shrugged. 'They will decide what action to take.'

I remained silent as we both considered the threat implicit in his last statement. 'I take it you want me to proceed with the transfer?' he asked finally.

'Yes, sir,' I replied in a small voice. 'Thank you, sir.'

My telephone call to Saad that evening was urgent. I could not tell him explicitly of my fears, of course – no doubt somebody was listening in – but he immediately understood the implications of what I told him. 'They are transferring me to Al-Mukhabarat in Al-Mansour,' I said as soon as the pleasantries were out of the way.

Saad fell silent. 'How long have you got?' he asked.

'I don't know, they haven't told me.'

My uncle quickly directed the conversation elsewhere. Some minutes later, however, quite out of the blue, he said, 'Next time you're home on leave, we'll pay that visit to your family in the north.' There had been no plans to visit anybody, of course. Saad was trying to tell me something else.

I spent the next few days in a state of the highest anxiety. The summonses to see the officer had come to a halt and I felt I was in limbo. I called Saad again a few nights later. 'You know that thing we were talking about?' he asked.

'Yes,' I replied apprehensively.

'I've found another way to go about it. We'll try it next time you're home.'

It was two weeks until my next leave, but I started to make my preparations long before that; Saad had given no more than a hint, but I fully expected never to see the unit again. I presented my leave papers to the *arif* for stamping in good time. 'Please,' I asked him, 'stamp it carefully.' It was a bold request, and he gave me an aggravated glance, but he stamped the flimsy piece of paper slowly and forcefully. I took special care to wait until the ink was dry before stowing it away with my military ID – I could not risk it smudging. The night before I was due to leave, I packed my bag with no regrets: I would not be sorry in the least to leave this place.

The following morning I did not loiter. At sunrise I left

the barracks, and as I passed through the gates I breathed the cool morning air deeply, barely able to suppress the excitement I was feeling. Without looking back at my unit, I walked straight to the bus station as quickly as I could – the hour-long trek took me no more than forty-five minutes – and boarded a coach to Baghdad. The coach was almost full, but I managed to find myself a seat towards the back.

We passed the first couple of checkpoints without even being stopped. As we approached the third, a number of my fellow passengers were snoozing – we had all been up with the sun to catch the early coach – but I was in no state to sleep. We were still 200 kilometres from the capital, and already my mouth was dry with anticipation. I did not know what Saad had lined up for me, but the quiet confidence in his voice the last time we had spoken had given me reason to expect that things had been put in motion. The driver sent his assistant – a young boy of about fourteen – around the coach to shake the slumbering passengers. 'Checkpoint,' he told them. 'Have your papers ready so that we can pass through as quickly as possible.'

Everybody fumbled around for their documents; mine were already held tightly in my fist, although I made sure I did not touch the stamp to avoid any risk of its becoming smudged by the sweat from my hand. As we approached the checkpoint, the coach slowed down, coming to a halt at a gesture from one of the Red Berets. The doors opened, and a large, unsmiling border guard came aboard. His skin was dark – swarthy, almost – and he had a thick and immaculately groomed moustache. Nobody spoke. The Red Berets were vile: often they reminded me of the villagers from Hamam Al-Aleel – vicious and uncaring. Ordinary Iraqis referred to them as *zanabeer* – wasps – because of the way they swarmed threateningly the length and breadth of the country. No good could come of a conversation with a *zanboor*. Slowly he walked the length of the coach, scrutinizing every passenger's papers carefully before handing them back and moving on. I had no reason to be nervous – all my papers were in order – but somehow the silence in the coach was enough to make even the most law-abiding citizen feel edgy. Finally he reached me. 'Papers,' he said curtly, and I handed him my documents. He gave them only the most cursory of glances before putting them in his pocket. 'Get off,' he instructed me.

'Why?' I asked. 'I've got—'

'Don't ask any questions,' he interrupted. 'Just get off.'

I left my bag in my seat – I was confident that I would not be detained – and asked the person sitting next to me to save my place. But the guard interrupted again. 'Take your bag with you,' he told me.

The side of the road was heaving with people – both guards and ordinary citizens, who sat in the dust eating food or talking animatedly. None of them paid me any notice as I stood by the side of the bus waiting for the guard to finish his checks. Eventually he alighted and indicated to the driver that he could leave; as the bus left, my hope left with it. The guard told me to walk over to a square concrete building. Once there I was led into his office, where he took a seat, leaving me to stand opposite his desk. Another Red Beret sat in the same office, not bothering to conceal his interest in what was going on. 'Haven't I seen you before?' my captor asked.

'No,' I replied.

'Yes I have,' he insisted. 'I saw you only last week. You're forging papers for leave.'

I shook my head as I felt my stomach twisting. 'No,' I assured him, 'these are genuine.'

'Forging papers,' the guard repeated as though he had not heard me. 'Very serious.' He looked at me expectantly.

I could not decide what he wanted me to do. My instinct told me that he was waiting for an offer of a bribe, but I could not be sure, and I did not want to land myself in further trouble by trying to bribe somebody who was not as corrupt as I imagined him to be. Even if I wanted to bribe him, I had no idea how to go about it – what should I say, how should I say it? I had never found myself in this position before; and besides, I didn't have a great deal of money.

'I'm going to conduct some enquiries,' he persisted, 'make a few phone calls. I know you're forging papers, so you might as well confess now. If you do, I'll send you back to your unit for three months' solitary; if you don't, you know where you're going to end up: military tribunal then Abu Ghraib. You'll probably be there for fifteen years.'

'I'm not confessing,' I said weakly. 'I haven't done anything wrong.' Then it struck me that maybe I had a trump card to play. 'I'm to be transferred soon to Al-Mansour intelligence compound.'

The guard scoffed. 'You? At Al-Mansour? Don't make me laugh.' He called through the thin door of his office, and another guard appeared. 'Put him in the cell,' he ordered.

The cell was about ten or fifteen minutes' drive from the checkpoint. *Mudireeat indibaat al-firka'a* was the compound for processing absconders from the Third Brigade. The small metal door was opened and I was hurled inside. I had never been in such a filthy place. In one corner was a communal lavatory – little more than a foul-smelling hole in the ground. There was a flushing mechanism above it that clearly hadn't worked for years, and a small bottle containing water for cleaning yourself. Two fans hung from the ceiling, providing a little welcome coolness, but also circulating the putrid smells from the lavatory. Graffiti covered the wall, and a few glum-looking prisoners sat at one end, hunched up with their arms around their knees. I stood for a few moments, not quite able to believe what was happening to me, before, in despair, I joined them. My face fell into my hands in utter desperation.

Some hours later, the door opened again and the guard who had detained me put his head into the cell. The moment he appeared, my fellow prisoners rushed up to the door like hungry children to a sweet-seller. They started begging him to let them leave. 'I can get my brother to send you some money! Please, let me out,' one of them implored.

The guard sniffed the air dramatically. 'I'm going home now,' he told us. 'When I get there, I'm going to sit under the shade of my vine and eat cold watermelon while my wife cooks me a delicious meal. You know,' he said regretfully, looking directly at me, 'all this could have been avoided if you had simply rustled up a few notes.' He smiled an insincere smile, then slammed the door shut.

I stayed in that stinking cell for a week while the army's interminably slow internal mail system verified that my leave papers were in fact genuine. During that time, other prisoners came and went, and as I talked to more experienced inmates I began to understand why the guard had picked on me. I was neatly dressed, for a start. I liked to take pride in my appearance, but all the guard saw was a young man from a good home who probably had a bit of money. The Al-Mansour address on my leave papers had confirmed this. My leave was for eight or nine days, and that too counted against me. The guard knew that I had to be returned to my unit before the end of the leave period; if I had had only a couple of days' leave, the threat of one day in the cell would not have been enough to encourage me to pay a substantial bribe.

I listened to what I was told, but I took in very little of it; after a while I even stopped noticing the revolting conditions. All I could think of was Saad and my mother. They were expecting me back home, and they had made arrangements – what they were I did not know, but they had probably cost money and they were most likely time-sensitive. They had no way of knowing what was delaying me. My mother would be sick with worry that some accident had befallen me, and driven to distraction by the constant questions from my brother and sister – 'Mama, when is Sarmed coming home?' Saad, I was sure, would be imagining something more sinister. And with every day I spent in the cell, my chances of leaving the country were becoming more and more remote: the longer I stayed there, the less chance I had of getting to Baghdad.

After a week, tired and dirtier than I had ever been, I was released into the custody of a military guard. Confirmation had come through from my unit that my leave papers were not in fact forged, but it had been decided that there was no point in my going on to Baghdad as I had only a couple of days' leave remaining. Wordlessly I was ushered into the back of a military truck along with seven or eight other soldiers. Two Red Berets sat at the back keeping watch over us.

I wanted to cry with frustration as the truck headed south again, trundling down the road that took me inexorably further from the place I needed to be. My companions kept their distance – I assumed it was because I smelled terrible after my week in the cell – and the Red Berets eyed me suspiciously. Clearly they had not bothered to find out why I was being returned to my unit, so they assumed the worst. As I sat there, driven crazy with frustration, wild escape plans formed in my head. Perhaps I could bribe the Red Berets to leave me by the side of the road? Perhaps I could act with more bravado, charge to the back of the truck and hurl myself out? But my mad plots were the stuff of the Western movies that occasionally found their way on to Iraqi television. This was real life.

After about an hour of travelling, the truck approached a roadside service area. As well as oil and water for the cars that had stopped, there was a mosque and a restaurant. A string of coasters – small coaches that acted like buses – were lined up ready to take their passengers away. The place was humming with people going about their business as the driver and his assistant went out to freshen themselves up. They came back with a jug of water and a steel bowl, and the Red Berets allowed us all a few gulps. I was the last to be offered the water; having drunk deeply from the bowl, I turned to one of the guards. 'I need to use the toilet,' I told him.

'Go and crouch down and piss in the desert.' Soldiers were perfectly used to doing that.

'No,' I said. 'I need a shit.'

The two Red Berets looked at each other. 'OK,' one of them said. 'You've got ten minutes. If you're not back then, I'll tie a rope round your neck and drag you all the way back to your unit.' He opened the back of the truck.

As I jumped down from the truck, I heard my fellow soldiers trying it on. 'I need to go! I need to go!' they clamoured.

'*Ukulkhara,*' the Red Beret shouted in no uncertain terms. 'Eat shit!'

I walked into the main restaurant area. It was teeming with people and I soon became lost in the crowd. In the far right-hand corner was the door to the lavatory; to my left was a partitioned-off area for praying. I weaved my way towards the lavatory, where I freshened myself up and splashed cold water on my face in an effort to wash away the grime and sweat of the past week. As I walked back into the restaurant, I looked out of the front window. The Red Berets were standing by the truck smoking cigarettes; there was no way that they could see me from that distance in the hubbub of the building.

What happened next occurred as if in a dream. It suddenly struck me that the coasters were leaving every couple of minutes. If I could board one without the Red Berets seeing, I could be speeding away from the service area before they even knew I was gone. It didn't matter too much which direction I went in – once I was away from them they would have no means of finding me. My leave papers still had a couple of days to run, so with the luck I was surely due by now I could get through any checkpoints and be in Baghdad by the end of the day. It was dangerous, but I only had a split second to decide. I chose to make a run for it.

With my head bowed, I hurried towards the prayer area, intending to walk out of a side entrance to where the coasters were lined up. To my right were three men, kneeling down with their faces to the floor, deep in prayer. On pegs by the door were their robes. Checking that nobody was looking, I quickly grabbed one. As I pulled it down over my uniform, I realized it was far too big for me, so I pulled up some of the extra material and held it between my teeth, as was the custom in the south of Iraq. My army boots were visible beneath the robe, and must have been a curious sight; but I reasoned that if the Red Berets were to come looking for me, I would have more chance of melting into the crowd like this. I took a deep, tremulous breath and stepped outside. I headed for the coaster at the front of the line, noticing that there weren't too many passengers and that there were seats free at the back. Out of the corner of my eye I saw the Red Berets:

they had finished their cigarettes and were looking impatiently towards the restaurant. I bowed my head once more, stepped on to the coaster and found myself a back seat.

Gradually passengers started to return to the bus after visiting the service area. One man approached me. 'Is that your seat?' he asked me curtly.

'No,' I apologized. 'I only just boarded.'

'Well, it's my seat. I was sitting here.' He pointed to a free place by the door. 'You can go and sit over there.'

'Please,' I whispered, not wanting to attract attention but equally anxious to stay well hidden at the back of the vehicle, 'let me stay here.'

The man looked pointedly at the boots below my robes. He raised his voice. 'I'm not giving up my seat for some shitty little soldier,' he shouted. I cringed as he did so, and looked out of the back window where I saw the two Red Berets scouring the area, talking to other members of the military with urgent looks on their faces. Please, I silently implored the driver, please just go!

'Why can't you sit over there?' one of my neighbours said to the other passenger, but it only infuriated him more. Before I knew it, a shouting match was taking place around me. As it reached a peak, I saw the heart-stopping sight of a Red Beret approaching the bus – it wasn't one of my two guards, but I most certainly didn't want him to start asking me questions. I pulled the huge robe tighter around me, even partially covering my face, and tried to make myself as inconspicuous as possible; but it took only a brief glance from the Red Beret for him to see how suspicious I was looking. The second he clocked me he jumped off the bus and called to his colleagues, my guards. Within seconds one of them was on the bus, striding down the aisle with a grim look on his face.

He grabbed me roughly by the front of my robes and hurled me towards the door. The passengers on the bus were shocked into silence by his vehemence; he kicked me hard from behind as I approached the door and I fell heavily on to the dusty ground, where he continued to kick me in the stomach until I had to beg him to stop. 'Get up!' he shouted at me. I scrambled to my feet. 'Where did you get the robes?' he asked abruptly. I pointed at the side door. 'Take them off!' I rolled the robes into a bundle and handed them to him as he pushed me towards the army truck. Once there, the second Red Beret opened up and threw me inside. He climbed in himself, locked the back door and sat there, his finger resting on the trigger of his Kalashnikov while his colleague replaced the robes.

The truck continued its slow, uncomfortable journey south; the nearer we came to my unit, the more sick I felt at what awaited me. My fate would be down to the whim of the officer in charge, and although he had treated me well in the past I had no reason to believe he would look at all kindly on my attempt to abscond. All the horror stories I had heard about soldiers in my position rang in my ears, and although the heat of the day was strong, I felt myself shiver as a cold sweat broke out across my body. I knew that as soon as I got to the camp I would be hauled up in front of Taha and told to explain myself, so I desperately tried to construct some sort of excuse for my actions. My head was muddled, though, and I found myself unable to think straight.

The journey seemed to pass more quickly than usual, and when we stopped outside the base an *arif* was called. 'He tried to abscond,' one of the Red Berets told him as he threw me off the truck.

The *arif* said nothing; he just pointed towards the door of Taha's office. The Red Beret led me there and knocked respectfully; when we were called in, he explained in a dead voice what had happened. 'Leave us,' Taha said.

Taha must have seen the fear in my face, and he did nothing to ease it. The look he gave me was cold, and for a while he didn't speak. 'You realize how serious this is, I take it?' He uttered the words without emotion.

'Yes, sir,' I mumbled.

He sat there playing with his pencil. Suddenly he let out a deep sigh. 'I don't understand. Why are you so reluctant to take advantage of your promotion?'

'I just wanted to see my family,' I lied, before explaining the events of the past week. 'I wasn't trying to abscond, I just wanted to see my mother while I still had a couple of days' leave left.' It was an unconvincing story, I knew, but it might be enough to spare me from the full force of the army's brutality.

It was impossible to read from Taha's face what he thought. I assumed he was weighing up the fact that I had been unfairly treated with the fact that I had tried to abscond. I closed my eyes and sent up a silent prayer to Allah that he would believe me. 'OK,' he said after a while. 'As you've already been imprisoned, I'll do you a deal. The very least you should receive for this is three months in prison.' I was astonished to hear him say that – I knew he didn't have the power to impose such a harsh punishment. But Taha was relatively new to his post, inexperienced and ruthless. I had seen him be so with other soldiers; just because he had been friendly to me didn't mean he couldn't change at any moment. Perhaps he was trying to frighten me; perhaps he was just trying to make sure I went through with the transfer. 'I'll give you three days in solitary, and all leave is cancelled until you are transferred to Al-Mansour. But any more games like this and you'll be up before a military tribunal. Understood?'

'Yes, sir. Thank you, sir.'

'Good. Now get out of my sight.'

4

A Shot in the Dark

Solitary confinement does strange things to your head. It was very rare for soldiers to be confined to solitary – it was generally just for political prisoners – but occasionally units would have a different way of doing things. The cell in which I was placed was a derelict toilet with two small windows and a metal door. I was only in there for three days, and compared to my previous accommodation it was positively luxurious, but after the events of the past week each day seemed like a lifetime. I went through periods of genuine rage: rage against the corrupt Red Beret who had scuppered my plans; rage against the *arifs* on guard outside who pelted my door with stones to amuse themselves; rage against anything and everything. I would hurl my shoes at the wall, and if I heard laughter from the base in the evenings as my fellow soldiers started winding down, I would literally yell with frustration. As the evening wore on, a few less charitable soldiers would use the door of my cell for target practice.

At other times I would be more introspective. I would examine the graffiti that previous incumbents of the cell had carefully carved into the wall with their belt buckles, and as I did so, my mind became focused on deciding how to deal with my situation. I was desperate to call Saad and let him know what had happened; but more importantly, having got away lightly with one escape attempt, I was emboldened to try another. I had to get away before I was enlisted at Al-Mansour. As I was denied all leave until that point, I would have to be more robust in my plans and make my escape directly from the unit. I also knew I did not have much time. The *arifs* would know what Taha had said, and I would be under more careful observation. They would not expect, though, that I would attempt to break out the night I came out of solitary, especially considering what I had just been through. I decided to use that to my advantage.

I was let out of the cell at six o'clock, and I made my way straight to the living quarters, where I had my first shower since leaving for Baghdad ten days earlier. I wanted to call Saad and tell him in some roundabout way that he would be seeing me in the next few days, but the queue for the telephone was too long. I couldn't exactly start packing a bag in preparation to leave, so I wandered to the outskirts of the unit. The barbed-wire fence stood between me and the desert, and about a hundred metres away, halfway to the road, was a pile of old, burned-out military vehicles that had simply been dumped there. In the distance, patches of bamboo rose out of what I knew were small pools of water. I gazed for a while, calculating the distances, and then examined the fence. It had been dug deeply into the ground, but I found one small area where it looked as though an animal had been burrowing. The rolls of barbed wire had slightly curled up from the bottom, leaving a small opening – by no means big enough for me to get through, but if I could find something to cut it with I could enlarge it a little.

I did not want to be caught loitering, so I went back to the dormitory. Keeping myself to myself, I rooted around in my locker and found my old leave papers. They were crumpled, and some of the stamps were not as clear as they could have been, but they suited my purposes well. I took a black pen and, as carefully as I could, doctored one of them so that it appeared to have a current set of dates on it. It would not stand up to close scrutiny, I knew, but I had to hope that it would only be glanced at briefly, if at all. My plan was to break through the fence, make my way to the road and flag down a car to give me a lift to the coach station. Once there, I would board a night-time coach to Baghdad in the hope that the checkpoint guards would be less thorough at that time.

I needed one more thing. I wandered out along the edge of the parade ground until I came to the unit workshop, where army vehicles were repaired. It was still open, and a few soldiers were working inside. I wandered up to someone I vaguely knew who was sweeping the floor. 'You're working late,' I commented.

'Fucking *arif*,' he said with venom – he was clearly on some sort of punishment. I stood by a workbench chatting with him; he kept looking round to check that nobody could see him slacking, and as his head was turned I grabbed a pair of pliers and slipped them into my pocket. 'I heard you got solitary,' he asked.

I gave him a rueful smile.

'What was the reason?'

'There has to be a reason?' I feigned surprise. He laughed and started sweeping again as I wandered out.

And then I waited.

The dormitory lights were switched off at ten, and I lay there for at least an hour until the usual banter died down. Gradually people started to fall asleep, and the quiet babble of the few radios that were still switched on faded away. Every few minutes somebody would get up to go to the lavatory, but by about eleven o'clock it sounded as though most people were deep in slumber. I lay on my back, my eyes pinned open, my breathing steady but deep, as I prepared myself for what was to come.

Noiselessly I removed my covers and slipped out of bed. I had placed my uniform neatly under the bed, and now I gathered it up in my arms. The jacket contained everything I needed: my papers, what little money I had and the pair of pliers. I had also packed a small nylon bag containing an apple and a torch. I left my Kalashnikov where it was – although it would have been comforting to take it with me, I knew it was too cumbersome for what I had in mind. Swiftly I walked out of the dormitory, knowing that anyone who was still awake would assume I was going to the lavatory, and stood silently at the door that faced towards the parade ground.

All was quiet. A light shone on to the centre of the ground, where the Iraqi flag was raised, but there was no wind so it drooped limply at the top of the pole. Beyond it I could just make out two guards chatting to each other. I took advantage of the fact that their attention was diverted and walked towards the bare room that was used as a mosque. Every part of my body screamed at me to run, but I knew that if I did so I would only draw attention to myself. I moved swiftly, but even so it seemed to take an age to reach my objective.

Once inside, I removed my pyjamas and put on my uniform; then, clutching my nylon bag, I slipped out again. Keeping close to the walls, and stopping at any corners to check whether I could hear footsteps, I hurried towards the boundary of the camp. When the buildings ended, I got down on all fours and crawled towards the barbed wire. It took me a few moments to find the hole as I did not dare turn on my torch, but once I reached it I stopped to regain my breath and look around me.

At one corner of the perimeter fence stood an observation post. Searchlights shone down from it, but for now they were all directed inside the camp, and although I couldn't see anyone at that distance I knew that the post was occupied by heavily armed guards. Beyond the fence, the desert was still. I stared out to allow my eyes to become accustomed to the dark, and could just make out the pile of wrecked vehicles that I had decided to head for. I took the pliers from my pocket and went to work on the barbed wire. It took a good fifteen minutes of effort to make the hole big enough for me to squeeze through. In places I managed to break the wire; elsewhere I simply rolled it up as far as I could force it, doing my best to ignore my bloodied hands and all the while checking behind me to ensure no guards were anywhere near. My luck held, and I slowly managed to wriggle my way through to the other side.

Once I was out of the unit, I saw no reason not to hurry. I crawled – like they had taught me under the barbed wire – as fast as I could in the direction of the vehicles, twisting my head occasionally to keep an eye on the observation post and its searchlight, knowing that if it were to fall on me I would be lit up like a firework – and shot down just as noisily. But its beam stayed safely inside the camp, and I continued crawling.

Suddenly I heard a gunshot. I froze, not daring to move an inch. It was followed by another one, which seemed to ring through me, and then silence. I remained still while I regained my composure, and I told myself over and over again that what I had heard was nothing out of the ordinary. Guards would fire random shots into the air all night: it quietened the stray dogs that fought each other in the area surrounding the unit, it maintained the threatening military presence and it gave them something to do. We just learned to sleep through it.

I started crawling once more, doing my best to keep quiet and ignore the attentions of the wild dogs. The distance to the burned-out vehicles was deceptive in the darkness, and it took longer than expected to get close. When I reached them, I would stop for a few minutes to gather my thoughts before moving on to the road. I was only a few metres away, however, when the gunshots started up again. This time they were different: not the familiar sound of single shots being fired into the air, but the steady repetitive thud of a machine gun. I looked back: the searchlight on the observation post was moving frenetically, illuminating not only the inside of the compound but also the surrounding desert. I crawled more quickly towards the vehicles, but suddenly I heard the high-pitched whizz of bullets speeding past my ear. Some of them were lost in the desert; others hit the metal chassis with a sickening clank and threw up the occasional spark. I raised myself up on to my knees and headed round to the other side of the military vehicles, where I would be protected from the shower of ammunition.

All of a sudden, my right leg collapsed beneath me and a pounding pain coursed through it. I let out a shout, then put both hands over my mouth to silence myself. I felt my pulse pumping in my leg as my face creased with the pain. 'You've been shot!' – I stated the obvious in disbelief as I fumbled for the wound with one hand, the other still covering my mouth as I bit deeply into the fleshy part of my palm. My inner thigh was wet with blood, and I felt around the other side to see if there was an exit wound: there didn't appear to be, which meant the bullet was still lodged deep inside my leg. My every instinct was to shout out but I knew that to do so would be suicide, so I bit harder on my palm as I forced myself to battle with the agony and lunged to safety on the other side of the vehicles.

I sat on the ground, trembling as I waited for the firing to stop. I did not think I had been seen – the searchlight had not illuminated me – but maybe they had discovered my absence earlier than I would have thought possible. Perhaps they were firing randomly into the darkness of the desert, knowing that that was my most likely escape route. Or maybe they would survey the landscape with their binoculars; generally they would use them to spot wild dogs in the desert at which they could take pot shots, but tonight they appeared to know they had a more interesting quarry. In either case, I had no option but to get to the road as quickly as I could and try to flag someone down. I had no idea whether the guards from the base were out looking for me on the road, so I had to trust once more to luck. By now my leg had gone numb, but it was still bleeding heavily and I felt dizzy and light-headed. I knew I had to stem the bleeding, so I stuffed my beret down my trousers to cover the wound. I then removed my belt and, panting heavily, tied it tightly around my leg, hoping that the pressure would staunch the flow of blood.

I could not linger long – the pile of scrap cars was an obvious place to hide, so I knew I had to move away as quickly as possible. I got down on all fours, and as my leg hit the ground I felt as though I had been stabbed with a needle-sharp dagger. And then I crawled for my life, through the dirt and the dust towards the road. How I made it there I don't know. The final few metres were the worst, as I had to climb up a bank of rubble, boulders and discarded car parts; it took all of my rapidly sapping strength to pull myself up. When I finally reached the side of the road, I collapsed into an exhausted heap.

By now my leg was throbbing again; when I checked

the beret it was saturated with warm, sticky blood. I was on a main highway, so cars were passing with some frequency and I couldn't risk being spotted by one of the military vehicles that I was sure would have been dispatched to find me, so I crouched down with my head bowed in the hope that an incurious driver would mistake me for a rock, or not notice me at all. All the while I kept looking for a taxi.

It took fifteen minutes for one to approach, the slowest fifteen minutes of my life. When I eventually saw the familiar white light, I pushed myself to my feet and furiously waved my arms. As he slowed down I saw that the interior of the taxi was highly decorated, as was the custom of the south: a picture of Hussein, the disciple of Muhammad, was surrounded by little fairy lights and multicoloured garlands. The car came to a stop and the driver wound down his window. He was an old man, his face deeply lined and weathered, and he wore a traditional white headdress. 'I need to get to the coach station,' I told him from behind clenched teeth. 'As quick as you can.'

The cab driver looked my uniform up and down. 'What are you doing sitting on the side of the road?' he asked suspiciously.

I had not even considered what I would tell him, so I said the first thing that came into my head. 'I was cleaning my gun in the barracks and I shot myself,' I lied.

'Why aren't they taking you to the hospital?'

'No vehicles,' I gasped. It was not as unlikely as it sounded – it wasn't a life-or-death situation and an ordinary soldier would not be driven to hospital after a minor injury – so the cab driver accepted my story. 'Please, take me to the coach station.'

'OK,' he nodded. 'Get in the back.'

'I need to lie on my leg to stop the bleeding,' I told him.

'No!' he shouted. 'The blood will get everywhere. Wait there.' He got out of the car and retrieved a blanket from the boot – silently I urged him on, terrified that a car stopped by the side of the road would attract unwanted attention. He laid the blanket over the back seat before allowing me to climb inside. He drove off to the sound of my heavy, shaking breathing in the back. 'Why don't I just take you straight to the hospital?' he offered. 'It's OK, I won't charge you.'

How could I tell him that the hospital was the last place I wanted to be? Hospitals meant impossible questions and awkward answers – he might as well drive me straight back to my unit. 'No, please,' I said weakly, 'no hospitals. The coach station is fine.' I don't know quite what I was thinking – there was no way I would be allowed on to any coach in this state. But amid the pain and the confusion, I remember saying to myself that Allah had sent me this taxi just when I needed it the most; he was protecting me, and would continue to do so . . .

The taxi driver drove on in silence for a few moments.

'*Ibni*,' he said suddenly, 'son, you need to get that wound looked at. I don't know why you won't go to the hospital but you must have your reasons. At least let me take you to a doctor I know in the next village. He is discreet, and he'll look at the wound for you.'

By now I was sick with the pain, and deep down I knew that my leg needed urgent attention. I did not know for sure if I could trust this man and I knew he wouldn't be a proper doctor living out in a village – perhaps an anaesthetist. But I didn't have much choice. 'OK,' I whispered. 'Take me to the doctor.'

The village was a good half-hour away, but once there it did not take the driver long to find the house he was looking for. All the while I remained lying down in the back of the car, steeling myself against any bumps in the road that would aggravate the pain of my injury. When the car came to a halt, the driver spoke again. 'Wait there,' he told me. 'I'll go in and get him.'

I lay in the back seat for ten minutes, becoming increasingly nervous. What was taking him so long? Were they making phone calls? Were they alerting the authorities? By now, though, I had put my trust in him and there was little I could do in this strange place. Eventually, to my relief, he came back with another man. The stranger peered into the car, but because of the darkness I did not get a good look at his face. He opened the door, then quietly and efficiently removed the belt I had strapped round my leg and my trousers. I shouted out in pain as he pulled the beret away from the wound and briefly examined it. 'You didn't shoot yourself' were his first words to me. 'You've been shot.'

'No,' I insisted, 'I was cleaning my gun . . .'

'My friend,' the doctor interrupted, 'if you had shot yourself at that sort of range with an AK-47, I would not be removing the bullet. I would be removing your leg. There's not even an exit wound. This bullet rebounded off something before it hit you – that's probably what saved your life.'

I remained silent, too scared to admit to him that he was right as I remembered the bullets sparking against the metal of the burned-out military vehicles.

'I don't know who you are or where you've come from,' he continued, 'although I have my suspicions, but your very presence here puts me and my family in danger. I'll remove the bullet for you, but I'll do it here, not in the house. You don't ask my name or anything about me. When I've finished, I never want to see you again. Do you understand?'

I nodded.

'Wait there then,' the doctor told me. 'I'll need some implements.'

He returned with a small bag, a torch and a steel bowl of orange liquid. The taxi driver held the light in place while the doctor rubbed his hands with the liquid which he then smeared over the wound. It stung horribly and my leg tensed. The doctor removed something from the bag. 'This will hurt,' he told me. The object in his hand was a large pair of metal callipers, with flat feet pointing outwards. 'Ready?' he asked. I nodded, and he plunged the feet of the callipers straight into my leg, then pulled them apart so that the wound was held wide open. The pain was indescribable – ten times worse than when I was shot – and I shouted out. 'Be quiet!' the doctor barked, pouring more of the orange liquid straight into my leg. The way it burned was almost as if he had poured boiling water inside. 'This will help stop any infection,' he informed me. Once more I shoved my palm into my mouth and bit hard.

Leaving the callipers in the wound, the doctor rooted around once more in his bag. He pulled out a thick swab which he soaked with the contents of a bottle of clear liquid. 'Hold this to your face and breathe it in,' he told me. 'It will help the pain.'

I breathed deeply. The smell was sweet and pungent, and made me feel slightly queasy. The doctor brought out a pair of long, pointed forceps. 'The bullet went in at an angle,' he told me. 'You're lucky it didn't hit the bone, but it has lodged itself several inches into the leg. It may take some time to remove. Are you OK?'

I nodded and breathed a little deeper. I felt him insert the tips of the forceps into the wound; as the cold metal touched my bleeding flesh, my whole body shivered with the pain. The bottom half of my leg went numb once more, and my head started spinning.

It took nine or ten minutes to pull out the bullet. All I remember was the light of the torch and the constant, muttering prayers of the taxi driver. '*La hawla walla kuwata illa billah*, There is no greater help than that of Allah . . .' I did not even see the bullet when it came out – the doctor flicked it on to the road almost contemptuously before stuffing a clean swab inside the wound, soaked with yet more of the agonizing orange liquid. He slowly removed the callipers and, taking a needle, carefully inserted a few small stitches in my leg. Then he dressed the wound with a clean bandage, ignoring my whimpers with the professionalism of a man who had clearly done this sort of work many times before. When he had finished, he packed up his tools and disappeared indoors, muttering a brief farewell to the taxi driver.

The driver closed the back door and returned to his seat. He said nothing for a moment, as though he were deciding what to do next. 'I don't want to know the details,' he said, 'but tell me where you need to get to.'

'Baghdad,' I told him. There was no point keeping anything secret from this man now.

He nodded. 'You can't make the journey in this state. You need rest. Come to my house – you can spend the night in the guest room.'

'What about tomorrow?' I asked. 'Can you take me to Baghdad?'

He closed his eyes, as though I had asked him the one question he wished I would not.

'I'll pay you double,' I pleaded.

The taxi driver looked straight out of the window. I knew I was asking a great deal.

'Very well,' he said finally. 'I will take you to Baghdad.'

5

Baghdad

Baghdad: the centre of Saddam's power. The one place in the world I was trying to escape was the one place in the world I had to get to. It wouldn't take long for the military to come looking for me, and the only people I could trust to help me now were my family.

We had passed several checkpoints on the way, where the taxi driver had shown my altered leave papers. One look at me laid out in the back of the car, white-faced and sweating and covered in blankets, combined with the fact that a taxi from the south up to Baghdad was seriously expensive, convinced the checkpoint guards that I was very ill, and we were waved through without problems.

The heat of the sun was becoming intolerable, and the bullet wound in my right leg – bandaged under the white *dishdash* the taxi driver had given me to wear – was throbbing. As we drove through the suburbs of the capital, I tried to distract myself by watching the ordinary Iraqis going about their daily business. Gradually we muddled our way through the traffic-filled streets and headed towards the central region of Al-Mansour – my home. I gazed out of the window, staring blankly at the familiar sights, lost in my own thoughts. My mother had expected me home on leave a week ago. She would be worried – angry, probably – with no idea of the trauma I had undergone. She would find out soon enough, though, when the military police came knocking on her door asking where I was. I had a couple of days' grace – it would take time for the inefficient Iraqi communications network to get word to the capital that I had absconded – but when they came, I knew I had to be far away.

The taxi driver – he had not told me his name and I knew better than to ask, so I just called him *Hajji*, a term of respect for an older person – pulled up outside my grandparents' house. For a moment we said nothing as I looked straight ahead, preparing myself for the explanations to come. To wake me from my reverie he coughed and, with a gesture of apology, I fished out the money I had promised him – double fare, and the last few notes I possessed. Once he had the notes safely stowed away, he turned to look at me. '*Allah wiyaak. Bilsalamah*,' he muttered quietly. 'God be with you. Safe journey.'

'*Shukran*, thank you.' I nodded at him and got out of the car, then watched the vehicle disappear into the midday haze. He was clearly eager to put some distance between us, and I didn't blame him.

Through the door of my house I could hear the sounds of my brother and sister, Hamoudi (Ahmed) and Marwa, playing in the hallway. They were often to be found there in the heat of the day as it was the coolest part of the house, and their banter instantly comforted me, reassuring me that, no matter how dangerous my life had become, at home everything was as it had always been. I rapped on the door, aware that my arrival was about to change things for ever.

They opened the door, and their shouts of enthusiasm were like a balm. There was no shock on their faces, no concerned questions – just joy at seeing their elder brother again. 'Mama, Mama!' they sang as we hugged and kissed. 'Sarmed is here! Sarmed has come!' I hugged them once more, and then left them in the hallway while I went to find my mother.

She was sitting alone; the look she gave me was puzzled. She raised a questioning eyebrow but, in accordance with the traditions of the Middle East, she refrained from asking me any questions just yet. It was hot; I had been travelling and was tired. All I wanted to do was have a shower, put on some clean clothes, eat a meal and gather my thoughts. Questions could wait until later, and my mother sensed and respected that.

It felt good to wash away the dirt and blood, rinse the mud from my hair and pull on some clean clothes. My mother prepared a hot meal of soup, rice and bread – humble fare, but so welcome that it tasted as fine as a banquet in the presidential palace, and I fell upon it ravenously. She watched me as we ate, but still I avoided telling her what had happened. Despite everything, I was still a teenager with a teenager's preoccupations, and I wanted to put my troubles out of my mind for a few moments.

I drank a cup of tea, then sat down in front of the television to relax – not easy given my bullet wound. My leg was throbbing and felt impossibly heavy, and shocks of pain were running from my thigh all the way up my back. I forget what was being shown – a movie, I think – but I remember clearly the intermissions. Every half-hour the film would stop, and a fat man with a large moustache would appear singing a song about Saddam, praising him.

> Sir, we are your servants,
> In life you are our prize!
> In moments of worry,
> Your hand gives us joy.
> Whenever we face difficult times,
> By your hand they become easy.
> You are the father of generosity and goodwill,

With you we have overcome the difficult times.

We are the joys of your life,

We are the candles of your victories.

The song would be intercut with pictures of Saddam in his white suit surrounded by children throwing petals at his feet, images of the army marching by the statue of the unknown soldier in Baghdad, tanks forming part of the procession, and servicemen saluting their leader. Fantasies from the warped mind of a tyrant; there was only so much of this I could watch. I switched off the television in disgust and limped off in search of my sister to catch up on local gossip. There was a girl I was interested in – what news of her? Had my friends come asking about me? What were our cousins and the rest of our family up to? The questions were inconsequential but it was a relief to me to be able to focus on such trivia.

And then I called my uncle.

'Uncle Saad,' I told him, 'I'm at home. I need to see you. Can you come now?'

Saad knew better than to ask any questions. I suppose he could tell from the tone of my voice that this was not a conversation to be had on the telephone. 'I'll be there as quickly as I can,' he assured me.

Saad's car pulled up outside the house an hour later. With difficulty, he manoeuvred himself out of the vehicle. He did not knock on my mother's door. Instead, he went first to my grandparents' house to say hello to them. It would have been unseemly had he not. His filial duties fulfilled, he made his way slowly over to my mother's house. My mother made tea and offered it to her brother along with a glass of cold water, before telling my brother and sister to go to their grandparents' house. And then, as the three of us were sitting round the table, I took a deep breath and broke the news to them.

As the story of my first, unsuccessful escape attempt unfolded, my mother started huffing and puffing, wringing her hands and displaying the warning signs that I knew heralded an explosive display of maternal rage! I told her that I had injured my leg, keeping quiet about the fact that I had been shot, but it was not enough to stop her shrieks and shouts when I reached the conclusion of my story. 'Sarmed!' she cried. 'How could you do this? They could have shot you on the spot.'

There was nothing I could say – other than that I knew full well what would happen if they caught up with me. I had a little time, however. I knew that the name of anybody who went absent without leave for three days would be put into a register of absconders. Your details would then be sent to Baghdad, where a judgement would be made in your absence and a punishment decided upon according to the gravity of your crime: imprisonment, removal of ears, sometimes execution. Your unit would then be informed of this decision, and a soldier would be dispatched to your home to inform your family of it. Soldiers would queue up to be given this job – it meant an extra few days' leave, time away from the unit. (No matter that they would be expected to pay their own way to do this official business – it was worth it.) All this took time. Meanwhile, if I came across any of the Red Berets and was unable to explain my absence from my unit, I would be instantly arrested and imprisoned.

My uncle tried to calm my mother down, but she was in no mood to be appeased. It broke my heart to see her in that state because of me, but I could not help worrying about the danger of her shouting like this. The walls of the house were thin; our neighbours were close and often nosy. A woman who lived in the immediate vicinity had sons who were in the Republican Guard, and I could not risk her hearing the shouts coming from the house and putting two and two together. Saad and I exchanged a glance. 'Sarmed,' he said quietly but firmly, 'come with me. We're going for a drive, just the two of us.'

It felt good to be alone with my uncle in the car. There were a number of checkpoints between my grandparents' house and his, but I knew I would be safe with him. He was a former high-ranking officer, and other officials would afford him respect. He also carried a Hawiyet Sadeeq Ra'ees al-Jumhuriya – a card stating that he was a 'friend' of the leader of the republic, which was given to all war heroes, currently in excess of half a million people. It gave him a certain authority.

It also felt good to unburden myself fully of my story. 'I took a bullet in the leg as I was escaping,' I admitted to him.

Saad nodded. 'I noticed you limping. You need somebody to have a look at that. One of your aunties, perhaps . . .'

I shook my head. 'No,' I told him. 'I don't want anyone to see it. The wound will heal in time. The doctor cleaned it well.'

We drove on in silence. 'They will come for you, Sarmed. And sooner than you think.'

'I know.'

'We have to get you out of Iraq. It is not too late to go through with the arrangements I have made for you. You will not be safe until you are beyond the jurisdiction of the Republican Guard. I have found some people who can help.'

Saad's four little daughters greeted us with much excitement. We kissed and hugged, and though it was good to see my cousins, I was eager to know what it was that Saad had in mind. We made our way into the guest room and sat down. Saad handed me some documents. There was a passport with my name, complete with an exit stamp to Jordan, and a yellow and green military service card stating that I had permission to be absent from the army for a period to travel abroad. Such documents did not come cheap – the corrupt officials who provided them knew that they could more or less name their price – and the risk my uncle had run in acquiring them had been considerable. I was suddenly overwhelmed with love for this man who treated me like his own son, and was seemingly willing to take any risk to help me in my bid to leave Iraq. 'These should be good enough to get you through any internal checkpoints,' he told me. 'They are unlikely to be checked in any detail. But they won't get you over the border. The guards there are more vigilant. They have the means to verify whether your leave of absence is genuine; it won't take them long to discover that it is not.'

I looked blankly at my uncle. 'Then what am I going to do?'

'Have you heard of the Al-Shemerry?'

I shook my head. 'Who are they?'

'A Bedouin tribe who live around the Jordanian border. Very powerful in that region. I have dealings with some of their relatives who live near here. I've been told that they are willing to help people across the border.'

'What about the border patrols? Even if I avoid the checkpoints, surely the patrols keep an eye out for people trying to cross elsewhere?'

'That's why we use the Bedouin. They have been crossing that border for hundreds of years in order to trade. No one would dare strip them of that right.'

'Can we trust them?'

'It's in their interest to get you across the border. If you don't make it into Jordan, they don't get the money I will have to pay them.' He looked me straight in the eye. 'I'm not pretending it isn't dangerous, Sarmed. It is – very. But I think it is your only chance.'

I had to make a decision, but in truth I knew the decision had been made for me. 'When do we leave?' I asked him.

'Tomorrow. You have to get to Jordan, and you have to get there quickly. If they apprehend you in Iraq . . .'

'What?'

Saad looked away. 'You will face the firing squad. And there will be nothing I can do to help you.'

We sat in silence while I considered my uncle's plan. 'What if I meet a corrupt internal checkpoint guard like before?'

Saad gave me a mysterious look. 'I don't believe that will be a problem.'

'Why not?'

He smiled. 'Because I will be coming with you.'

I slept badly that night, although I relished the coolness of the primitive air-conditioning system as I lay on one of the grey metal beds in the bedroom I shared with the rest of my family. My thoughts were a whirlwind. Finally I had a chance – a real chance – of getting out. Over the years I had watched my peer group dwindle as, one by one, unhindered by obstacles as I was by my father, they disappeared to make a new life for themselves elsewhere. Eventually all that remained of my group were the ones who simply had to stay in Iraq because of their family, and the ones who were too scared to take the risk. And me. Now, despite everything, I was being given the opportunity to make a new life for myself as my friends before me had done.

My excitement was tempered by fear. Not a vague, unfocused fear but a genuine knowledge that there was still so much that could go wrong. I didn't know quite how many military checkpoints there were between Baghdad and the Bedouin village, but each one was dangerous – I knew that well enough from my past experiences. My uncle's chilling reminder of what would happen if I was caught resounded in my head. I would be placed against a wall with other absconders, my hands tied and a blindfold covering my eyes, and shot down by a firing squad. Then an officer would shoot me in the head at point-blank range to make sure I was dead. This was the punishment for those who had absconded twice – and that is what an unsympathetic accuser might well deem that I had done.

Even if we made the journey to the Bedouin village successfully, how did I know I could trust my guides? I would be putting my fate into the hands of people I had never met, and that made me nervous. And there were dangers even closer to home. I did not really suspect that the military would come knocking on my mother's door just yet, but in the quiet of the night even my most unlikely fears were compounded tenfold.

But there was also cause for relief. When Saad had told me that he would be accompanying me to the Bedouin village, it was as if a weight had been lifted off my shoulders and I felt more optimistic than I had for weeks. He would be wearing his decorated military uniform and a suave, confident smile. Surely, if the first of these was not enough to get us past the internal checkpoints, the second would be. I could not wish to be in safer hands.

My leg throbbed. Medicine was hard to come by, and painkillers were especially scarce. All I had been able to lay my hands on had been some paracetamol, and it certainly wasn't enough to stop the pain of a bullet wound. I tried to put it from my mind by running over the events of that evening. I had stayed late at my uncle's house, going over and over the plan for the following day. Around midnight he had driven me back to my grand-parents' house. My mother, brother and sister were still up when we returned, and the house was shrouded in the nervous quiet of anticipation. I could tell from the look on my mother's face that she was still angry with me. I hated to see that expression, but I knew there was nothing I could do or say to make her feel better. My uncle took her into the guest room, and they remained there for some time. I heard the gentle murmur of voices through the door, and I knew that Saad was explaining to her what it was that we were intending to do. Gradually my mother's voice became louder; Saad's, by contrast, remained perfectly calm. Once she had fallen quiet, he came out of the room and smiled at me. 'You'd better go and get your stuff together,' he told me. He glanced at my mother's anxious face. 'Take your brother and sister.'

I took Ahmed and Marwa by the hand and led them across the courtyard to the separate flat they shared with my mother. There I began putting together the things that I would be taking with me out of the country. I would not have room for much – there was no way I could carry huge bags with me across the desert; but my possessions were few in any case, and I limited myself to photographs, cassettes and other trinkets, items that would sustain me in a foreign land away from my family, as well as the small amount of money I had.

My brother and sister watched me pack. 'What is happening, Sarmed?' Marwa asked me. 'Where are you going?'

I knew I had to tell them the truth, and so we sat down together. 'I'm leaving Iraq,' I explained to them. 'Saad has arranged it. We go tomorrow.'

'How long will you be gone for?' they asked.

I shook my head. 'I don't know.'

'Are you going to go and see Uncle Faisal in Manchester?'

'I'm going to go to Jordan first. From there, I'll see if I can make my way to England.' I didn't tell them that what I was doing was illegal.

'Will you write to us?'

'Of course I'll write to you.'

'Will we see you again?'

I looked into the enquiring eyes of my brother and sister. How could I tell them that I did not even know if I would make it as far as the border? 'Of course we will see each other again,' I told them. 'I promise.'

I finished packing and went out into the courtyard. It was August 1994, I was eighteen years old, and I needed a few moments to myself, time to say goodbye to the place that had been my home when I was a young boy. Standing in the moonlight on that hot night, I remembered happier times. I remembered the hours I had spent caring for my menagerie – the dogs, the budgerigars, the tortoises and pigeons. I remembered the happy days I had spent climbing our date tree when its branches were heavy with fruit, gathering its harvest in a small basket. I remembered the times I spent with my family planting flowers in our garden, trying to create our own little patch of colour in the huge sprawl of Baghdad. I allowed myself a smile as I remembered my grandmother, bent with age, vigorously hurling a raw egg against the inside of the front door before anybody brought a piece of electrical equipment across the threshold. It was a common custom – where its origins lay, nobody knew – meant to ward off evil spirits and bless the equipment, but it brought great hilarity to the household every time she did it.

Suddenly it seemed very difficult to leave this little house, and perhaps, if circumstances had been different, when it came to this moment I would have decided to remain. When I was surrounded once more by the love and care of my family, the rest of the world seemed lonely and dangerous; but now I had no option. I allowed my hands to linger on the whitewashed walls, trying to absorb something of the place before I left it, most likely never to return.

The lone voice of a muezzin penetrated my sleep as it floated around the rooftops like a tendril of smoke disturbed by a gentle breeze. Its quiet monotone was punctuated by moments of lilting musicality: '*Allah u Akbar,*' it sang, 'Allah is great! I bear witness that there is no divinity but Allah! I bear witness that Muhammad is Allah's messenger! Hasten to the prayer! Prayer is better than sleep! Allah is great, *Allah u Akbar!*' A similar sound would be emanating from every mosque far and wide across the Middle East, calling the faithful to prayer. There was no time for me to visit the mosque, but my prayers that morning were fervently, if silently, said nevertheless.

My mother had prepared breakfast, but as we ate the tension between us was still strong and we spoke only a few words. When we did speak, we avoided the matter in hand, talking instead of more mundane things. Suddenly I heard a shout from my grandparents' house. It was one of my little cousins. 'Sarmed, Sarmed!' he called. 'Uncle Saad is here!'

I felt a momentary hesitation, a reluctance to go through with our plan, but I put my worries firmly from my mind. I knew how limited my options were. Without saying a word, I stood up from the table and went about gathering my things. Then, my small case in my hand, I made my way over to my grandparents' house, my mother, brother and sister following behind me. Saad had given my grandparents a bag of peaches. He always brought them something, some small gift to cheer their day – a watermelon, perhaps, or some dates. My uncle was wearing the trousers and shirt of his military uniform – the jacket, with its medals and honours, he had left in the car – and he had attached his false leg rather than have to move around clumsily with his crutches. They sat in the front room of the house, waiting for me.

It was a quiet farewell. Although my grandparents did not know the full details, they knew I was making a bid to leave Iraq, and they clearly felt the need to help me in whatever way they could, whether it was by a kind word or something more material. My grandfather sat nodding in his chair. He gestured to me to approach him.

'Yes, Jidoo?'

'Good luck, Sarmed,' he muttered in his quiet voice. 'May God be with you, and *inshallah* you will reach your uncle Faisal in England. Do not forget your family.' Few words, but well meant.

My grandmother had been preparing food for Saad and me to eat in the car on the way – kebabs and fruit, traditional Middle Eastern fare – and as she finished packing up the meal, she signalled to me. 'Come here, Sarmed. Come with me.' I followed her. In her bedroom was a cupboard which, when I was a child, had always been a place of great mystery to me. In it my grandmother kept what seemed to my childish eyes to be great treasures: sweets, old letters, gadgets, tools, videos and a VHS player, jewellery, packets of cigarettes. With a twinkle in her eye, she started to rummage through the cupboard. She had clearly hidden something in there, and hidden it well because it took her some time to find it. Eventually, and with a smile, she pulled out a woolly sock containing a thick wad of notes – American dollars.

'This is your auntie's money. It is what she earned from selling her gold.' Carefully she peeled off a hundred dollars. 'This is for you. It is only a loan, but it will help you get started.'

I did not want to take money from my family, but I knew my grandmother would not be refused, so I gratefully placed the notes in my pocket. 'Thank you, Bibi,' I said. A hundred dollars to start a new life. At the time it seemed like all the riches in the world.

My grandmother placed the remaining money back in her cupboard and turned to give me a big hug. 'The world is a dangerous place, Sarmed,' she whispered. 'Be careful.'

'I will, Bibi.'

Back in the front room, Saad was anxious to make a move. It was a long way to the border and we couldn't afford to delay. I hugged my mother and my brother and sister and then we walked out to my uncle's car. Under other circumstances, the sight of uncle and nephew limping together might have been comical. But there was no comedy here. My mother started to cry. I knew nothing I could say would make our farewells any easier, so I just held her tight and then climbed into the car. Through the window I could see that my sister was also crying, and I felt the tears well up behind my own eyes. I wound down the window. 'I'll be in touch as soon as I can,' I told them gently.

Then I turned to Saad, who was waiting for me to give him the word. 'Let's go.'

6

A Journey at Night

I did not look back as we drove away, and Saad was discreet enough not to speak until long after my home had disappeared into the distance.

The road out of Baghdad was long and busy. It was early but the sun was already hot, and I was glad Saad's green Toyota automatic had air conditioning. He didn't use it all the time as it would be expensive to replace; but this was a special occasion, and the fact that he had it would give him more authority if we were stopped at any checkpoints. As we struggled down the congested streets, flustered pedestrians looked hopefully at Saad. In Baghdad there were lots of official taxis, but never enough to satisfy demand at the busy times of day. Today I saw only the occasional familiar white-and-orange taxi, the battered 'taxi' sign on its roof – as if the gaudy colouring were not enough to make clear that it was for hire. Some taxis were decorated with garlands and religious symbols in the same fashion as the one that had brought me up from the south; others had a photograph of Saddam fastened to the dashboard – either an expression of their Ba'athist sympathies, or after a threatening word from a passenger who was a member of the security services. 'I see you have a picture of Muhammad. What about our leader, may God protect him and bless him? Why do you not have a picture of him?' More often than not, the terrified driver would waive that particular fare.

When cabs were scarce, anyone with a car would suddenly switch professions and become a taxi driver for an hour. Saad's air-conditioned Toyota was popular, and he could always be sure of a good fare if times were lean. He would pull up to a crowd of people waiting for transport and ask who was going in his direction. Intense negotiations would follow – money would be discussed, certainly, but potential customers would also want to be sure that this opportunist chauffeur had the right intentions and was not some bandit with a false smile, fully prepared to murder them for the few dinars in their pocket. During the day this might not have been that likely, but late at night it was an alarmingly common occurrence: while the penalty for absconding from the army could be horrifically severe, the punishment for murder – if you could show that it was done in self-defence (easy enough with a few bogus witnesses) – was six months' imprisonment.

But there would be no fares today, nothing to hinder us in our objective. Our journey would take us first around the outskirts of Fallujah, and the road that would lead us there was good and full of traffic. It was unlikely that we would encounter any difficulties on that early stretch and it would only take us about an hour. Once past Fallujah, however, things would become more problematic. It was about 450 kilometres from there to the village where we were heading. Although the highway that continued west to the Jordanian border crossing was relatively new, in places where heavy military vehicles had left their mark it was in poor repair, and the going would be slow. We did not expect to get to our destination until the following day.

The state of the highway, however, was the furthest thing from my mind. I could think of nothing but how we were going to talk our way through the internal check-points. I asked Saad how many there would be. 'Three, perhaps four,' he said with a shrug.

I kept quiet. I did not want Saad to know how scared I was about approaching them, but I think he sensed my fear. 'Don't worry about it,' he told me calmly. 'If they stop us, leave everything to me.'

I was dressed neatly in a pair of jeans and a T-shirt, and together we looked perfectly respectable. 'We want to give them the impression that you are my son.' He gestured at the jacket of his military uniform, which was neatly folded on the back seat. 'When they see that, it will instil some kind of respect into them,' he told me. 'If they assume that you are my son, that respect will rub off on you. Let me do the talking.'

It did not take long for us to approach a checkpoint. My uncle slowed down, and a look of intense concentration passed over his face. 'Give me my jacket, Sarmed,' he said. I reached into the back, handed him the jacket and he wriggled his way into it, keeping one hand on the steering wheel. 'Good,' he said. 'Now, open the glove compartment.'

I did so. Stashed inside was a 9mm Beretta handgun. This was not an ordinary Beretta. For a start it was an Iraqi-made *tarek*, and it had been given to the officers of the Iran–Iraq war who had been awarded bravery medals as a 'gift' from Saddam. It bore a small insignia on the handle that identified it as a special-issue weapon; the owners of such items were afforded particular respect by other members of the military. Saad took the gun from me and placed it prominently on the dashboard.

As we approached the checkpoint, I saw the usual hubbub of activity. Coaches were parked by the roadside, as were white-and-orange taxis – more modern than the one in which I had journeyed the previous day. Their occupants were hanging around outside, talking, drinking, cooling down and generally taking a break from their journeys. The checkpoint itself was little more than a bunker on the side of the road, there to protect the guards from the sun. The Red Berets gripped their AK-47s firmly, and their light-armoured vehicles stood nearby as they looked through the papers of those drivers they had decided to stop.

I saw all this from a distance. My uncle continued to slow down and as he did so I felt my heart in my chest. I did my best to look straight ahead and appear calm. But as I strained my face into a look of sombre innocence, I could not help but feel that to the trained eyes of the Red Berets I showed all the signs of a guilty man. For a split second I thought I caught the eye of one of them. He had clocked me. Surely the look of fear on my face would arouse his suspicions. I breathed deeply.

'*Lat khaaf*, Sarmed,' said my uncle. 'Don't be afraid.' He kept looking straight ahead as if he didn't have a care in the world, but I could not take my eyes off the guard. As we passed him, I foolishly turned my head and our eyes locked; I saw him begin to raise his arm before I jerked my head away. My uncle kept the car moving slowly forwards, ignoring the guard's attention, and, suddenly, the checkpoint was behind us. I looked in the rear-view mirror, fully expecting to see one of the light-armoured vehicles pull away. I wanted to tell Saad to drive more quickly, but I knew that would arouse suspicion; and gradually the checkpoint faded behind us. We had passed our first obstacle, it seemed, without incident.

As we drove further from Baghdad, the traffic became less and less heavy. From my point of view, this was not good. The fewer vehicles there were along the road, the more chance we had of being stopped at the next checkpoint. Although the Red Berets would be more likely to stop any coaches or taxis, they would still pull over a substantial number of ordinary vehicles, and that could mean us. Perhaps I should have felt more relaxed, having made it through the first checkpoint safely; in fact I grew more terrified.

It did not take us long to reach the western deserts – bleak, sandy terrain on either side with no sign of civilization. We approached a second checkpoint. It was less busy than the first, but our luck held and we were waved past with no questions asked.

It was late afternoon by the time we reached a rest stop known as Kilometre 160, just west of Al-Ramadi. Part restaurant, part garage, part mosque, this place catered for the most basic needs of the travellers along the road. We ate a meal in the restaurant, which was the least filthy part of the whole complex, and then made our way to the car to spend the night. I tried to sleep, but without much success.

We left early the next morning. Continuing west, we eventually reached a fork. One road led up towards

Markiz Al-Waleed Al-Hudoodi, the checkpoint with Syria; the southernmost fork was the one we took, towards Jordan via Al-Rutbah, where the Al-Shemerry lived. Gradually the traffic, which had been sparse, became heavier. It did not take long to see why this was happening: there was a checkpoint up ahead, and to my horror they were stopping every car that passed. Terrible scenarios flitted through my brain. Did they know Saad and I were heading west? Had the military police been to my mother's house and extracted a confession from my family? Why would they be stopping every car that passed if not to look for us? Whether such thoughts were going through Saad's mind, I cannot say. He simply put on his military jacket once more and made sure his Beretta was in full view. We were silent as we sat in the line of cars awaiting our turn, but the time we spent in that queue gave me the opportunity to imagine increasingly awful explanations for the delay.

Eventually, two Red Berets walked up to the car in front of us. They stood there for some minutes asking questions of the driver, then asked him to pull over to the side of the road. As he did so, one of the guards followed him; the other unsmilingly waved us forward. He appeared at the driver's door and gestured at Saad to wind down the window. He took one look at his military uniform and saluted him, but there were no pleasantries. 'Where are you going, sir?' he asked.

'We are going to see family in Rutbah.' My uncle smiled at him.

'Is this your son?'

Saad nodded.

'Your papers,' the Red Beret said to me.

Nervously I handed him the fake military pass. He studied it carefully. The seconds ticked by. Out of the corner of my eye I could see the driver of the other car being frisked and then taken into the guards' hut. There was an anxious silence; even Saad could not think of anything to say. The Red Beret looked at me, looked down at my papers, and then handed them back. 'Do you always keep your Beretta on the dashboard, sir?' he asked my uncle.

Saad flashed him a grin. 'Why?' he said. 'Are you looking to buy one?'

That was all it needed. The Red Beret smiled for the first time. 'You can go, sir,' he told us. Saad inclined his head politely, they saluted each other and we were waved on. As we passed the checkpoint, I let out an explosion of breath, and Saad and I laughed with relief. We were through.

We arrived at a small Bedouin village at around seven o'clock that evening. There were perhaps twenty houses made of mud and brick. We knew that the tribesman we were looking for lived in this area, but we had no means of finding him. There was nothing for it but to go knocking on doors. 'Do you know Abu Mustapha?'

To start with we were met with blank faces – either they did not know this man, or they did not want to let on to somebody in military uniform that they did. But eventually we found someone who was willing to help. He pointed to a small road leading away from the settlement. 'Take that road,' he told us. 'It will lead you to another village. He is well known there. Ask anybody and they will point you to his house.'

We returned to the car and followed the road he had indicated. As we drove, the silence of the desert gradually impressed itself upon us, and we grew quiet ourselves. Sure enough, after about half an hour, we came to another village. A group of children were playing in the street, so we stopped and asked them the same question. 'Do you know Abu Mustapha?' With typical childish exuberance they shouted that they did, and pointed us towards what seemed to be a more modern house than the others. As we made our way to it, a few children who, barefoot and filthy, had been playing in the driveway at the front of the house came out to the car.

'What do you want?' they shouted. 'Who are you?'

Saad limped up to them. 'Is your father at home?' he asked.

The children scurried indoors, calling for their mother, who soon appeared at the door. 'Who are you?' she repeated, suspiciously.

'My name is Saad Al-Khatab,' my uncle replied, 'and this is my nephew Sarmed.'

'What do you want?'

'We are here to see Abu Mustapha.'

'Are you sure it is him you want? What makes you think he lives here?'

'I am a friend of relatives of his in Baghdad. They described to me where he lives. I have a business proposition for him.'

Reluctantly, the wife nodded. 'Wait here,' she said and went inside.

We waited for several minutes before a huge figure appeared at the door. He had a thick white moustache and white hair, and was wearing a black gown; in the failing light of the desert evening he was an impressive sight. He stood in the doorway and said nothing, so my uncle repeated the words he had already spoken. 'My name is Saad Al-Khatab, and this is my nephew Sarmed.'

Suddenly a smile lit up the tribesman's face; it was clear that he understood why we were there. He clapped his hands and shouted at his children to stop playing and make themselves scarce. Then he called to his wife. '*Ya marr'a!* My dear wife! Prepare supper!' he shouted. He extended his arms to Saad and me, and ushered us inside. Our presence did not seem to surprise him. Maybe he had been forewarned of our arrival; maybe people like us arrived on his doorstep out of the blue on a regular basis.

We were led into Abu Mustapha's guest room. It was a peaceful place: there was no television, and the walls were covered with embroidered religious texts. The seating, of course, was all Bedouin-style, with cushions scattered across the floor. We sat down, and tea was brought in to us, along with sherbet – concentrated fruit juice diluted with water. We were thirsty after our long journey, and the drinks refreshed us. Abu Mustapha sat opposite Saad and me, a huge imposing figure shrouded in his flowing gown. I glanced at my uncle and saw a look on his face that I recognized, a calm, almost humble aura he emanated before engaging in any kind of negotiation. As we sat there, there were frequent moments of silence as my uncle and the tribesman smiled and nodded to one another. Each knew what the other wanted but there was a ritual to such meetings, and nothing was said yet of the real reason for our presence. Tradition dictated that we should wait until after we had eaten together – or at the very least finished our first round of drinks – before we even began to discuss business.

Abu Mustapha fingered his *sibbha* – a string of beads – and continued smiling knowingly at us. Every few minutes he would shout '*Allah bilkhair*' – 'Welcome! God is good!'

'*Allah bilkhair*,' we would intone. It was the traditional reply.

Gradually my uncle engaged the tribesman in small

talk. He explained that he was acquainted with his relatives in Baghdad, that he had had business dealings with them before now. 'You are interested in guns?' the tribesman asked out of the blue.

My uncle shrugged. 'A little,' he replied.

Abu Mustapha stood up suddenly, left the room and returned with a *berrnaw*, a rifle with an extra-long barrel. It was the traditional weapon of the Bedouin of that area, and could shoot over hugely long distances – two to three kilometres. The tribesman had a look of pride on his face as he handled it, mixed with a glint in his eye that spoke volumes: he was, he was demonstrating, a man who could take care of himself.

We admired his gun for a short while, and then food was brought in. His wife presented a steaming dish of *baagillah*. It was a favourite of mine, an Iraqi dish of lamb, naan bread and beans traditionally served on Fridays after prayers. Saad and I fell upon this feast as hungrily as politeness would allow.

When we had finished eating, more tea was brought. This was the sign for us to get down to business. I had expected my uncle to explain the situation in more round-about terms than he did; after all, we did not know yet that we could trust this man sitting opposite us. He was full of smiles, but who knew what those smiles could be hiding? 'My nephew here, Sarmed, has absconded from the army.' I gave Saad a sharp look, but he held a restraining hand up to me and continued. 'He needs to leave the country and he wants to go to Jordan. Your relatives told us this might be something you could help with.'

For a while Abu Mustapha just sat there, expressionless. The silence in the room was thick, broken only by the sound of him fingering his *sibbha* and the constant whirr of the fan above us. We had come all this way, but I had never imagined that this man would say no to our request – and he certainly did not seem to be jumping at the chance. I had an uncomfortable feeling that we might have to drive back to Baghdad that night. He looked carefully at me, and then at my uncle. It was impossible to read his eyes. Finally he spoke. 'I do not recommend that you go to Jordan.'

In that moment I knew we had a chance of persuading him. He had not turned us down outright, so it was clearly something he was prepared to consider. But why not Jordan? And if not Jordan, where? As if in response to my unspoken question, the tribesman said, 'Syria.'

Saad shook his head. 'Syria will be too dangerous for him.' He was right. The relationship between Iraq and Syria at that time was bad. Iraqis were not allowed to work in Syria for a start – in Jordan, there was at least a chance. More worryingly, if I was apprehended, the likelihood was that I would be taken for a Ba'ath Party spy and imprisoned for I don't know how long.

Abu Mustapha shook his head. 'There are many border patrols between here and Jordan. The government spends a great deal of money on surveillance in that stretch of desert. The Syrian border police are poorly paid, and there are fewer of them. There are landmines near the border with Jordan too. We think we know where most of them are, but . . .'

Saad was adamant. 'It is a risk we are prepared to take.'

Abu Mustapha looked uncomfortable. Maybe he was more familiar with the crossing into Syria, I don't know. He let out a heavy sigh. 'If you choose that route, we will have to make the journey at night. And I cannot guarantee you safe passage. There are wild animals in the desert.' He looked straight at me. 'They do not much care what they eat.'

I shuddered, but Saad stood his ground. 'If he is captured in Syria, the treatment he will receive will be just as bad as any he can expect in Iraq. Jordan is more civilized, and from there he has a much greater chance of finding his way to the West.'

Again there was a silence. Finally Abu Mustapha closed his eyes and slowly nodded his reluctant acquiescence.

He shouted for one of his children. Almost immediately one of his sons entered the room. 'Go and find your uncle,' his father told him. The boy said nothing, just left the room swiftly. The three of us remained seated; barely a word was spoken between us. From the corner of my eye

I looked at Saad. He seemed as calm as ever, his expressionless face indicating none of the panic Abu Mustapha's reluctance to take the route to Jordan had instilled in me. The Bedouin knew this stretch of land better than anyone – certainly better than Saad or me. They had crossed these borders all their lives, and their ancestors before them had done so for hundreds of years. They knew where the dangers lay. If they were worried about our plan, should we not also worry? I tried to push such thoughts from my mind. I had trusted my uncle this far; he had not let me down. And as I looked at the imposing figure of the tribesman before me, I could tell that he would be able to look after himself – and me. That, at least, was some small comfort.

After about half an hour, the door opened again and another burly tribesman walked in. 'This is my brother,' said our host. We shook hands in greeting as more tea was brought. 'My young guest,' he gestured towards me, 'is of a mind to travel to Jordan.'

Immediately his brother shook his head. 'No,' he said emphatically. 'Too dangerous. We can't take you all the way into Jordanian territory, but we can take you into Syria.'

It felt as if we were back at square one. His look was stern, and he did not appear to be open to negotiation. I think my uncle must have seen that in him; without delay he played his trump card. 'My nephew is not going to

Syria. It is Jordan or nothing. If you are unwilling to take that route, we must leave now. It is a long way back to Baghdad.' He sat back without taking his eyes off the Bedouin, and sipped his tea.

The two men looked at each other, aware that their lucrative business arrangement might be disappearing before their eyes. Eventually the brother nodded in agreement. 'We have details to discuss,' he told Saad.

My uncle nodded. 'Wait here, Sarmed,' he told me as the three of them stood up and went outside. I heard the murmur of hushed negotiations through the door, and I knew that they were discussing what Saad would pay them to undertake this illicit venture, along with terms and guarantees. My uncle would then have to persuade them that I would not be a liability in the desert – that I knew how to take care of myself. When they returned, there were smiles all round: a deal had been struck. 'The arrangements have been made,' Saad told me simply, his tone altered now from one of concern to one of confidence. 'You will stay here tonight, and you will make the journey after sundown tomorrow.'

'What about you?'

'I must leave,' he told me quietly.

'Now?' I asked him. The moment seemed to have come upon us very quickly.

'There is no reason for me to stay, and I have business to attend to in Baghdad.' He smiled. 'Don't worry,

Sarmed. You are in good hands. Everything will be fine.'
He turned to the tribesman and his brother. 'You have my
thanks, and the thanks of my family. *Inshallah*, as soon as
we hear that he has made it across the border, I will give
the remainder of the money to your relations in Baghdad.'
With that he left the room.

I followed my uncle to the car in silence. To say goodbye to this man who had risked so much for me was
almost more than I could bear. Neither of us had spoken
of the one thing that was foremost in our minds throughout this eventful journey: we might never see each other
again. And now, standing by the car in a strange village
somewhere in the Iraqi desert, the time had come to say
our farewells. As I removed my things from the boot,
Saad fished a piece of paper out of his pocket, on which he
had scribbled a name and an address. 'When you arrive in
Amman, find this person. His name is Wissam, and he is
a friend of mine from many years ago. He will help you in
any way he can.' My uncle put his hands on my shoulders.
'Be strong,' he continued, 'and trust no one. You have to
have your guard up all the time.'

He went to the car and came back with something
wrapped in material. 'I want you to have this. Handle it
with care.'

Gingerly I unwrapped the package. Inside I felt cold
steel. It was a black Beretta handgun – not the special-
issue Beretta that he had positioned on the dashboard but

another weapon from his collection. 'You might need it to protect yourself after the Bedouin leave you,' he explained.

I said nothing while Saad hugged me, holding me close and breathing deeply, smelling me as if trying to absorb something to remember me by. 'Goodbye, *habibi* Sarmed,' he whispered, 'and may Allah be with you. You are my son, and you always will be. I will miss you very much.' For the first time ever I heard his voice waver, and I saw his eyes filling up. I did not trust myself to speak; nor could I think of anything to say.

How long we stood locked in that embrace, unwilling to leave each other, I couldn't say; but eventually, reluctantly, Saad climbed into the car and started the engine. He wound down the window and looked me straight in the eye. 'Be careful,' he told me solemnly. 'And remember, the genuine man never forgets his family. We are sending you to freedom so that one day you may rescue them from this place.' Then he slowly pulled away.

I stood on that weathered track in the near-darkness, my eyes full of tears and a small bag at my feet containing everything I now possessed in the whole world, and I watched my uncle's car as it became a cloud of dust settling in the distance. And then I turned back to look at the Bedouin house where I was a stranger.

I had never felt so alone in my life.

* * *

I made my way back to the guest room. Abu Mustapha and his brother were still there, and I tried, half-heartedly, to make conversation; but it was clear to them how upset I was at having said goodbye to my uncle, and that now was not the time for polite chit-chat, so they made their excuses and left me alone. I was grateful to them for that: I needed time to compose myself.

I faced a picture of Mecca that adorned the wall, and prayed. I prayed that my uncle would make it back to Baghdad safely; I prayed for my family; and I prayed that the next thirty-six hours would not be filled with the dangers that haunted me. I opened my bag and looked through my things. The trinkets I had brought with me seemed out of place so far from home, but it was a comfort to have them as a reminder of what I had left behind. I took a pen and a piece of paper and tried to write a letter to Saad, but somehow I could not find the words to express what I wanted to say, and the letter was abandoned almost before it was begun.

Behind me I heard the door open, and Abu Mustapha entered with his wife. She laid a mattress on the floor so that I could rest. 'It would be best if you tried to sleep,' he told me. 'We wake early, and there is much to do tomorrow in preparation.'

I nodded, and thanked his wife for her kindness. Alone again, I redressed my wound with some clean bandages I had taken from home, wincing as I removed the doctor's professionally inserted swab and replaced it with the limited skill my military training had afforded me. It still hurt beyond belief, but I had other worries to occupy my mind now: as I lay down and closed my eyes, I knew that when sleep came – if it came – it would be fitful and disturbed.

Sure enough, I awoke early the next morning. Abu Mustapha entrusted me to the care of his nephew – the son of his brother who had been with us the previous evening. It was explained that the three of them would be accompanying me that night, and I was to spend the day learning as much about their life as I could. If we were stopped by border patrols, it was essential that I was believed to be one of them.

The Bedouin are nomads of the desert. Traditionally they would herd and trade livestock – sheep and goats – moving across the desert according to the seasons. Divided into tribes, each tribe historically led by a sheikh, the Bedouin take no account of international boundaries. They had – and still have – a disregard bordering on contempt for anything or anyone that attempts to tamper with their centuries-old traditions, and especially for governments that try to impose nationalities upon them. That concept is meaningless to the Bedouin. Their concern is not with the outside world. They are still traders, wandering across the desert from village to village to buy and sell their livestock, crossing borders at will, often travelling at night to avoid the scorching heat of the desert sun. They are, as they have been for hundreds of years, an accepted feature of the Middle East landscape and nobody – not even Saddam – would contemplate removing from these desert wanderers the right to travel where and when they please. The Al-Shemerry tribe had a huge number of settlements in the area around the Iraqi, Syrian and Jordanian borders.

This did not mean, however, that they were above suspicion. The authorities were not so naive that they did not realize that certain Bedouin tribesmen took advantage of their nomadic status to earn themselves extra money. The border guards in this region allowed the Bedouin to wander at will, but they kept close tabs on them. If we had travelled by car, we would have been stopped and searched without question; walking was our safest option. There was no guarantee that we would not be stopped and questioned as to our movements, however, and if this happened it would be essential that I looked and acted like one of their tribe.

Abu Mustapha's nephew was a little younger than me – perhaps sixteen – but the ravages of life in the desert had not been kind to his features, which were weathered beyond his years. We sat together in a communal court-yard around which the village's houses were built. In the middle of the courtyard, the burned-out shell of an old car lay in the dusty earth, and thin-looking sheep and goats wandered around at will. The nephew quizzed me about myself and my life in Baghdad and Mosul, and I did my best to answer his questions patiently, aware that the world I was trying to escape might well seem strange to him, just as his world did to me. But my mind was focused on the path that lay ahead, not that which lay behind, and I was eager to talk to him about our evening's work. 'What will I have to wear tonight?' I asked him.

'Come with me,' he said. We went inside and he found me a dark, embroidered *dishdash*. He also gave me another, heavier robe. 'This will make you look the part.'

I put the garments on. They had a heavy, musty smell to them, but they fitted well enough. He then handed me a long stick. 'On the first part of our journey we will have sheep with us,' he explained. 'This is what we use to herd them. It's not difficult. If you tap them on the right, they will turn left; if you tap them on the left, they will turn right. Come with me, we can practise.'

We returned to the courtyard, and he identified the sheep that belonged to his family. The families would mark their animals on a particular part of the body, either with henna or with some other dye, so that they could distinguish which beast belonged to whom. Together we practised herding the sheep that we would be taking with us, while the nephew explained to me that if I was spoken to, I would have to try to speak in their dialect. This would be difficult for me – the accent was different from that of Baghdad, more like the accent of Samarra or Tikrit, and I did not believe I would be able to fool anyone. I did my best to practise with the nephew, but I could tell by the look on his face that I was unconvincing. I would have to hope no border guards spoke to me.

The day passed slowly. As the sun was setting I sat in the guest room waiting for my guides to tell me it was time to leave. When Abu Mustapha arrived with his brother and nephew, I saw that they were wearing headdresses tied tightly round their heads and their chins, and they had strapped bullet belts in the shape of an X around their bodies. Both of the older men were carrying their evil-looking *berrnaws*. I looked at them enquiringly. 'In case of wild animals,' Abu Mustapha said. 'Come, we need to get moving.'

I put on my Bedouin garb, grabbed my bag and followed them outside. My belongings were strapped to one of the sheep, and the place was full of activity – primitive bells around the necks of the cattle clinked as they wandered freely; children ran around and the wife was cooking bread in the courtyard. It was a heady, homely smell, and under other circumstances it would have made me hungry; but even though the journey ahead was long, my stomach was churning from apprehension and I had no thought for food. We left the bustle behind us and set off into the silence of the desert, four Bedouin tribesmen and seven sheep, a common sight in the deserts of Jordan and Iraq and one which I hoped would pass unnoticed.

As soon as we were clear of the village, Abu Mustapha spoke to me. 'In that direction,' he pointed away from him, 'if you walk for twenty miles, you will hit the Syrian border. But the border with Jordan lies this way.' He pointed straight ahead. 'We are heading for an area where there are fewer Iraqi patrols,' he told me. 'I hope we do not encounter any, but if we do, you must leave it to me to do the talking. Do not attract attention to yourself.'

'What if they ask who I am?'

'We will simply tell them that you are our relative and you are coming with us to visit family.'

It didn't seem very convincing to me, but I could do nothing now but trust my guides. I nodded, and looked ahead. Even in the twilight I could see the desert stretching out before us, and I wondered how on earth these people could navigate their way through such a featureless expanse of land. Behind us, the lights of the village twinkled in the distance; ahead was a barren, hilly landscape. Small bushes dotted the desert sands, spiky cacti of various sizes, some small and unassuming, others huge and gnarled. 'We will take you across the border and point you in the direction of the road that will take you to Amman,' Abu Mustapha continued.

'Can't you take me to the road itself?' I asked him. I didn't relish the idea of being left alone in the desert.

He shook his head. 'It would be too dangerous. The Jordanian border guards know that we would never travel along that road – we need to make them believe we are travelling between villages and the road is completely out of the way. If they catch us heading towards it, they will be sure to ask questions that we do not want to answer, and they will check us out thoroughly. It won't take them long to find you.'

After a couple of hours, we arrived at a neighbouring village. This was where we were to deliver the sheep and, as was the custom, we were expected to sit and have tea with Abu Mustapha's relatives. It was about eleven thirty, and very, very dark when we left.

It was impossible to see what lay in front of us, but the Bedouin seemed in no way unsure of their route. This was not the darkness that I was used to in the city, or even in the desert surrounding my unit; here we had only the light of the moon. We carried torches, but used them only when absolutely necessary, to avoid drawing attention to ourselves. We could still just see the village behind us, and somewhere, far away, the distant lights of another settlement. The tribesmen used these landmarks as points of reference, and occasionally consulted a compass by the light of a match; but their most important navigational tool was their own knowledge of the desert.

As time wore on, I became aware of the engulfing silence, the stillness of the desert. The Bedouin talked in low voices ahead of me, but other than that and the sound of our own footsteps, there was no noise.

Suddenly the silence was broken. In the distance I heard an unfamiliar sound, somewhere between a bark and a high-pitched whine. It shocked me, and I stopped walking for a moment. 'What is that?' I asked nervously. 'What was that howling?'

Slowly Abu Mustapha turned to look at me. He was smoking a cigarette, and the light from the tip vaguely illuminated his face, giving him a sinister aspect. 'They are the wolves,' he said quietly, in an almost sing-song voice.

'If they catch you,' added the nephew, as if sensing my tension, 'they will rip you into little bits!' He grinned at me.

I gave him a flat look. For some reason he was clearly enjoying my discomfort, but I would not let him relish it for too long. I turned away and continued walking; but though I tried to remain nonchalant, beneath my studied calm was a terrible sense of panic. As we continued our slow march, the howling grew nearer. Whether the wolves had sensed our presence, I couldn't tell; but it was not something I wanted to find out. Abu Mustapha clearly had the same thought. He lifted his hand, and we came to a stop. Swiftly he raised his rifle in the direction of the howling and fired a warning shot. It seemed to do the trick. The howling receded, for now at least.

The later it got, the more edgy I became. The sound of

the wolves had worried me, and in the dark I became increasingly aware that there might be any number of other hidden dangers in the desert that night. I was wearing my army boots, which was a relief because I trod on all manner of unknown, unseen objects and textures. My great fear was that I would tread on a slumbering snake. Had I been wearing my army trousers, it would have been less of a worry as they were made from tough material; but under my Bedouin *dishdash* I was wearing only thin jeans which would not have been robust enough to withstand a snakebite. Snakes had always been my greatest phobia, and I do not think I would have been able to continue my journey if I had encountered one.

Every so often the wolves grew closer, and Abu Mustapha would fire a shot towards the animals to keep them away. The sound of the *berrnaw* was twenty times louder than any handgun, so it encouraged them to stay clear. But I also had reason to be nervous of the gunshots. Each time the tribesman fired, it announced our presence to any border guards who happened to be in the vicinity. It seemed unlikely that we were going to avoid their notice for long.

It had been fully dark for about an hour when we first saw the lights of a patrol vehicle. Rather than head straight for us, it drove round us in a circle, and then disappeared from sight. 'Perhaps they didn't see us,' I said to Abu Mustapha.

'No,' he replied. 'They saw us. They will be back.'

He was right. We continued through the desert, and some time later we saw lights from a different direction. Whether or not it was the same patrol I couldn't tell, but it seemed likely that they had been circling us, perhaps to make us nervous. Eventually what looked like a pick-up truck approached us head on, stopping directly in front of us with the headlights beaming straight into our eyes. In the back was a large spotlight, and a guard sat there operating it. I froze momentarily, but then remembered what Abu Mustapha had told me: 'Do not attract attention to yourself.' I lowered my head and stood at the back of the party, keeping quiet. Abu Mustapha approached the patrol vehicle. '*Allah bilkhair! Allah bilkhair!*' he called congenially into the night.

Three patrol officers got down from the car. They did not look friendly. 'Who are you?' the driver asked roughly.

'My name is Jaffar Muhammad Hassan, known as Abu Mustapha, from the Al-Shemerry tribe,' the tribesman replied smoothly.

'I see,' replied the driver. 'One of my brothers-in-law married into your tribe. Where are you going, Abu Mustapha?'

'We are visiting relatives in a village nearby, but we have no truck so we travel on foot.'

The driver did not seem to find this odd – it was

common enough for the Bedouin to travel in this way. He turned his attention to the rest of us. 'And who are these people?'

'This is my brother, and these are his sons.'

The driver looked closely at us; I avoided his gaze, worried that if I caught his eye he would ask me a question.

'You should come to our house,' Abu Mustapha said suddenly to divert the driver's attention. 'On behalf of my village, you are most welcome!' It did not seem an odd invitation – such gestures of hospitality are central to Bedouin tradition – but the other two border guards seemed particularly unmoved by it. It served its purpose, however, as the driver shifted his focus from me and back to the tribesman.

'Abu Mustapha, I expect you all to return to your village, and I do not expect any of you to go missing.'

The tribesman smiled. 'Of course,' he told the driver. 'If only my vehicle hadn't broken down.' The two other border guards eyed him suspiciously, then they all climbed back into their vehicle. 'You are welcome any time in our village,' he called after them as they screeched away across the sands.

I watched them disappear behind a hill. 'Do you think they will come back?' I asked.

Abu Mustapha shrugged. 'Who knows?' he answered me non-committally. 'We had better keep moving. The border is very close.'

We walked for another hour, and gradually in the distance I began to notice moving lights. 'What are they?' I asked nervously. I was still terrified that the patrol would return, and any sign of movement compounded those fears.

'That is where you are headed. It is the road into Amman. We must leave you soon.'

Slowly the lights ahead grew imperceptibly closer, and once more Abu Mustapha raised his hand to call us to a halt. 'We can't take you any further,' he said. 'We have bypassed the two main border checkpoints on the road. All you need to do is continue in that direction towards the lights and you will be OK.'

I nodded.

'If you hear the wolves, fire some warning shots into the air. It should scare them off.'

'Thank you for your help,' I said. It seemed inadequate, but what else could I say?

'*Bilsalamah*,' he replied in acknowledgement. 'Be safe.' He hugged me perfunctorily and quickly kissed me on each cheek. The others followed suit, before silently turning to retrace their steps. It did not take long for my guides to disappear into the blackness, leaving me with nothing but my bag and my gun.

Never had I felt so vulnerable. As the sound of my guides disappeared, I stood perfectly still and tried to accustom myself to the solitude and the silence. It was some minutes before, with renewed determination, I started to make my way towards the road. Now I was alone, my senses became heightened as I strained my eyes and my ears to judge if any unknown danger was close. Occasionally I would look back and think I had caught a glimpse of the patrol cars' headlights; but if I did, they were distant – they would not be able to see me from so far away. I could just see the road from where I was, and there were no patrols ahead; I would be very unlucky to meet anybody now – unless I was forced to fire the Beretta, and as all seemed reasonably silent around me I decided not to do that.

I soon realized, however, that sounds in the desert could be deceptive. More than once I stopped still because I thought I had heard an unfamiliar noise alarmingly close, but I told myself over and over again that it was a faraway sound carried to me by the gentle but fickle night breeze. I kept the pace as fast as my wounded leg would allow, my eyes fixed on the occasional light from the road ahead, and I realized that it was not only sounds that could be deceiving, but distances also. Although I had no conception of time, the road did not appear to be getting any closer, and the longer I hurried through that dark expanse, the more unnerving my solitude became. As I walked painfully, I could feel the swab around my bullet wound become wet – clearly the stitches had opened slightly from the movement.

Then, out of the darkness, I heard a sound I could not ignore, a sound that immediately stopped me dead. It was not new to my ears – it was unmistakably the same howling that I had heard with the tribesmen – but it was shockingly close. I stood still for some moments, aware only of the trembling whisper of my own heavy breath, before hearing another howl that made the blood stop in my veins. It was as loud as the first and no less desperate, but it was not its closeness that filled me with a sickening sense of horror: it was the direction from which it came. The first howl had been somewhere to my right, the second to my left.

I have never known fear like it. A cold wave of dread crashed over me; I felt nauseous and all the strength seemed to drain from my body. I know I should have fired my gun in the air, but in that minute some other impulse took over, an impulse that forced any faculty of reason from my head and replaced it with blind panic. Foolishly, I ran.

I could never have outrun them. They were lean, desperate with hunger; this was their territory. I was limping and terrified. The more noise I made, the more I attracted their attention. I became aware of more wolves around me – I don't know how many, but it was clear they were hunting as a pack and I was their quarry. Blinded by my tears, I stumbled, and their baying became more frenzied. Then, as if by some prearranged signal, the pack fell silent.

About twenty metres ahead was a bush. In the darkness I could scarcely make it out, but I could tell there was movement close to it. I stood absolutely still. Vaguely I saw silhouettes ahead, creeping towards me. There were three, maybe four of them. I gripped my Beretta nervously; despite my fumbling I managed to release the safety catch and load the chamber, but my hand was shaking too much for me to be sure of an accurate shot even if I had known precisely where I was aiming.

Suddenly the moonlight caught in the eyes of one of the animals, and for a moment it was illuminated. I will never forget its appearance: this was not a furry white wolf like those I had seen in pictures; this one was thin, bony almost, and dirty. There was a madness in its eyes that suggested it was riddled with rabies, and it was more vicious than anything I had ever witnessed, or hope I ever will. Its eyes seemed disproportionately small for its face, but there was something almost human about it; as our glances briefly locked, it snarled and pawed at the sand, revealing its teeth. I wanted to run, but I knew there was no way I could get away from these fast, hungry beasts; and in any case my legs had frozen to the spot.

And then, as one, the wolves started to run towards me, the momentary silence broken by the wicked sound of their barking and snarling. Almost as a reflex, I opened fire.

The magazine of the Beretta contained only nine

bullets. In quick succession I fired several shots blindly as the wolves hurled themselves towards me. The first few shots disappeared into the night, and although the noise of the gun stopped their charge for a moment, the animals had clearly worked themselves into a frenzy at the prospect of fresh meat so close; rather than turn and run as I had hoped they might, they scampered round in a circle before continuing their approach. They were close enough for me to smell – a sickening, rotten stench.

Once more I fired, all my skill with a gun dissolved by fear; it was more by luck than judgement that I hit some of the animals when they were only metres away from me. I heard them yelp as the bullets seared into their flesh, but I knew I was not safe yet. There was at least one more out there, and suddenly everything had fallen silent. I spun round, my arm outstretched and my quivering hand gripping the handle of the gun with all the strength it had, trying to spot whatever wolves remained as I stepped backwards, away from the animals I had hit. How long I continued like that I cannot remember, but gradually I became aware of another sound. I stood listening for some moments before I realized what it was: one or more of the wolves were biting into the carcasses of their injured – but not yet dead – colleagues.

The animals had been distracted by easier meat, and I had no option but to run. I circled round where I thought the beasts were, and headed as fast as I could towards the road. I was shivering and sweating from the fear; the wound in my leg made me limp and slowed me down completely; at one point I stumbled and, thinking in my near-delirious state that I had fallen upon a sleeping snake, I started shouting into the darkness for help. I lay on the ground, trembling, for about five minutes until behind me I became aware of the noise of more wolves fighting over the dead animals. I did not know how long it would take them to strip the meat off the bodies, but I wanted to be well away before they did so. That was the impetus I needed: I pulled myself up and continued to hurry – half running, half limping, always glancing behind me and occasionally firing one of my few remaining bullets in the direction of the wolves – towards the road.

For forty-five minutes I ran, stopping only occasionally to catch my breath and to vomit on to the sand through fear, propelled more by a horror of the wolves than a desire to reach the road. Eventually I got to it. There were very few cars, and I was in no state to tell whether those that passed were military vehicles or not. I collapsed. The wound in my leg hurt more than ever, and I could feel the sticky wetness of the blood beneath my trousers. I was in shock. I was freezing cold. I was unable even to speak. The lights of the cars on the road blurred before my eyes into a sea of movement, and as nervous exhaustion and delirium set in, I became vaguely aware of what looked like a white border-control vehicle stopping a few metres past me. I heard voices around me, but could not make out any faces. Out of the confusion I heard a man's voice. 'Get him in the car,' he said in an accent I didn't recognize, 'and we'll take him back to the border crossing.'

'No,' I rasped, not even knowing who I was talking to. 'I can't go back to the border. I need to get to Amman . . .'

But as I spoke the words, my head fell heavily on to the ground, and blackness engulfed me.

PART TWO

NO GOING BACK

7

Amman

When I regained consciousness – perhaps it was seconds later, perhaps minutes – they were looking me over and talking in hushed tones. I could tell they were male by the sound of their voices, but their faces blurred in and out of focus as I lay there stretched out on the road, and I heard myself repeat the words I had already spoken: 'Please, I can't go back to the border. *Don't* take me back to the border.'

The blurred faces looked at each other. 'What are you doing by the side of the road?' one of them asked without disguising the suspicion in his voice. I tried to answer, but the words that came out of my mouth were confused and incoherent, and suddenly I felt myself being picked up by the arms and dragged along the road towards the car. The wound in my leg throbbed as my heels scraped along the rough surface, but soon enough they gently lowered me back down to the ground.

I looked around me, my head starting to clear. It was still dark, and the lights of the car seemed overly bright to my tired eyes, blinding me and still preventing me from seeing exactly who these people were. I felt a knot in my stomach at the thought that they must be border patrol guards, and the conversation that followed did nothing to ease my concerns.

'We'd better search him.'

'What for?'

'Find his papers, see who he is. Look at him – he's in no state to tell us himself.'

Almost involuntarily I clutched the bag I was holding. I didn't want anyone to rifle through my things, although I could hardly deny anything to these officials – if indeed that was who they were.

'We haven't got time for this,' one of the men said impatiently. 'The sun is coming up soon and it's a long way to Amman. I don't want to be driving in the heat. Let's just take him back to the border and let them deal with him.'

'No,' I whispered hoarsely, causing them to look round in surprise that I had spoken again.

The other man bent down in front of me. He was wearing a *dishdash*, and I remember his dark eyes sparkling in the beam of the headlights. 'What's your name?' he asked me quietly.

'Sarmed,' I told him.

He nodded mutely. 'And what are you doing lying by the side of the road, Sarmed?'

I peered more closely at the man. Everything about his demeanour was wrong for an official: his clothes, the way he spoke in a concerned voice rather than harshly demanding immediate answers to his questions. But still I couldn't tell him the truth. It would have been reckless of me to come clean, especially when his companion – the driver, presumably – seemed so keen to get rid of me and continue his journey.

As I decided how to answer him, I heard one of the car doors open. 'What's going on?' a voice asked – a woman's voice, which instantly put me more at ease. Suddenly it seemed much more likely that this was just a family group. 'Who is he?' She walked round to where I was sitting and gently put her hand on my cheek. 'You need water,' she told me. 'I have some in the car.' Seconds later she was handing me a bottle, and I drank from it gratefully. The driver was pacing about in the background, clearly wanting to be off, and as I finished drinking his friend repeated his question. 'What are you doing here?'

I looked straight into his eyes with all the sincerity I could muster. 'My car was stolen,' I told him shortly.

He raised an eyebrow, as if urging me to tell him more.

'There were two guys by the side of the road,' I continued, lying with a little more confidence. 'They flagged me down and I pulled over to give them a lift, but they had a gun and they forced me out of the car, beat me up and then drove away. That's why I'm in such a state.'

The man nodded his head, scanning my face for any signs that I was not being truthful. Whether he found any or not I can't say, but I felt that there was still an air of mistrust around him. 'So why don't you want to go back to the border? It's not far – you can report the crime there.'

I shook my head violently. 'I'm Iraqi,' I stated, though it was clear that he already knew that from my accent. 'Those guys stole all my papers. If you send me back to the border, I'll never have any chance of finding my car again and I won't be allowed to stay in Jordan.' In the end, I knew, I would simply have to appeal to his better nature, and that of the woman who seemed to have taken a shine to me. 'Please,' I begged. 'I can't go back to Iraq.'

'But . . .' he started to protest, but I interrupted him immediately.

'Give me a lift to Amman. *Please*.'

'We can't give him a lift,' the driver barked from the darkness on the side of the road. 'The car's too full of people as it is. Where are we going to put him?'

The others were quiet. Awkwardly I pushed myself up on to my feet, wincing as a shock of pain ran through my gunshot wound, then peered into the car. The driver had a point. In the front passenger seat was a small, sleepy child – clearly he had been travelling on the lap of whichever adult was sitting there – and in the back seat was a girl of about eight, another older man and a young man of about my own age. It was full to capacity, but I knew I had to persuade them to take me. My only other option was to wait for a coach, but the road was almost empty – I had no idea how long it would be until a coach passed, and even if one did I was worried about how I would flag it down. I walked round the car, desperately trying to come up with a solution. As I did so, I heard the woman start chanting a prayer in a light, monotone drone. When she had finished, she began entreating the driver. 'Don't send him back to the border. Can't you see how scared he is?'

'No.' The man was adamant. 'There's no room.'

'We can squeeze up,' she offered.

'Don't be foolish.' The driver glanced over at me and then turned back to the woman. 'Look at him,' he said distastefully. 'He stinks.'

He was right. I looked down over the heavy *dishdash* the Bedouin had given me and saw the stains where I had vomited down my clothes in fear. Added to the fact that I had sweated like never before, I can't have been an appealing prospect. But I couldn't let that get in my way. 'I'll hold on to the roof rack,' I told them out of the blue.

The three of them stared back at me uncertainly. 'It'll

be easy,' I said, trying to persuade myself rather than them. 'I'll sit here.' I indicated the small metal frame that was attached to the boot of the car and on to which their luggage was strapped. 'I'll hold on to the roof rack here.' I climbed on to the luggage to show them. It was uncomfortable crouching there, but I thought I could manage it for a while.

The man who had been questioning me walked over. 'What if you fall? I could bind your hands to the roof rack with rope,' he suggested. 'That way you'll be safer.'

I shook my head. 'It's OK,' I told him. 'I'll be able to hold on.' I didn't much like the idea of being shackled to the car – I was used to being on the run now, and I didn't want anything to hinder me if I had to escape.

'This is stupid!' The driver stormed back into the fray. 'I can't drive to Amman with him clutching on to the back of the car like that. I'll have to drive slowly, and it will take us all day to get there. He'll fry in the heat.'

'We won't have to take him all the way.' His colleague was backing me up. 'Just until we find another vehicle to take him. A taxi or a bus – there's bound to be something coming along soon.'

The driver looked pointedly along the road. There were no other cars in sight. 'Whatever.' He shrugged. '*Yalla*. Come on. We haven't got all day.' He stomped off and after a few seconds I heard the unmistakable sound of him urinating against one of the low scrub bushes that lined the road.

The woman looked after him with amusement in her eyes. 'Now we've stopped,' she said lightly, 'we should eat something. Are you hungry?'

I nodded keenly, then sat down again to reserve energy for my next ordeal. Meanwhile, the others got out of the car and eyed me suspiciously without speaking. The woman placed two bowls in front of me, both wrapped in muslin cloth and tied together at the top with a heavy knot. She unwrapped them and offered me the food they contained. In one bowl was *kofte* – ground meat mixed with onions and herbs – and in the other was bread. '*Tafadal*. Go on,' she said, encouraging me to help myself. 'Eat.' I took some food and devoured it quickly while she offered it around to the rest of the party.

We had been there for about half an hour when my rescuers decided to set off again. 'Are you sure you'll be able to hold on?' the woman asked me, worry etched on her face.

'He had better be,' the driver muttered. 'I'm not going to travel at a snail's pace on his account.'

'I'll be fine,' I assured the woman. I climbed up on to the back of the car once more, hitched my bag on to my shoulder, pulled my Bedouin robes tighter around me, then clutched the roof rack as firmly as I could while the others clambered back into the car. I closed my eyes, mumbled a quick prayer, and we set off.

At first the driver took things slowly and carefully, making sure he did not drive over any bumps in the road. But as his confidence, and mine, increased, so too did his speed. Grimly I held on as the wind blew in my face, my eyes half closed to protect them from the elements. It didn't take long for my arms and the rest of my body to become stiff and uncomfortable, so I occasionally allowed myself to let go with one hand as I shuffled into a less stressful position, then held on tightly again as the car shuddered at high speed over the less than perfect road surface.

As we drove, my mind was turning somersaults. How had I got myself into this position? The wolves were still fresh in my thoughts, and as I squinted out at the bleak expanse of desert that was just starting to lighten up with sunrise I wondered how many more of those awful beasts were out there. It wouldn't do to find myself alone again at the side of the road – I clutched on to the roof rack with renewed vigour and tried to put all notions of falling from my mind.

The road remained fairly empty. Occasionally a car would pass us travelling in the opposite direction, its headlamps announcing its presence on the long, straight road a long time before it was actually upon us; but whether their occupants found the sight of a frightened young man clutching on to the back of the car they passed a strange one, I can't say – nobody stopped to look, and our car was travelling too fast for anyone to overtake us from behind. It was a far cry from how things would be a few miles up the road in Iraq, where the fear of check-points and border guards would have made this way of travelling impossible. Here there was just the possibility of random spot checks. The scenery around me might have been practically identical, but already I could sense the differences between the two sides of the border.

We drove like this for about half an hour, by which time my arms and wrists were aching from holding on so tightly, and I was becoming nauseous. My robes were wrapped tightly around me, and the sleeves had blown up like a parachute from the speed. Every time we hit a bump, the shock, unsoftened by the car's shoddy suspension, would reverberate through my whole body. Occasionally my mind would wander as I reflected on the almost dreamlike events of the night; but I would be brought harshly back to earth when I realized that my grip on the roof rack had begun to slacken.

I felt the car slow down slightly and the driver veered into the middle of the road, so I had to steel my body against the pull in the opposite direction. I swore under my breath – what was he playing at? – but then I noticed that the driver had put his hazard lights on. I peered over my shoulder. Behind me were the unmistakable lights of a coach's headlamps, and in the instant I became aware of it there was a deafening noise, a screech of a horn as the coach driver tried to warn this strange car ahead against driving so dangerously. My nerves already frayed, I wanted to cover my ears with my hands, but it wasn't an option as I had to maintain my grip on the car; instead I scrunched up my face and focused on holding my position. The car's driver, however, remained firm. He stayed in the centre of the road, gradually slowing down and waving his arm out of the window to indicate to the coach driver that he should pull over. Whether it occurred to him that this was strange behaviour – like a bandit trying to hijack the coach, or a couple of drunks fooling around – I don't know; certainly I remember feeling relief that I might soon find myself a more comfortable mode of transport. After a few minutes of driving like this, the two vehicles gradually came to a stop in the middle of the road.

The two men climbed out of the front of the car and walked towards the coach. 'Stay there,' one of them told me as they passed. 'We'll do the talking.' I did as I was told.

There was a hiss as the doors to the coach opened up, and after a few seconds' pause two other men climbed down – the driver and conductor, I presumed. One of them, a short, squat man with an ugly face, was carrying what looked like a piece of heavy metal piping strapped to his hand with a sturdy length of leather. From the way he held it, it was clear that this was a weapon and that he was prepared to use it. For a moment nobody spoke. 'What do you think you're playing at?' the man holding the piping finally growled at my two new acquaintances.

The man who had been sitting in the passenger seat pointed at me. 'He needs a lift. We can't travel with him like that for much longer.'

None of the suspicion left the other man's face. 'Does he have any money?'

'I don't know. I'll ask him.' He walked back to me. 'Well, do you?' he asked.

'A little,' I said warily. 'American dollars.'

He reported this back to the coach driver, whose eyes softened slightly although he maintained his grip on the metal piping as he walked up to me. 'OK,' he asked, 'what's your name?'

I told him.

'You're from Iraq?'

I nodded.

'Which tribe?'

'The Al-Samarrai.'

'And what happened to you?'

I repeated the story about my car being stolen, taking care to make the details the same as those I had given earlier. The driver listened without much interest. 'Where do you want to go?' he asked.

'Amman.'

'It will cost you fifteen American dollars.'

Fifteen dollars. A sizeable chunk of the money my

grandmother had given me only three days before, but I wasn't in a position to haggle. I fished inside my bag and brought out the hundred-dollar note my grandmother had given me, then handed it to him. He nodded curtly and indicated to me with a flick of his thumb that I should board the bus.

Painfully, but with some sense of relief, I climbed down from the car and approached the two men who had given me the lift. 'Thank you for your help,' I told them simply.

The driver didn't respond – he just walked back to the car. But his friend gave me a little more time. '*Bilsalamah*,' he said. '*Inshallah* you'll find your car.' We exchanged a meaningful look, and as our eyes met I realized he hadn't believed a word of my story.

'Thank you,' I said again as he walked back to the car. I stood there for a minute, watching the car head off along the road, before the conductor hurried me on to the bus.

It was packed with maybe forty people. They all looked at me curiously as I climbed on, but by this time I was too exhausted to allow their stares to worry me. There was no chance of a seat – even the conductor was sitting in the aisle – so I dumped my bag on the floor and prepared myself for a long, uncomfortable journey to Amman.

It didn't take much time for the other passengers to grow used to the sight of me, for the mild excitement caused by my arrival to subside, and now that it was clear to the conductor that I was not a threat he became a bit more friendly, asking me questions that I didn't really want to answer. What was my name again? How many people were there who robbed me? What did they take? What was I going to do? His questions were well-meaning enough, I suppose, intended just to pass the time, but I was in no mood to answer them with anything but the curtest responses, and eventually he left me to my own thoughts.

Everything had happened so quickly in the last few days that I had scarcely had the chance to organize the events in my head. It seemed impossible that only five nights ago I had still been in the army barracks near Basra, a place that seemed a million miles away from me now. As I thought back over the events that had followed my escape, I realized how lucky I had been – had the coin fallen differently on any number of occasions my circumstances would be very different to those in which I found myself now. It made the discomfort of the cramped coach that bit more bearable. Every time the vehicle slowed down, though, I had to suppress a shudder of fear, and I realized that I had been living with a constant terror of being stopped and searched. Just because I had managed to cross the border didn't mean that I could simply shrug off that terror. My passport, with its fake Jordanian entry stamps, would not stand up to prolonged professional scrutiny, and although checkpoints and security guards were not a part of daily life in Jordan as they were in Iraq, I did not find it easy to escape the paranoia that had been with me for most of my life.

It was not just fear of capture that knotted my stomach; it was fear of the unknown. Up until now I had focused solely on making it across the border into Jordan. All my energy had been channelled into that one aim, and I had not given much thought to what I would do once I arrived here. I had very little money and I knew nobody. Had anyone asked me, I would have told them that my plan was to travel to England to live with my uncle; but at that moment England seemed like an impossible dream.

The coach trundled on, and I remained lost in my thoughts.

I was awakened from my daydream by the sound of a woman's voice. I looked up to see her sitting there – an old lady, clearly an Iraqi, next to a young child – telling him to move and let me have his seat. I shook my head. 'It's OK,' I told her. 'I'm fine. Don't worry.'

But with quiet firmness she insisted. 'Come and sit here. You're tired, you've had a rough night. The boy can swap with you – he'll be fine.' The child looked at me with wide eyes and nodded, so I gratefully accepted the old woman's offer and took the seat by the window. We started chatting, but somehow I did not find her questioning as intrusive as the conductor's – I told her my name, and repeated the story of my car being stolen, and even told her proudly that I was travelling to Amman en route to England. It made me feel better to tell her that, almost as if I was making the plans in my head more concrete. I refrained from asking her too many questions about what she was doing in Jordan, because I knew she was unlikely to have had much difficulty in obtaining permission to leave Iraq. That was the way with elderly people – too old to be of any use in the country, they were allowed to leave so that they would not be a burden. Saddam had no use for old ladies; it was fit young men like me that he wanted.

It was much lighter by now, and as we journeyed on I found myself gazing out of the window. Every now and then we would pass a hostel of some description on the side of the road, and it was only then that it suddenly sank in that I was not only in a different country but almost in a different world. It was small things that spoke to me, things the Jordanians no doubt took for granted; but they jumped out to me as sights that I would never see in Iraq. Some of the hostels were advertising ice cream; others had bananas hanging from the walls. I was astonished. Bananas on display? Nobody in Baghdad would be so idiotic as to do that – someone would steal them within minutes, and probably attack the owner for good measure. But the thing that made my eyes pop out were the crates of Coca-Cola full of one-litre bottles piled high outside the hostels. Flashing signs advertised the distinctive logo. I hadn't seen Coca-Cola for years, not since the sanctions had been established against Iraq in 1990, just before the first Gulf War, and the sight was as curious to me as piles of gold bars would have been to a Westerner. If crates of Coke had been spotted in Baghdad in such proportions, thirsty young Iraqis would have fallen upon them like vultures on dead meat. It was that, more than anything else, that brought home to me the fact that I was no longer in a military state. This was a place where tourists came, with their sunglasses and their disposable income to spend on luxuries like ice cream and Coca-Cola. I found the sight vaguely comforting. Resting my head against the window, and watching these places as they sped past, I soon fell into a deep sleep.

By the time I awoke it was about nine o'clock, and the scenery around me had grown more urban as we drove through the outskirts of Amman. The road was better here, and modern-looking buildings intermingled with white tenement blocks and the colourful domes of the many mosques. Expensive cars shared the road with more run-down vehicles, and I even saw other coaches full of tourists. It was an unfamiliar sight: very few people came on holiday to Baghdad.

Eventually the coach pulled up outside a line of white buildings. 'The hotel,' my new-found companion said shortly. I looked at it through the window – there was nothing to indicate that that was what it was, but everyone

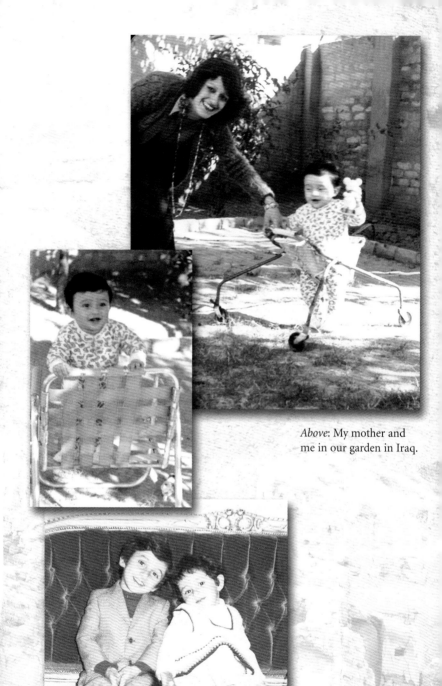

Above: My mother and
me in our garden in Iraq.

Left: With my sister at
home in Iraq in 1981.

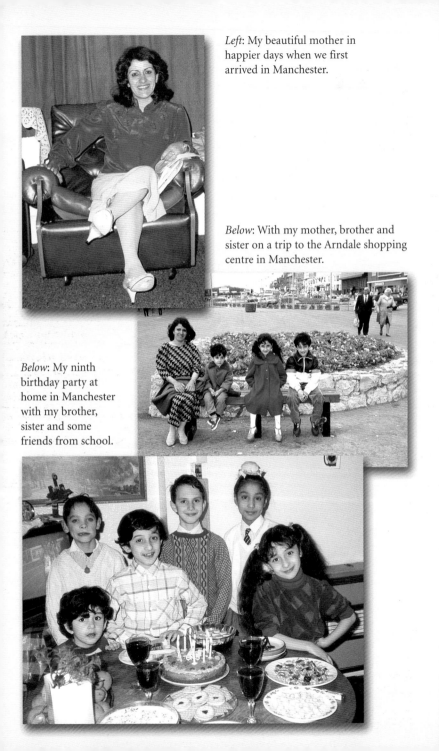

Left: My beautiful mother in happier days when we first arrived in Manchester.

Below: With my mother, brother and sister on a trip to the Arndale shopping centre in Manchester.

Below: My ninth birthday party at home in Manchester with my brother, sister and some friends from school.

BISHOP BILSBORROW PRIMARY SCHOOL

Princess Road
Manchester
M14 7LS

J.4.

Mathematics	C+	A satisfactory result but Samad finds problems quite difficult. He must concentrate more and when in difficulty seek teacher help and not rely upon his friend
Reading and Language Development	B	Has made good progress in his reading which has been reflected in his written work
Science	B	Samad works well in a group situation and takes an active part in discussion and investigation activities
Environmental Studies		Has enjoyed the visits and produced some good work which has been displayed.
Physical Activities		Always tries hard and applies himself well to team games. Progress has been made in his swimming
Creative Activities		Has potential in art and craft showing a special talent in modelling in clay. Has used this talent in other subject areas
Social and Personal Development		A pleasant boy who enjoys school. Samad will talk about any problems he has and not become anxious about them
General Comments on Year		A reliable and trustworthy boy who has worked hard this year to do well. If he continues this approach he will progress at St Thomas Aquinas.

teacher ...A.M.Roman...........

Top and left: The party to celebrate our last day at primary school in Manchester.

Background: My report from my final year at primary school.

Above: A photo from secondary school.

Above: My uncle Saad on his return from the Iran–Iraq war in 1982. He had been in a coma for over a week.

Right: With my physics teacher and high school classmates in Mosul.

Below: The counterfeit student ID card I used to get out of Iraq in 1994.

Left: With two of my friends in Mosul at the medical clinic in the College of Agriculture and Forestry.

Below: With my biology teacher and two of my best friends in high school.

Below: My military ID card.

Left: At work in Jordan.

Right: My ID card with the fake name from the counterfeit UAE passport that I used to travel to Malaysia.

Below: In the office at the company I worked for in Jordan.

```
The British Council

      LIBRARY
ADULT MEMBERSHIP

Family Name ;  MOHAMED AHMED

First Names :  MR AADEL

Expiry Date :  27 . 11 . 96
                              No.  0664
```

Left: Working out at the gym in Amman – a home from home.

Right: In Hashemite Square in 1995, just before I left Jordan.

Below left: The picture of myself in Amman I sent home to my family in Iraq.

Below right: The certificate from my biology O-level, which I took in Amman in preparation for medical school.

University of London

General Certificate of
Education Examination

May/June 1995

This is to certify that

SARMED AL-SAMARRAI

AMMAN, JORDAN

obtained the grades indicated in the following subject(s):

ORDINARY LEVEL   (ONE SUBJECT)

BIOLOGY   GRADE   C (6)

Signed on behalf of the University of London

Dean, University of London   Chief Executive, University of London
Examinations and Assessment Council   Examinations and Assessment Council

Candidate's Signature

Centre No.   Candidate No.   Date of Birth   Certificate No.
93540   8212   6/02/76   86012600

(Explanatory Notes are printed overleaf)   012811

Left: In *United 93*, playing the role of the lead hijacker.

Below: My first reunion with Uncle Saad in Syria in 2007.

Right: Outside my house in London.

in the coach was getting their belongings together and making for the door. It was clear that this was some sort of package deal in which accommodation at the hotel was included, which suggested to me that it would be cheap. If I was going to stay there, it would have to be – my money was already dwindling and I had only been in Jordan for a matter of hours. I approached the hotel with the old lady and her young companion, and we waited our turn at the reception desk. 'How much for a room?' I asked the bored-looking hotel employee.

He quoted me a figure, too much for my meagre budget, and the concern must have shown on my face because the old lady instantly came to my aid. 'It's OK,' she told me. 'You can stay with us.'

My eyes flickered to the receptionist, but he was un-interested in my sleeping arrangements. 'Thank you,' I told the old lady. 'I'll give you some money . . .'

But she dismissed my offer with a wave of her hand as though she were brushing off a troublesome insect. 'For a night or two it will be fine. But perhaps you would be good enough to help us carry our luggage upstairs.'

The hotel was far from glamorous. A small lift took us up several flights to our room, which was sparsely furnished – a couple of beds and a wooden table. I put the old lady's luggage down, then rather sheepishly laid my putrid robes on the floor as a makeshift mattress. 'You look tired,' the woman told me, and it was true – my few hours' snooze on the coach had done nothing to alleviate the exhaustion I was feeling, but I knew there was no chance of sleeping now. For a start, my mind was dancing with the excitement and apprehension of being in a new city; but I also had something urgent to attend to.

My bullet wound had not been dressed since the Bedouin house; since then I had gone through a punishing amount of physical exertion and I knew from the sinister throbbing in my leg that it needed cleaning. The last thing I wanted to do was take myself to a doctor or a hospital, so I realized I would have to attend to it myself. I made my excuses to my benefactor and went in search of a pharmacy, where I spent a few of my precious dollars on clean bandages and an alcohol solution to disinfect the wound. Back at the hotel I was relieved to find that my roommates had gone out, so I sat on one of the beds and removed my jeans. The wound was as bad as I would have expected: blood had seeped out and stained the bandage a dirty brown, then dried in streaks down the length of my leg. I gingerly unwrapped the bandage, wincing slightly as it unpeeled from the wound, then steeled myself for the inevitable sting as I dabbed the alcohol solution on to the raw, exposed flesh. As I did so, the memory of falling in the desert, not knowing if the wolves were ahead of me or behind, flashed in front of my eyes; I felt giddy as the enormity of what I had gone through in the last twenty-four hours hit me yet again. It took a moment for me to regain my composure, then I tightened a clean bandage over the wound and pulled my dirty jeans on once more.

Again it struck me how tired I was, that perhaps I should try to get some more sleep. But time wasn't on my side. I couldn't stay in this room for ever, no matter how benevolent the old lady might be feeling. I had to make arrangements for myself, and to do that I needed to get my bearings and make enquiries. I needed to head to downtown Amman.

8

The Comfort of Strangers

Amman is a city of refugees. Palestinians from the west, Iraqis from the east, it is a melting pot of cultures. For some it is their new home, for others simply a staging post on the way to somewhere more hospitable. For me it was ideal – it meant I would blend into the scenery, and without the constant fear of the Republican Guard round every corner I could perhaps allow myself a little breathing space. But I couldn't become complacent. My passport was fake, as were the stamps on it that allowed me entry to Jordan. Even if they fooled people, I was only allowed to be in the country for six months, after which time, if anybody scrutinized them, I risked deportation back to Iraq. I needed to start work immediately on gaining passage to the West, to a place where I could claim political asylum. To England.

Nevertheless, I was a stranger in a strange country. I had no friends, little money and no idea where to go to get the help and information I needed. I had overheard some of the Iraqis on the bus saying that when they arrived in Amman they would head immediately for an area called Hashemite Square, and the hotel receptionist confirmed with something of a sneer that this was where the Iraqis in Jordan tended to congregate. His manner suggested to me that he had opinions of his own about such people. I followed his directions.

Hashemite Square seemed to me to be a lively built-up area. Along the side of the main road was a vibrant collection of shops, behind which rose a hillside covered with a crowded jumble of white houses and tenement blocks. On the other side was a verdant park with trees and lakes. A stark white modern clocktower stood in the middle, and at its base groups of young men sat talking animatedly. The whole area was full of people milling around, and the air was thick with the distinctive Iraqi dialect of Arabic. Nobody paid me any attention whatsoever – to them I was just another face, and I found that blanket of anonymity a comfortable one. I realized how thirsty I was, so I took a seat in a nearby fast food joint and ordered a milkshake – cold and sweet, just what my body was craving. After my first few gulps, I slowed down and pulled out a piece of paper from my pocket. Crumpled and dirty, it was the scrap on which Saad had written the name and number of his friend Wissam. I remembered his words: when I arrived, I was to hunt him out.

I felt uncomfortable making the call. I had no idea who this man was, and I didn't even know what I was going to ask him. Surely my call would seem suspicious? Surely he would want nothing to do with this unknown Iraqi boy with nowhere to stay and hardly any money, never mind who his uncle was? I didn't know what kind of favour Saad had afforded this man to make him so sure he would help me, but I did know that some favours were soon forgotten and reluctantly repaid.

Still, experience had taught me that I could trust Saad's judgement in these matters, and besides, I didn't have any other options. That crumpled-up piece of paper was the only collateral I had. I slurped the remainder of my milk-shake and went to find a telephone service shop.

The phone rang several times. In fact, I was on the verge of hanging up when it was answered. 'Hello?' The voice at the other end growled its greeting rather unenthusiastically.

'Good afternoon,' I replied as politely as possible. 'My name is Sarmed Al-Samarrai. I'm the nephew of Saad Al-Khatab from Baghdad.'

The sound of his voice was like the sun coming out. 'Saad Al-Khatab!' he exclaimed. 'Of course! How is he?'

'He's well, and he sends his regards.'

'Saad is a good man. What can I do for you, Sarmed?'
His voice was booming and jolly.

I lowered my voice slightly, though for what reason I
can't say – probably it was out of habit. 'I've just arrived in
Jordan from Iraq. I don't know anybody here, so Saad
suggested I call you . . .' My words trailed off.

'Of course.' His voice became more sober. 'Where are
you now?'

'In Hashemite Square.'

'And where are you staying?'

'In a hotel on the outskirts.'

I heard him sucking on his teeth in thought. 'OK,' he said
finally. 'I'll tell you where I live.' He recited an address and
explained which bus I would need to get there. 'It's a little
way outside of Amman,' he told me. 'Let's meet tomorrow
and we'll see what we can do for you.'

I thanked him profusely, and put the phone down feeling more confident than I had in days.

Before I could walk away, there was one more phone
call I had to make. I lifted the receiver, dialled the
operator and waited half an hour to clear the bureaucratic
red tape needed to make a call to Baghdad. Before long a
familiar voice answered. As I spoke, I could hear my own
voice cracking. 'Uncle Saad,' I said quietly. 'It's me.'

Saad was silent for a moment, as though he did not dare
hear the answer to the question he had to ask. 'Where are
you?'

'In Amman,' I told him, unable to withhold a grin even though he couldn't see it.

Saad let out an explosive breath of air. 'Thanks be to Allah,' he whispered. 'Did you have any trouble?'

'A little,' I told him, not wanting to worry his mind with the realities of what had happened since I last saw him. 'I am meeting with your friend tomorrow.'

'Excellent,' Saad replied. 'He is a good man. I'm sure he will help you.' I had the feeling that he was not entirely confident about that. 'I'll tell your mother that you are well. In the meantime, keep your head down and don't get into trouble. And Sarmed?'

'Yes, Uncle Saad?'

'Don't forget what I told you.'

His parting words echoed in my mind. *The genuine man never forgets his family. We are sending you to freedom so that one day you may rescue them from this place.* 'I won't forget, Uncle Saad,' I told him sincerely. 'Hug my mother for me.'

The conversation lasted no more than a minute.

I spent the rest of the day enjoying being able to walk around without fear. As evening fell and the heat of the sun dissipated, more and more young people appeared. There were all sorts of nationalities – Jordanians, Iraqis, Syrians, Lebanese, Saudis – and they congregated in groups, laughing, eating ice cream, having a drink. Not having eaten since early that morning by the roadside, I approached a stall selling street food. A group of young men about my age were hanging around there, and somehow we fell into conversation. 'Where are you from?' one of them asked me.

I looked around nervously. In Iraq, you would take care before entering into conversations with strangers on the street, as you never knew who had the ear of the authorities. The idea of spilling my secrets to some random person I had just met was anathema to me, but there was something about his demeanour – a lack of interest that suggested he was making idle conversation rather than pumping me for incriminating information – that made me feel I could trust him. 'Baghdad,' I told him. 'I arrived today.'

'Staying long?'

I shrugged. 'I don't know. I want to get to England.'

'To claim asylum?' He sounded as if it was the most natural thing in the world, and I nodded a little warily.

'Have you been to the UN yet?'

'The UN?' The question surprised me. 'No. Why would I want to do that?'

The guy smiled at me, as if indulging a naive child. 'To get yourself on their lists. Sometimes they provide refugees with passage to a safer country. You never know, it might be quicker than whatever else you had in mind.'

One of his friends interrupted. 'Be careful, though.'

'What for?'

'There are all sorts of rumours going around that the place is watched.' Without taking his eyes off me, he took a slurp from the bottle of Coke he was drinking.

'Who by?'

'Spies,' he said shortly. 'Military police from Iraq or wherever, put there to keep an eye out for people who have skipped the country illegally. Not that I'm saying that's what you did.' He smiled and winked knowingly.

'What about the Jordanians?' I asked, a bit disconcerted by this news. 'Is it worth asking them to grant me asylum?' It wasn't something I had planned to do, but I figured that it was best to know what my options were.

The guy laughed, a short, ugly bark that betrayed his contempt for the Jordanian system. 'Sure, you can try,' he told me. 'They'll put your name on a list and you'll never hear from them again. At best you'll be forgotten, at worst you'll be alerting them to the fact that you're here illegally. Don't let yourself feel too welcome in this town, my friend. They only tolerate our presence because of the free oil they've been getting from our country for years – if it wasn't for that, we'd be out of here faster than you can say "Abu Ghraib".' He laughed again, at his own joke this time, before wandering off with his friends.

It had been a sobering conversation. In my overwhelming desire to get to Jordan, it had not really crossed my mind that such tensions would be something I would encounter, but now that it had been spelled out to me it made perfect sense. And as if to confirm my new discovery, an incident occurred as I was wearily making my way back to my hotel that underlined how careful I needed to be. I had just left Hashemite Square and was looking around me, drinking in the sights and sounds of the quarter where I would no doubt be spending a fair amount of time, when I passed a group of young men and women not much older than myself. Suddenly one of them called out to me, and it was clear from his accent that he was Jordanian. '*Alaa waaish bidahik?*' he shouted. 'What are you looking at?'

I stopped, frozen by the aggressive tone of his voice, and didn't immediately answer.

I shook my head. 'I'm not,' I mumbled.

'What is it? Do you want to fight me?' He was walking towards me now, his gait lurching in a way that suggested he had been drinking. I took a step backwards, but he continued to bear down on me. He pushed me heavily in my chest and I stumbled.

'Look, my friend,' I started to say. 'I'm not looking for trouble . . .' But as I spoke I caught sight of a uniform at the other end of the street. Immediately my fear of the confrontation was supplanted by my inbuilt horror of uniforms. Every instinct in my body shrieked at me to get away, to avoid being questioned by a figure of authority.

I walked briskly away, with the words 'Fucking Iraqis!' ringing in my ears.

* * *

First thing the following morning, having showered at the hotel so that my body at least was a little cleaner, I made my way to the UN headquarters. I had not forgotten the warning I had heard the previous night but I had decided to take a calculated risk – if these talked-about Iraqi spies were real, how would they spot me among the tens of thousands of other Iraqis in Amman? My passport was good enough to pass a cursory examination, and after all this was the UN – if I didn't feel safe there, where would I?

The headquarters were housed in a quiet residential area of Amman, surrounded by pretty gardens and tall metal railings. A number of people were milling around outside, but as I approached the gate with as great an air of confidence as I could muster, I avoided meeting anybody's eye. I didn't want to betray my nervousness. I have legitimate business, I kept telling myself. I have a right to be here. Nobody approached me as I walked in.

The scene inside the headquarters could not have been more different to the calm of the exterior. It was bedlam. Despite the early hour, all sorts of people were there – refugees from Sudan, Somalia and all over the Middle East – chattering loudly in languages that I did not understand. I stood for a moment in a daze, not quite sure what to do, before joining a queue marked 'Asylum Requests'.

When my time came, I sat down at the desk nervously.

'Fill this in,' the official in charge said without even looking at me. I scrawled the few details that were required of me on the sheet, then handed it back. Finally the official looked me in the eye, his contempt and boredom written plainly across his face. 'Where are you from?' he asked in a tone of voice that immediately reminded me of the corrupt checkpoint guard who had detained me on my way to Baghdad.

'Iraq,' I told him, shifting uncomfortably in my seat. This was not the welcome I had expected from the UN.

'Do you have permission to be here?'

I shook my head.

'Why do you need political asylum?'

'I believe my life would be in danger if I returned to my home country.' I thought this sounded dramatic, but the official had clearly heard it a thousand times before. He looked at me with suspicion, as if deciding what to do with me – though in truth I don't suppose he had the authority to do anything other than process me as he had everyone else. Finally he stamped my form and gave me a date several months hence when I was to return for further interviewing. He beckoned the next person in the queue before I had even stood up to leave.

I left the room feeling slightly bemused. I had expected the UN headquarters to be a haven, a place where I would feel safe, where my past would be something to invoke sympathy, not suspicion. In reality, I was just another number, an illegal alien, a statistic. Nobody was interested in me as an individual. With a thump I realized that I couldn't rely on anybody but myself to ensure my safety – and the fulfilment of my dream to make it to England.

Hitching the small bag that contained everything I owned further up on to my shoulder, I stood at the gates of the UN to gather my thoughts, this time taking in my surroundings in greater detail. There seemed to be more people outside now than when I had gone in, and I took a brief moment to scan the faces of those around me. Some of them were hanging around in groups, others sitting on benches across the road. On the corner of the street I noticed one man just standing there, loitering. He was wearing Western clothing, and he would have been entirely unremarkable were it not for the fact that he was staring directly at me. I tore my gaze from him and tried to look nonchalant, but when I glanced back his eyes were still fixed on mine. Immediately I found myself short of breath, with nauseous waves of panic crashing over me as the warning I had received the previous night rang in my head. I started walking briskly away in the opposite direction. I tried not to look back but in the end I couldn't stop myself.

The man was no longer on the street corner.

I stopped, turned round and scanned the crowds to see if he was still among them. No sign – until suddenly he walked out from behind a group of people. He was

ambling coolly towards me, and even though I had no
way of knowing whether he had any interest in me or not,
I was overcome by a paranoia that would let me do only
one thing: run. Not caring how conspicuous I made
myself, I turned and fled, losing myself in a maze of back-
streets. I ran with a painful limp for five or ten minutes,
all the while glancing back over my shoulder to check that
I wasn't being followed. I invited curious looks as I hur-
tled down the streets in my filthy clothes, seemingly
running from nothing and with sweat moistening my
skin, but when I stopped it was not out of a desire to stay
still. Out of the blue I was almost floored by an excruciating burning sensation in my stomach. I stumbled to a halt,
then bent double as I gasped for breath – half on account
of my exertions, half on account of the terrible, piercing
pain that was ripping through my abdomen. I collapsed
on the side of the road, unable to move, and waited until
this sinister pain had subsided.

The relief I felt when it had done so was like a balm. I
touched my hands to my cheeks and realized they were
wet from unnoticed tears, so I wiped my face and tried to
regain my composure. Part of me felt foolish, as though I
had been running from shadows; but I knew that in the
same situation I would do the same again. I had come too
far to throw everything away through carelessness. What
the pain in my stomach had been I had no idea. Probably
just hunger, or maybe stress, but I couldn't worry about it

now as there was too much to do. I went to find someone of whom I could ask directions back to Hashemite Square, from where the buses left to go out of Amman. It was time to meet Saad's friend.

Wissam lived in a well-to-do Christian area some miles out of the city with his wife and children. After an uneventful bus journey there, I approached his house with some trepidation – it was a large, beautiful place draped in grapevines and with fruit trees in the courtyard, not the sort of place I had expected to find myself on my second day in Jordan. I knocked rather timidly at the door, unsure what to expect. The man who greeted me was friendly, if formal at first, tall and good-looking with piercing green eyes. He introduced me to his family, his wife brought us some tea and we sat down to talk. As we dealt with the necessary pleasantries, I gained the impression that despite his friendliness he was a firm man, somebody who knew what he wanted in life and was comfortable with the position he had achieved. I could trust him, I knew; but I must not overstep the mark. He would help me so far, and no further. 'Now I think about it, I remember you,' he told me mysteriously when we had made ourselves comfortable in the shade of the vines that grew in a canopy over the courtyard. 'When I came to Baghdad to study in the late seventies, you were just a little baby.' He smiled at the reminiscence. 'Your uncle took care of me when I was a stranger in a strange land. He showed me where to go and what to do, and even let me stay with him for a while. I would be repaying him poorly if I did not do the same for you.'

'Thank you,' I said sincerely.

He sat back in his chair. 'Why don't you tell me everything?' he asked.

I closed my eyes, took a deep breath and began to tell my story. How they had wanted me to join the intelligence services; how I had escaped the barracks; how Saad had helped me to get out of Iraq. Certain things I kept to myself – the shooting, the journey across the desert with the Bedouin – so as not to make myself sound too dangerous a charity case. All the while I spoke Wissam stayed silent, nodding gently, and I realized that although there were some Jordanians – like the youths with whom I had had a run-in the previous night – who resented the presence of Iraqis in their territory, there were others, like the man in front of me, who understood the reality of life in our country, and were prepared to help us. It was a reassuring moment.

When I was finished, he was silent for a while, as if he was mulling my story over in his mind. Finally he spoke. 'Do you have money?'

'A few American dollars. Not enough.'

'And what is your plan from now on?'

'To get to England and study to become a doctor.'

He nodded silently. 'And how do you propose to do that?'

'I don't know. There must be a way, but I'll have to make enquiries ...' I knew it sounded feeble even as I spoke the words, but it was the truth.

Wissam waved his hand, as if to indicate that he didn't want to hear about such things. He knew that I was alluding to an underground world of false documents and people-smugglers, and he clearly didn't want to go down that path. He clapped his hands briskly to divert me from the subject. 'You'll need a job, then,' he said in a businesslike fashion. 'What can you do?'

Of all the questions he could have asked me, that was the one for which I was the least prepared. I had never really had a job, and my academic qualifications, such as they were, seemed next to useless now. 'I can speak English,' I told him with a shrug.

'OK,' he told me. 'That's good. Tomorrow I'll take you around, speak to a few friends. We'll see if we can find you some work. In the meantime, until you get a place for yourself, you can sleep here.'

As he promised, the following day he started taking me round places he knew that might be able to offer me a job. We started out at a baker's shop, but when they found out that I had never worked in a bakery before they rejected me out of hand. 'I'm sorry,' Wissam was told. 'He has no expertise. We've got Iraqis who know how to bake bread queuing up for jobs.' Everywhere we went it was the same story, and as the day progressed I began to grow demoralized – and so, I think, did Wissam. 'It looks like there are a lot of Iraqis trying to find work,' I said to him at one point. 'Too many. What if I'm not successful?'

He didn't answer.

Eventually he took me to the last place on his list. 'It's a company I know,' he told me vaguely, before explaining that it was run by three Iraqi brothers. The law stated, however, that you had to be Jordanian in order to own a company, so foreigners would pay Jordanians to front their affairs for them. The man we were about to meet was the Jordanian front for the company. 'Their business is imports and exports, and they have offices in Baghdad. I'm sure they'll be impressed that you speak English, but I imagine they'll want to know if you have any degrees or more advanced qualifications. Just tell them you have.'

I nodded. Dissembling was becoming second nature to me now, and I knew that if I could lie my way through Iraqi checkpoints, I could lie about a few examinations. Besides, I liked the sound of this place. A proper company. There would be desks and carpets, people doing business – it sounded a lot better than the sweltering kitchens of the bakery I had been to see, and maybe I would learn something useful. I wondered why Wissam had left this place till last.

The man we were led in to see was enormous – one of

the fattest people I have ever met – with a long, scraggly brown beard. He had the unusual and slightly off-putting habit of placing his left thumb under his left armpit and digging it into his ribs, almost as if he was massaging his overstrained heart. His name was Khalil Bakir, and he looked at me in utter disdain. I had the impression that Wissam was a client of his, and that was the reason I was being given so much as the time of day. 'Can you make tea and coffee?' he asked in response to Wissam's enquiry after vacancies, slightly wrongfooting me as I had been preparing myself to answer much more complicated questions than that.

'Yes,' I replied meekly.

'Good. You can start the day after tomorrow. One hundred dinars a month.'

And so it was that I became an employee of the company.

On my first day at work they took a photocopy of my passport without paying it much attention – it was little more than a formality to them, as Wissam had vouched for me and clearly his word was trusted, and in any case they were in no position to tell a genuine passport from a fake one. My job was to make the tea and coffee for Bakir and his brother, do a bit of washing-up and run a few errands, and it wasn't long before I learned more about the company and its workings. The first thing that struck me was how little work everybody seemed to do. The office was staffed by Bakir's family as a condition for him fronting the company – clearly he had told his Iraqi colleagues that if they wanted to set up in business, his nearest and dearest would have to have pay cheques. His family members were illiterate – they neither read nor wrote Arabic, which was not such an uncommon thing – and they did literally nothing other than sit around chatting and drinking the tea I made them, and I remember thinking, perhaps naively, that the import-export business must be a very profitable one in order to allow the management to keep on such a large number of unused staff. It was not up to me to say anything, however, because Bakir, their benefactor, had me under his thumb. There was something about his demeanour that terrified me. I can't explain what it was, but I do remember wondering why it was that I, who had escaped the army, been shot and chased by wild wolves in the desert, should be so scared of this one man. Perhaps it was the fact that he now held my livelihood in his hands. Iraqis were treated like scum in Amman – I was lucky to have this job, and it was the only means available to me to earn enough money to continue with my plans. He knew he had a hold on me, and he capitalized on that to make me work hard: his gaze was ferocious, and his eyes would follow me around the office as I went about my business, keeping me well and truly in line. I exercised all the politeness I had on him, but most of the time he seemed impervious to it, like a smooth, fat rock that would not shine no matter how many times it was buffed.

Deep down, though, Bakir had a heart. On occasions his sons, who were younger than me – one about fourteen, the other perhaps ten – used to come into the office. They were well dressed, and their full faces spoke of a healthy, plentiful diet and privileged lifestyle – a stark contrast to my ragged and undernourished features. I used to envy them, and wonder why it was that life had not rolled the dice for me a bit differently; and sometimes, after his sons had been to the office, I would catch Bakir looking at me thoughtfully, as though the difference in our circumstances was not lost on him. And so, although he treated me with brusqueness, he also did his best to help me. He knew that I spoke English – he himself spoke very little – and after a while, once it had become clear to him that he could trust me, he started giving me little jobs to do. Writing a letter, translating something – just little tasks that an English-speaker would be suited to. And after about nine months, when I had demonstrated my ability, he sacked his secretary and put me in her place. It was a brutal move, and one that did nothing to dispel my fear of the huge man, even if what he had done was a help to me. I felt as if I was strangely favoured, but had a sword hanging over me nevertheless. I shuddered to imagine what Bakir's reaction would be if he knew the truth about my past – doubtless nobody in the company really expected this young Iraqi man to be around for ever, but every instinct informed me that my story was best left untold.

But now I had more responsibility and a slightly bigger pay cheque. Because the company had offices in Baghdad, they allowed me to divert some of my pay there, so that my family – normally Saad – could pick it up when times were lean. I was not the only Iraqi to do this – it was a common way for my fellow countrymen to send money home, and as a result I met quite a few other Iraqi immigrants. Some of them paid me little attention; others I grew friendly with. There was an architect, whose name was Abu Firas, who seemed to take a particular shine to me. Whenever I saw him at the company offices, we would chat; and now and then I would see him outside his favourite café in Hashemite Square.

Occasionally, when Bakir was not looking, I would use the company phone to make calls home and speak to my mother or to Saad. Sometimes they would even phone me. These conversations were short and non-specific, as we couldn't be sure that nobody was listening in. Personal household telephones could be – and frequently were – tapped; and if you wanted to make a call from a communal phone, you would have to submit all your details, including your civil registration card, then wait for two hours before making the call. Anonymous calls were practically impossible. And so everyone was careful not to disclose anything that might give away where I was – they would just ask after my well-being and thank me for the money I had sent – or tell me that they were OK this month and that I should hold on to my earnings. They knew how important it was that I saved up.

As time went on, however, these phone calls home became more sinister and traumatic. At first all I had was a vague sense of misgiving, the uncertain impression that something was wrong. Gradually, however, I managed to piece together from our coded conversation that a soldier from my unit had, about three months after my escape, arrived at my grandmother's house to deliver notice that I had gone AWOL. A month or two later, however, things escalated when my mother, my brother and Saad were apprehended by Al-Istikhbarat and taken to Division 5 in the area of Al-Kadhimiya.

What happened to them there, I did not know at the time. I had to piece it together from snippets I gleaned and from what I knew went on in that place. They were told that I had to return to my unit immediately. If I did, they said, I would be dealt with leniently. My ears would not be cut off, and I would not face the imprisonment or even worse that I would be expecting; I would just be made to complete my military service in the usual fashion. My family knew, of course, that they were lying, and remained adamant that they knew nothing. So the interrogators threatened them with economic sanctions. If he did not help them, Saad was told, they would arrange for him and his family to be cast out of the house in the Al-Zaafaraniya compound which he had been given because he was an amputee from the Iran–Iraq war. Still Saad insisted he did not know where I was. And so they took his gun from him, held it to his head, and cocked it. 'How would you feel,' he was asked, 'if we shot you with your own gun? Now tell us where he is.'

Saad remained silent.

At that point, the interrogation was handed over to somebody else. The two officers who had apprehended Saad had seen him in his home environment, with his parents and sister. Perhaps they would have been inclined to treat him with undue lenience – to treat him like a human being – if it had been their job to take the questioning to the next stage, so a specialist was brought in to complete the job. Someone who could do so without emotion or mercy. Someone who did this kind of thing day in, day out.

My uncle was brutally beaten across the face and chest with a thick iron bar. The fact that he had suffered so much for the sake of his country meant nothing to his assailant. Whether he asked for pity I don't know, but I doubt it: his pride would have been too great for that. His skin was then branded with a hot iron – a common way of reminding people of the pain they had undergone. My mother and brother underwent similar brutality. And then they were released, but not before the intelligence officers had reiterated their demands: I was to return immediately, otherwise the consequences for my family would be dire.

It was only later that I found out the details of what had happened to them, but through my coded conversations with Saad on the phone I deduced that I was being pressured to return, and I knew such pressure would be far from lenient. I fell to pieces. I suppose I had always known it was possible that my family would be questioned in some way, but I really didn't expect it to go to that extreme. Saad had filled me with his confidence, and I felt sure that he would be able to protect everyone from the full force of the security forces' predilections. It seemed I was wrong. The treatment that Saad had undergone did not bear thinking about, and it was all because of me. There was only one thing that I could ethically do: turn back. Return to my unit and hope that I was afforded the leniency that Saad had been promised. But when I made my thoughts known to my uncle, I was shot down in coded flames. 'Forget my studies over here,' I had told him. 'I'm going to come back. I'll finish them another time.'

'No,' Saad told me sharply. 'Think of all the money we've spent sending you abroad to study. Just remember what I told you when you left.'

I wanted to ask him how he would deal with this situation, but of course I couldn't. I knew the answer in any case. It would come down to money. A few dinars in the pockets of the right people and perhaps he could keep the military police away from my family, for a while at least. It wasn't foolproof – after all, there was no record of whom he had bribed – so he might have to grease the palms of different people in the future, but for now he sounded confident, despite his horrible experiences. 'You just concentrate on what it is you have to do,' he told me, 'on behalf of your family.'

And so, with misgivings, I gave up all thoughts of returning; but the terrible prospect of my mother and siblings being harmed did not leave my mind for a single waking moment.

I stayed with Wissam for a couple of weeks, but it was not long before I gained the impression that he considered his debt to Saad to be repaid. It was nothing spoken, just a vague subtext, but I certainly did not want to outstay my welcome. There was an Iraqi working at the company, and I stayed with him for about two weeks. He was a very religious man, an engineer who had grown up in the States and spoke fluent English. He was very kind to me. When I felt I could no longer stay with him, I asked if I could sleep at the company offices for a while and arrangements were made for me to do so, but after a couple of months I discovered that the company owned a flat in the prime area of Amman and I was offered the opportunity to stay there. Excited by the prospect, and expecting it to be something rather special, I made my way to the place, only to find that it was quite different to what I had in mind. About twenty backward and illiterate itinerant Iraqis were living in the three-bedroom flat. The floor was covered with tattered cushions that had been gathered into makeshift beds, and everyone seemed to keep their few belongings in old nylon bags. It was none too clean, and as I stepped into the flat I became aware of the musty smell of too many people living in too cramped a space. The occupants eyed me suspiciously before asking me a barrage of questions. Who was I? Where did I work? Who had given me permission to stay there? I answered the questions honestly and in good humour, not wanting to fall out with these people who were clearly going to be my flatmates, but they didn't make it easy, closing ranks like a group of frightened criminals. They worked at the head office of the company, it transpired, and since I wasn't working there and wasn't a threat to their jobs, they grudgingly accepted me into the fold.

As part of my job, however, I would occasionally make trips to the head office, running errands for Bakir, and it was there that I started to learn more about the company's business. It was a large building – eight storeys high and all owned by the company – and in the reception was a large picture split in two, with Saddam Hussein on one side and King Hussein of Jordan on the other. The company wore its Iraqi origins firmly and even proudly on its sleeve. I had learned from chatting to the people in the office where I worked that the driving force behind the company was an Iraqi, a member of the Al-Bu-Nimer – the Tiger tribe from the Sunni Al-Anbar region near the Jordanian border. Although Al-Anbar was a long way from Saddam's power centre, the members of this tribe were very loyal to him, and were afforded favours as a result. The main man was called Mushtaq, and he had something of a reputation as a flamboyant character. Occasionally I would see him at the head office – from time to time he would come to work in a football shirt, but usually he wore brightly coloured yellow or pink suits and a wide smile. Even from a distance he had a magnetic personality – good-looking, confident and suave – and I was keen to meet him.

One day I got my chance, when I was sent on an errand to Mushtaq's office. He was friendly enough, gregarious but clearly without much time to devote to a lowly secretary from one of his other offices. His own office was huge and richly appointed, but as I stood there answering his half-interested questions, my attention was not grabbed by the furniture: my eyes had fallen on something that to me seemed much more sinister. On Mushtaq's desk, in pride of place, was a picture of him shaking the hand of Uday Hussein, and another of him with Saddam. I was transfixed – they looked so easy in each other's company, clearly theirs was a relationship that went a long way back. What would Mushtaq do if he knew that one of his employees was in Jordan on a fake passport with fake entry stamps, having gone through everything I had gone through in order to leave Iraq? I felt my skin prickle and realized that I had not taken in a word of what Mushtaq had been saying to me. I made my excuses and left.

That night, back in the flat, I couldn't sleep. I lay there listening to the heavy breathing and snores of my room-mates, unable to get those pictures out of my head. By this time, my bullet wound had largely healed up. It still bled occasionally, but it had crusted over and grown much smaller. It should still have served as a reminder for me, though, to be constantly wary. In the time since I had started at the company, I had allowed my guard to drop a little. I hadn't been careless, but I had slotted into this new life with surprising ease. The picture I had seen in Mushtaq's office, however, brought home to me the fact that I must never forget I was on the run. I was grateful to the company for having given me a job, but I knew without question that the business interests of my employers would always come before their charity to me, so I could never let them know the truth about my situation. Part of me wondered if I should look for other work, but I soon dismissed that idea. Having started to make acquaintances with other Iraqis who congregated around Hashemite Square, who had to make do with filthy jobs for scant wages, I knew that I was lucky to be in my position. I was able to put money aside for my ultimate escape from Jordan, and even send a little back home to my family. I would just have to be on my guard.

As I lay there that night, I felt sick. Then I felt scared. Then I steeled myself to continue working hard to earn the money that would buy me my passage out of Jordan.

9

Caught

The months passed. I would procrastinate, putting off making calls home and feeling terrified whenever I did because I dreaded hearing terrible things. But I heard no more bad news. It seemed as though the military police had decided to forget about me, for now at least.

I moved out of the company flat and used some of my earnings to rent a place of my own, deep in the Palestinian quarter of Amman. It was on the side of one of the hills on which Amman is built, where years before Palestinian refugees had set up camp and formed what could only be described as a ghetto. Back then the hillside was covered in tents; now it was more permanent than that, and the area was perfect for me: cheap, and a place where I could melt into the background whenever necessary. The room was nothing to speak of: situated on its own on the roof of a high-rise building, it was a former laundry room with little in the way of facilities and disproportionately expensive; but it was my own space, somewhere I could hide away whenever I wanted or needed to.

One morning I woke up to the sound of rain. The rainy season had arrived and such downpours were not uncommon. I lay in bed for a while, mustering the energy to get up. It had been a broken night, but that was nothing unusual for me – my dreams were filled with gunshots and wild animals and Republican Guards around every insubstantial, shadowy corner, and I would wake several times a night wide-eyed and sweating. Occasionally my dreams would be accompanied by the same excruciating stomach pains that I had experienced the day I ran from the UN, and I would lie there in a darkness that multiplied my fears tenfold.

But just as the sun dispels shadows, so the daylight would banish my night-time anxieties into a far corner of my mind. I woke up, ate some breakfast, put on my suit, grabbed my umbrella and left for another day at work. The rain was still heavy, and I was glad of the umbrella as I trod the familiar route. Just then, someone walked up from behind me and strode ahead. She was about the same height as me, with long brown hair; as she passed I caught a glimpse of her face, with its dark skin and the most stunning green eyes I had ever seen. Hers was the kind of beauty that made me catch my breath a little. Almost without thinking I stepped ahead and began walking beside her. 'Would you like to share my umbrella?' I asked. My invitation was uncharacteristically forward.

She smiled, a modest and appealing smile; I held the umbrella over her head, allowing it to protect her from the rain far more effectively than it did me, and we fell into slightly awkward conversation. Her name was Shireen and she was perhaps a couple of years older than me. She was studying to be a fitness instructor. I told her that I had a job at a large company and tried to make it sound rather grander than it was, and by the time we had introduced ourselves we had arrived at my work building. I handed her the umbrella. 'Take it,' I told her.

She smiled that smile again. 'But when will I be able to give it back to you?' she asked.

I waved my hand nonchalantly. 'It doesn't matter,' I told her. 'I'll see you around. Give it to me then.' She started to protest but I wouldn't allow her to, and I stood in the pouring rain watching her walk away. Just before she disappeared around the corner, she turned her head and smiled at me.

'You're soaking wet,' Bakir barked when I got into the office.

'I'm sorry, Mr Bakir,' I muttered.

'You're also late. I don't pay you to be late. Fetch me tea with honey.'

But even Bakir's reprimand couldn't dampen my spirits that day. The picture in my mind of Shireen's smile was enough to ease my other worries, at least for a little while. As the day wore on, I began to curse myself for playing it cool and not arranging to meet her again, so I determined that the following day I would leave my flat at exactly the same time in order to try to run into her again.

I woke earlier than normal the next day and spent a little longer getting dressed. Stepping out into the street wearing a cloak of confidence that I did not really feel, I looked around me, hoping to see the adorable sight of Shireen walking along the road. She wasn't there. I kept my eyes peeled all the way to work, but by the time I arrived I was crestfallen. It looked like I had blown it.

I went about my business, making Bakir his tea, shuffling papers around without much enthusiasm. It wasn't until mid-morning that someone called out to me. 'Sarmed, you have a visitor!' There was a slightly mocking, sing-song quality to his voice, and as I looked up I saw why.

There was Shireen, holding the umbrella. 'I thought you'd like this back.' She was smiling.

I did my best to keep cool, thanking Allah that she couldn't feel the beads of sweat forming on my palms, or taste the sudden dryness of my mouth. 'I looked out for you this morning,' I told her non-committally.

She nodded mysteriously. 'I went a different route.'

'Do you always go a different route?'

'Not always,' she told me. 'Perhaps I'll see you another day.'

'Perhaps.' I grinned, and spent the rest of the day walking on air.

A couple of times a week I would see Shireen on my way to work. Sometimes she would be with a friend, sometimes alone; but each time we met we would fall into easy conversation, and in no time at all I became besotted with my new friend. I learned more about her. She had been born in Jordan, but her family were of Palestinian origin and she still considered herself a refugee. Somehow I felt that brought us closer. On the mornings I saw her, I would be happy for the rest of the day; when I missed her, my day was ruined. I even found myself writing poems to her that I knew she would never read. It was an entirely innocent relationship, and looking back I have no doubt that the obsession I felt for this woman was not reciprocated, but to me it was more than just a teenage crush. It was something that made me feel as if I belonged. Now and then I would ask her out; she always turned me down with a smile that made me want to redouble my efforts the next time. In a perverse kind of way, her rejection gave me confidence, the impression that I had something to work towards – I was sure that one day she would accept. Who knows, perhaps when the time came she would join me in leaving the country. But somehow that time seemed a long way off. I had started to feel a sense of community, with my workmates, with the Iraqis in Hashemite Square whom I had befriended, and even elsewhere.

One afternoon after work I was walking aimlessly around a quarter of Amman with which I was not familiar when I passed a run-down building standing on its own that had clearly once been a block of flats. On the top was a billboard announcing that it had been newly converted into a gym, and on an impulse I went in to investigate. The staircase leading up to the gym was horribly shabby – I almost turned back, thinking I had made a mistake and people couldn't possibly be working and training there – but I persisted and eventually found myself in a hot, sweaty room. Mirrors were on the wall, music was blaring, and bodybuilders were working out. No doubt with my mind on the fact that Shireen wanted to be a fitness instructor, I joined there and then.

Gradually the gym became a home from home. I would go there every day after finishing at work, and I became friendly with the gym owner, a former Olympic body-builder who seemed to take a shine to me. I think he was impressed with the enthusiasm with which I threw myself into this new hobby, so when I decided that I was spending so much time at the place that I might as well be working there, he was sympathetic to the idea. 'You have the right to work here?' he asked perfunctorily.

'I already have a job at a respectable company,' I reminded him.

'Very well,' he said. 'I could use someone to help me tidy up the gym at night. I can't give you much, though. Free membership, and a few extra dinars in your pocket . . .' But that was all I wanted – I still had my job at the company, and as I was earning more than most of my fellow Iraqis I wasn't about to be greedy.

Gradually, though, I found myself becoming settled. When the time allowed me by my fake Jordanian entry stamps had passed without comment from my employers or anybody else, I suppose I even began to feel blasé. In the back of my mind I knew that this was going to make things difficult for me when the moment came, as it surely would, to leave; but for the first time ever I was beginning to enjoy myself a little bit, earning my own money and living my own life free of any interference. And even though I knew I had to be careful, to keep a low profile so that the Jordanian police who patrolled the streets never requested my passport, nevertheless I was experiencing the kind of freedom that people in the West took for granted, and it was a genuine liberation. I found that I didn't especially want to leave the life I was making for myself in Amman; I didn't want to leave my friends at the gym; I didn't want to miss out on my morning walks with Shireen.

Despite everything, however, I was illegal, as were

many of my acquaintances; as such I could not help but become schooled in the underground business of people-smuggling. When I met up with the Iraqis in Hashemite Square, more often than not the conversation would take that direction: voices would become hushed, and people would pass on the latest rumours about forged passports and large sums of money changing hands to facilitate border crossings that sometimes were successful and sometimes weren't. I would feel something approaching a sense of peace when I heard of contemporaries who had made it to a safer place; but for every good-news story there was one to go with it of a deportation back to Iraq. It didn't bear thinking about what had happened to the poor souls who were unlucky.

It was a shady, illegal business, but rife, and as such it attracted its fair share of dishonest characters. I had acquaintances who were so run-down by the life they were living in Amman – working in bakeries for twelve hours a day in the burning heat for a third of the wage that I was fortunate enough to receive – that they would throw caution to the wind and listen to the honeyed tones of crooked smugglers who would promise them the world. Sometimes you could spot the conmen a mile off – young Iraqis who were grafting every waking hour in poorly paid jobs were clearly unlikely to be the high-flying smugglers that they sometimes claimed. Others played the game more subtly. 'I can get you to Canada in three weeks,' they would state confidently. 'It will cost you a thousand Jordanian dinars, but you have to give me the money up front now.' They talked a good talk, but whoever was foolish enough to pay in advance seldom saw the smugglers – or their money – ever again. I realized very early on that in such matters it was important to avoid the flash, confident braggers, the people who would spend their time partying and drinking and smoking. As I watched my contemporaries trying to leave, it became obvious that the ones who had the greatest success were those who put their faith in more sober members of the community – religious people, professional people, people who were doing what they did because they truly wanted to help others break free of the political shackles that kept them in that part of the world rather than out of a desire to make a few easy and dishonest dinars.

And so I learned to be patient. I knew it would take a while for me to amass enough money and find the right person to help me to fulfil my dream and get to England. For the moment, I decided to make good use of my time – although there wasn't much of that. I would finish one job at two in the afternoon, then start my second at four. When I wasn't working at the company or at the gym, though, I would go to the British Council to learn what I could about English culture and history. They had VHS tapes, magazines and newspapers that enabled me to study the country I wanted to make my home, and a large community of pro-Western Arabs frequented the offices. I threw myself wholeheartedly into that environment. While I was there I made enquiries about the possibility of taking some basic exams with a UK college – I was still determined to study to become a doctor if and when I managed to get to England. 'No problem,' I was told. 'Just write to the college whose course you want to follow, they'll advise you what books to read and you can do your exams here. If you pass you'll get your award.' I couldn't believe it was that simple – if I did well I'd make the grade, unlike in Iraq where my exam results were compromised by the fact that my parents had no military connections.

I bought the books, I studied hard and I passed the examination.

The sense of elation and achievement was something I had never experienced before. I had done this off my own bat, without the need for subterfuge, and I had succeeded. I wanted to celebrate, so the day I received my results I took the day off work and met up with a few friends. Jolly Bee was one of the places where the young people of Amman would hang out – a burger joint with MTV screens blaring loudly and a special nursery area for younger children. I spent some time there with an Iraqi friend I had made called Duraid, and Muafaq, a Jordanian who worked as an administrator for Mushtaq at the head office of the company. We had a good time, laughing, joking and stuffing ourselves with the fast-food treats Jolly Bee had to offer us, toasting my recent academic achievement with a succession of milkshakes. When we left we were in high spirits, boisterous even. I had always made a point of trying to be inconspicuous when I was out and about, but today that seemed uncalled for. Duraid, Muafaq and I ran down the street chasing and shouting at each other, and laughing just a bit too loudly. I don't remember what it was that had caused such hilarity – perhaps I had said something about Shireen to my friends, or perhaps it was nothing more than high spirits. Whatever it was, for a few moments it caused me to forget myself, to forget that the main focus of my life should have been to keep a low profile.

Muafaq and I sprinted round the corner into a much smaller side street – and practically ran into a policeman, unmistakable in the summer uniform of the Amman police force. It was as if he had materialized out of nowhere. He had just bought himself an ice cream, and was about to put the cone to his mouth when we almost knocked him flat.

I stood absolutely still. We both did. In the few seconds of silence before the policeman spoke, a panic of thoughts went through my head. Not once in all the months I had been in Jordan had I been stopped by the police. I had been too careful for that. What would he do? We hadn't done anything wrong exactly, so maybe he would just tick us off and tell us to be on our way. But it was also within his power to question us, to ask for our papers and check that we were who we said we were. It was entirely down to his frame of mind. I did my very best not to look as though I had any reason to be scared, but no doubt my face was a picture of the concern I was feeling. I had turned from jubilation to desperation in an instant.

He looked us up and down, his face impassive. 'What are you two doing?' he asked. His voice gave nothing away.

I was aware of Muafaq gently making his way to the front of our little group. He was Jordanian, so I suppose he thought that if he spoke for us the officer might not think he had encountered a couple of Iraqi tearaways. 'We're just on our way home, officer,' he told him soberly.

The policeman eyed him up and down. 'Your ID card.' It was an order, not a request.

Muafaq smiled as he pulled his ID card from his jacket and handed it over. 'And this is a very good friend of mine . . .' he started to say, hoping to defuse the situation, but he was instantly interrupted.

'I'll come to him in a minute,' the officer snapped.

He scrutinized Muafaq's ID card, and as he did so I considered running. The main road was busy so I could lose myself in among the crowds – but the officer would still have Muafaq. I couldn't put him in the position of having to hide my identity from the Jordanian police.

Besides, I had noticed the weapon swinging from the officer's belt. I would just have to try to talk my way out of the situation, and pray that he didn't ask me for the one thing I couldn't supply: proof of residence. The officer handed Muafaq's ID back to him, then turned his attention to me. 'Can we go now?' I asked, affecting a Jordanian accent as best I could. It didn't fool the officer for a moment.

'Where are you from?' he asked with thinly veiled contempt.

'I live here,' I told him, avoiding his question.

'I didn't ask you where you live. I asked you where you're from.'

'Iraq.'

The officer nodded, as though I had confirmed his worst suspicion. 'In that case, I'll need to see your proof of residence. Where's your passport?'

'I don't have it with me,' I stuttered. 'Maybe I could bring it to you later?'

He shook his head. 'Where is it?'

I had to think fast. In reality it was safely locked away in my tiny apartment, but I couldn't tell him that. For a start I suspected I might have to take him there, and I certainly didn't want the authorities to know where I lived. More importantly, however, my Jordanian entry stamps had expired. Even if he didn't notice that it was a false passport, the fact that I was illegal was clearly stated there in black and white. I didn't know what to say. The officer looked at me, one eyebrow raised as my uncomfortable silence spoke louder than any excuses I could make up.

'It's at work,' I stammered, for no reason other than that I thought it might buy me some time.

The officer narrowed his eyes. 'And where do you work?'

'I have a job at a company,' I said. I didn't mention the name of the firm but told him the general area where the office was situated, adding that I was a secretary to the Jordanian owner. Perhaps that would give me a little leverage.

The officer thought for a moment. 'Very well,' he said finally. 'Take me there.'

As though in an awful dream that I couldn't wake up from, Muafaq and I were escorted to a patrol car in which another officer was sitting, and we were driven through the traffic of Amman towards my office. We stayed silent. We didn't even look at each other, not wanting to betray our nervousness. The minutes passed and I felt the hotness of genuine fear creeping down the back of my neck. What were my employers likely to do? Sack me on the spot, most likely; leave me to the mercy of this aggressive policeman, who clearly had the bit between his teeth as far as I was concerned. There was certainly no reason for them to stick their necks out for me; indeed, there were many reasons for them not to. I was popular at work, but they had a successful and profitable business – why on earth would they risk a run-in with the authorities on my account?

As the patrol car edged slowly towards the district where the company had its offices, I became increasingly certain that I was heading into the lion's den, and so, without thinking it through properly, I blurted out: 'Actually, my passport isn't there.'

The officer who had arrested me looked over his shoulder. 'What do you mean?'

'I have another job,' I told him. 'At a local gym. I had to give them my passport.'

'Why didn't you say so before?'

'I forgot,' I said rather unconvincingly. 'It was a while ago.'

It was scant relief when the policemen directed the car towards the gym. The gym's owner was still a Jordanian, still ran a business and still didn't want any kind of trouble with the authorities. I just felt slightly more comfortable with the idea of the officers confronting him rather than Bakir.

It was about two o'clock when we arrived, and the gym was pretty much empty – the regulars would not turn up for at least another hour, maybe two. Nevertheless, loud Western pop music was blaring through the stereo speakers as I led the way across the gym mats towards the owner's office, closely followed by the officer who had arrested me. Muafaq had stayed in the car with the other policeman, which was an extra worry for me: he was not known for his discretion, and I worried that he would inadvertently say something incriminating. But all that was out of my control; I had to concentrate on the matter in hand.

I will never forget the shock on the owner's face as he watched me being marched across the gym towards him. Abu Sameer had been so kind to me, helping me out with work and friendly advice – now it must have seemed that I was not the person I had pretended to be. As we entered, he put down the pen with which he was filling in some paperwork, sat back in his chair and gazed warily at us both. 'Sarmed,' he muttered by way of greeting.

I nodded, then the officer stepped in front of me. As Abu Sameer was clearly Jordanian and much older than him, there was no way the officer would speak to him in the same dismissive tones he had used with me, but he was stern nevertheless. 'The boy says he works for you.'

Abu Sameer nodded.

'How long has he worked here?'

'A few months, nothing more.' I saw his eyes flicker towards me as he spoke.

'He's from Iraq,' said the officer, stating what the owner clearly already knew. 'We're clamping down on illegal immigrants at the moment, especially young males, so I need to see his residency permits.'

'You think Sarmed might be illegal?' His face gave nothing away.

'Yes,' replied the officer, 'I do. He's been acting very suspiciously. He tells me you have his passport. Is this true?'

The question hung in the air. Once more I saw Abu Sameer's eyes flicker towards me, and from behind the officer's back I slowly made a signal to him, imploring him not to give the game away. It was a futile hope, I knew – what could he say when put on the spot like this? My future depended on his answer. Still, this burly Jordanian had no reason to help me.

Finally he spoke. 'Yes, I have his passport.'

'Then perhaps you could show it to me,' the officer asked almost politely.

I held my breath.

'I'm very sorry, officer, but I'm afraid I can't do that.'

'What do you mean?'

Abu Sameer stood up from his desk and pointed to a large safe in the corner of the room. 'I keep his passport in that safe. You have to be careful with so many people around, and I wouldn't want to lose it. Anyway, my wife has the key. She's not here today, but I'd be happy to bring Sarmed's passport to you tomorrow whenever it's convenient for you.' He smiled, his face lighting up with such honesty that surely nobody would suspect he wasn't telling the truth.

The officer shifted from one foot to the other, glancing from me to Abu Sameer in sequence. Then he shook his head. 'No,' he said firmly. 'I'll be back this time tomorrow. Then we'll have a look at these documents of yours.'

I inclined my head, but didn't say anything. The officer lowered his voice. 'Consider yourself lucky I'm not taking you with me. The cells at the police station are very uncomfortable. Just make sure you're here tomorrow,' he told me, and turned to leave.

Abu Sameer and I remained silent as we watched the officer cross the gym towards the exit, the clomping of his heavy shoes echoing against the mirrored walls. Even when he had closed the door behind him, Abu Sameer refrained from speaking. It was as if we were both holding our breath, waiting for the officer suddenly to walk back in and catch us discussing what we shouldn't have been.

Eventually he spoke. His voice was quiet, threatening almost. 'Can you bring me your passport to show this guy?'

I bowed my head and gently shook it. 'No,' I whispered. 'I can't do that. I'm sorry.'

Another pause, and then Abu Sameer banged his formidable fist against the table. 'Do you have any idea what sort of situation you've just landed me in?' he hissed.

What could I say? After all he had done for me I knew he had every reason to be angry, so I wasn't surprised when he pushed past me and stormed into the main area of the gym, striding around furiously for a couple of minutes while I was left to stew. Now more than ever I was at this man's mercy – he had lied to protect me, but there was nothing to stop him from going back on his subterfuge should he realize that he was in too deep.

Finally he returned to his office where I stood waiting for him. 'You're a good boy, Sarmed,' he said gruffly. 'I don't know why you lied to that policeman, and I don't want to know. But he's going to come back, so you can't be seen round here again.'

'What will you tell him?' I asked meekly.

'I don't know.' He seemed irritated by the question. 'I'll deal with that. You just leave this place and keep your head down.'

I nodded in agreement.

'I don't blame you for not wanting to go back to Iraq, but you can't live like this for ever, Sarmed,' he told me, more calmly now. 'It's madness. If you're illegal here, they're going to catch up with you eventually. I don't want to know what your plan is, but if you're going to stay safe, you'd better have one.'

'I know,' I said. 'I'm hoping to—' But he held up his hand to stop me giving him any information he didn't want to have. Then I watched him as he removed a string from around his neck on which a key was hanging. He walked over to the safe and used the key to open it – I couldn't help a flicker of a smile as I remembered the earnestness with which he had assured the policeman that his wife held the key. He took out a small pile of notes and started counting them out. 'These are the wages I owe you,' he said, then counted out a few more. 'And here is a little extra, to help you on your way.' He handed them to me, then wrapped his enormous arms round me in a bear-like embrace. 'I'm sorry it's not more,' he said. 'Stay well, Sarmed, and be safe. I never want to see you here again.'

I took a trembling breath as I struggled not to cry in front of this man who had quite possibly saved my life. Then I muttered a few inadequate words of thanks before turning and leaving the gym, knowing that I could never return.

10

The Smuggler

I ran all the way home, tears of frustration blinding my eyes. What had started off as a day of jubilation had suddenly turned into the worst day I had endured so far in Jordan. When I arrived back at my tiny apartment, I frantically rummaged through my clothes to find where I had hidden my passport, then pulled it out to look at it. I sat staring at that document for some time, as if by willing it to be so I could make it genuine, or at least extend the time left on my fake entry stamps by a few months. But of course it remained just as it had always been: a fake passport for an illegal alien. I felt a crushing sense of loneliness – I might have started to make a few friends here in Amman, but in that moment I realized that any sense of belonging or stability I might have felt in the past few months had been entirely misplaced. Nothing could change the fact that I was an outsider, on the run from the country that I considered home and not tolerated by the authorities in this halfway house. In the back of my mind I realized I had harboured a vague desire to stay in Jordan for a long time, to continue working at the company, to continue seeing Shireen; but it was suddenly clear to me what a futile hope that was. Abu Sameer's parting words had sounded in my ears like a wake-up call: *You can't live like this for ever, Sarmed. It's madness.*

I looked out of my window over the roofs of Amman, and not for the first time my thoughts took me back to the house in Al-Mansour where my family were still living. It was around dinnertime. My mother would have hosed down the front yard to cool it after the fierce heat of the afternoon sun, and the air would be thick with the humidity and the aroma of the food my grandmother would be cooking. Ahmed and Marwa would be playing; perhaps Saad would have arrived, bringing my grandparents a gift of watermelon or peaches as he always did. Perhaps my mother would speak proudly of her son who was making a new life for himself: he is successful, she would say; he sends money home.

'He's a good boy,' my grandfather would mutter. '*Inshallah*, all is well.'

And Saad would sit quietly, keeping his own counsel.

It made me feel even lonelier, knowing that I could

never travel back to the place that I missed so much, that little house that was to me an oasis of peace and hospitality in the centre of the city I had fled. Inside its walls, I could just be myself – no lies, no pretences, no need to be constantly on my guard.

Suddenly the irony seemed too horrible to consider. I had run away from home, never to return, and yet I missed it with every bone in my body. I ached to be with the people I loved, the people who loved me. And somewhere deep down I felt guilt too. Saad had made it clear to me that I was being helped out of Iraq so that I might help my family out, yet I didn't seem to be any closer to achieving that aim than I had been the day I arrived. Sure, I sent money home, but freedom was more expensive than that. I rummaged in a cupboard for something to eat, but gave up when I found nothing that tempted me. I wasn't really hungry anyway.

As night fell, I took to my bed; but as had been the case so often in recent weeks, I barely slept. My eyes, wide open, stared at the blackness of the ceiling as I considered what options I had. My savings were scant: I had been putting aside a little every month to fund my eventual escape from Jordan, but the rest had been spent on my accommodation and on sending something home to my family as often as they needed it. Even had the coffers been full, however, I wasn't about to announce my desire to get out of the country to just anyone in Hashemite

Square – the conmen would have been on me like hyenas, and I would never have been able to tell the genuine offers from the bogus ones. Occasionally I would sit up straight in bed, struck by an overwhelming sense of panic, and with these thoughts rushing through my mind the night passed fitfully.

The next morning I hoped more than ever to run into Shireen on the way into work. I felt that more than anybody else she accepted me for who I was, not what it said on my documents, and I had always found that her presence calmed me, despite her refusal to meet me at any time other than on our morning walks; and if ever I needed soothing, it was now. But she was nowhere to be seen, so I shuffled my way to the office with a renewed nervousness that did nothing for my state of mind. All day I moped around, dark rings under my eyes and a constant frown on my face. Bakir noticed it, and would bark out instructions occasionally to keep me alert; but at other times I saw him looking at me thoughtfully, as if wondering what was going through my mind. It unnerved me even more. I was thankful that I had not mentioned the name of the company to the police officer, but it didn't mean that I felt safe at work. Suddenly I didn't feel safe anywhere, or with anyone.

Except one person.

I had maintained my friendship with Abu Firas, the Iraqi architect whom I had met through working at the company. He had legitimately made his home in Jordan, and was always neatly dressed, quietly spoken and modest – my very first opinion when I had met him some time previously was that he was a reputable and honest man, not at all a charlatan. He would often come to Hashemite Square and drink lemonade in the evenings as the heat of the sun faded, and sometimes we would talk. Gradually he learned the general nature of my situation – although as always I had refrained from telling him the whole story – and one day he had quietly said to me, 'When the time comes, Sarmed, and if you need any help, I know a few people.' Nothing more – no brash claims or demands for money that would have instantly marked him out as a crook. It was no surprise to me that he knew about such things. Maybe he did make a little money arranging for people to smuggle themselves out of Jordan, but my impression was that he kept abreast of such matters because, although he had a good job in Amman, he knew that the Jordanian authorities could deport him at any time on a whim, so he had to know the best ways of getting to the West. I had nodded gratefully and stashed his offer of help away in my mind for the moment when I needed it. Now that moment had arrived. I decided to hunt him out that evening.

Sure enough he was there, sitting alone at his usual table on the pavement outside his usual café, an ice-cold drink and a small plate of tempting *baklava* placed neatly in front of him. He seemed perfectly content watching the daily hustle and bustle of Hashemite Square unfold before him, and didn't notice me until I was almost upon him. He smiled as I approached and gestured for me to sit down. 'I haven't seen you in a long while, Sarmed,' he complained.

'I've been busy, Abu Firas,' I explained, my eyes flicking nervously around me. 'Work.'

'And chasing pretty young Palestinian girls, from what I hear.' He winked at me as I felt a blush rising to my cheek.

We sat there in silence for a while. Abu Firas watched me as he took a sip from his drink, clearly waiting for me to say whatever it was I had come to tell him.

'I had some trouble with the police yesterday.'

He seemed unsurprised. 'Is it all sorted out now?'

'Kind of. But I think the time has come for me to leave.'

'I'll be sorry to see you go,' he replied, as though wilfully ignoring the subtext of what I was saying. I felt momentarily confused – perhaps I had misunderstood or misremembered the offer he had made?

'You said a while ago that you might be able to help me.'

'It's possible.'

'How much will I have to pay you?' I thought I might as well get the question out in the open.

Abu Firas took another sip from his drink. 'I am an

architect, Sarmed, not a people-smuggler. If I help you, it won't be because I want your money. It's because I understand what you are running from.'

My eyes narrowed slightly. This was not quite what I had expected.

'You're suspicious,' Abu Firas noticed. 'Good. You need to be. The circles in which we move are full of corruption, Sarmed, and you need to be careful. If you are going to make it to England, you will have to take great risks. Plenty of people will give you advice, me included. But at the end of the day, every decision you make must be your own. Do you understand?'

I nodded mutely.

'Good. Do you have your passport with you?'

Fortunately I had thought to bring it, thinking he might ask me that. Abu Firas took it from me, held it surreptitiously between himself and the table and spent some time flicking through it.

'This is a very good fake. In fact I would say that it was originally a genuine blank passport from Baghdad. The only people who will be able to spot it is not official will be the Iraqis themselves. But your Jordanian entry stamps have expired.'

'I know.'

He shook his head regretfully. 'That was foolish, Sarmed. It makes things much more difficult.'

'What am I going to do?'

Abu Firas thought for a moment. 'You need to get to Malaysia.'

'Malaysia?' It seemed like a crazy route, halfway across the world in the wrong direction. 'Why?'

'Because you can, Sarmed. Look, the Iraqi passport is the most disregarded passport in the world. There are very few places it will get you, but Malaysia is one. As soon as you can, you need to go to the Malaysian Embassy and apply for a single-entry visa. The Malaysians won't care that your entry stamps into Jordan have expired. They should give it to you there and then.'

I stared at him as if he was mad. 'But Abu Firas, this is a fake passport. What if they find out?'

'They won't be looking out for it. Like I say, only the Iraqis will know that this isn't genuine. And in any case, only an idiot would apply for a visa in person on a forged Iraqi passport. They'll never suspect anyone would do such a thing.' He flashed me a smile that did nothing for my confidence. 'Trust me, Sarmed, this is your only option.'

'What will I do when I get to Malaysia?'

'I have contacts in the West who can supply you with a fake United Arab Emirates passport. That, I'm afraid, will cost you money – not for me but for the counter-feiters. UAE passport holders can travel directly between Malaysia and the UK without visas. It should be enough to get you out of Malaysia.'

'Can't I just use this UAE passport to leave Jordan?'

'No,' Abu Firas replied sharply. 'I can help you fake Jordanian entry and exit stamps on the UAE passport just in case you get questioned in Malaysia, but it would be best if the Jordanians did not see them. They would only need to tap the details into their system to establish that the UAE passport is fake. If they do that, you'll be looking at a long prison sentence. It's much more difficult for them to establish the authenticity of your Iraqi passport.'

'How will you fake the entry and exit stamps?' I asked him.

'I told you, Sarmed, I'm an architect. I draw things and make designs. Forging a little stamp like that won't be a big problem for me. But listen – keep that to yourself.'

I sat there quietly for a moment as I tried to absorb everything I had been told. Abu Firas's plan seemed to me to be fraught with risks. So many things could go wrong, but one concern worried me more than any other. 'If I leave Jordan on my Iraqi passport, what will the border guards do when they see my entry stamps have expired?'

Abu Firas sighed. 'I don't know, Sarmed. The truth is it will probably be up to the mood of whoever interrogates you.'

'But they won't deport me?'

'It's possible.'

'Then I can't do this.'

Abu Firas's face became serious. 'I don't think you have

a choice, Sarmed. The longer you leave it, the more difficult things will become for you. I know you haven't told me everything about why you had to leave Iraq, but I sense that things would go very badly for you if you were forced to return. That's why I wouldn't suggest this if I didn't think it was the only way. I know what I'm suggesting is risky, but if you sit around waiting for risk-free methods of leaving the country, you'll be an old man before you get out.'

He winked at me, a curiously upbeat gesture given our conversation.

'Or at the very least,' he said, 'I will be.'

My meeting with Abu Firas left me in two minds. On the one hand I was glad I had him to advise me – he seemed to know what he was talking about, and that was encouraging. But at the same time, he had been eager to point out to me the risks I was going to have to take. What he had told me represented progress, but it did nothing to ease my mind.

It all seemed so complicated, and I wondered if there might not be an easier way. I had heard that the British Embassy would sometimes issue foreign nationals with a study visa so that they could travel to the UK in order to attend university. I had shown my capacity for study – perhaps they would take me on? I arranged an immediate appointment for a study visa application, and the fact that they agreed to see me so soon filled me with confidence.

As I was waiting there, I fell into conversation with an Iraqi woman who was obviously several months pregnant. She told me that she was a British citizen through her marriage to an Englishman, but she had come to inform the embassy that she was returning to Iraq in order to have her baby there.

I was astonished. 'Why do you want to do that?' I asked her. 'What if you don't get back out again?'

'That's why I'm informing the British Embassy,' she told me, her serious face full of concern.

'Aren't you scared? You know what it's like there now. It's not a safe place.'

'Of course I'm scared,' she said plainly. 'But despite everything it's still my country, and I hope that some day I will be able to return for good. But in the meantime I want my child to be born on Iraqi soil.' She smiled at me. 'You're very young. One day, perhaps, you'll understand.'

Deep down, I think perhaps I did.

I was ushered into a stark room in the embassy by an official carrying a cup of coffee – I remember thinking how strange that was, as officials in Iraq carried nothing but a stern face and a glower for whomever they had to deal with. 'What can I do for you?' he asked as we both sat down.

I handed him an application form. 'I'd like to apply for a study visa,' I told him.

'I see.' His face was inscrutable. 'And how do you propose to pay for your course?'

'I have an uncle in England,' I told him. 'I'm sure he will fund me for the first year.'

'And after that?'

'I'll have to get a job,' I told him honestly.

The official shook his head. 'No,' he told me. 'I'm afraid it doesn't work like that. I need to see that you have the funds to pay for your entire course and your living expenses *before* I issue you a visa.'

'But that could be sixty or seventy thousand pounds,' I protested.

'Yes,' he replied shortly. He looked down at my application again. 'You're from Iraq, I see. Why don't you finish your education in Iraq?'

'It's not as simple as that,' I told him.

'Have you completed your military service?'

I shook my head.

'Why not?'

'Because I don't want to serve a criminal.'

He looked at me with undisguised disapproval. 'I suggest you return home and continue your military service,' he said, ignoring my previous statement. 'Then you can complete your studies there. We can do nothing for you here.'

I couldn't believe what I was hearing, that a British official could be so naive. But it was clear from his demeanour that there was nothing I could do to change his mind, so I made my excuses and left.

Knocked back, I was still reluctant to follow Abu Firas's advice, and so I quietly let it be known among a few of my acquaintances that I was looking for someone who could help me leave. Suddenly I was inundated with offers, shady characters pretending to be my closest friend and promising that they could get me anywhere in the world in return for more money than I could pay them – in advance. But without exception, when I probed a little deeper into their plans I found that they were either nebulous or non-existent; and when I suggested that I would only pay them once I was successfully in England, they melted away, never to be seen again.

And so I contacted Abu Firas once more, to tell him that I intended to go ahead with his plan.

He agreed to make arrangements for the UAE passport, while I prepared myself for the first hurdle: a trip to the Malaysian Embassy, false Iraqi passport in hand, to apply for a visa. To my astonishment, and just as Abu Firas had predicted, it was issued without question. Suddenly I began to have a little more faith in my benefactor.

There were other problems, though. Along with my photograph, I had given Abu Firas half the money, the other half to be handed over on delivery of the passport, and this would all but wipe out my savings. Somehow I was going to have to raise the money to pay for my flights to Malaysia and to England, and I could think of no way of doing so. My friends couldn't help me out, and asking Abu Firas for a loan seemed to me to be a favour too far. Still, until I had the UAE passport in my hands it was all just a dream anyway. I had no idea how long it would take, so I kept my head down and continued my work at the company, squirrelling away as much of my pay as I possibly could.

Days became weeks, and the passport did not arrive. Occasionally I would see Abu Firas and ask him if there was any progress. His response was always the same: 'These things take time, Sarmed. It will come.' But it didn't come, and I even started to wonder if Abu Firas had been stringing me along after all. The stress of waiting was becoming almost unbearable. My nights were increasingly wakeful, and I continued to suffer the mysterious stomach pains that had been plaguing me over the past few months. I did my best to distract myself by redoubling my efforts with Shireen. Our morning strolls were just as frequent and just as cherished. We had fallen into the easy companionship of good friends, but still she refused to meet me at any other time. In my eagerness to be with her, though, I started plotting a wild scheme in my mind. 'Do you ever think about leaving Amman?' I asked her one day as we were walking together.

'Sometimes,' she replied enigmatically. 'Why?'

'Oh, I just wondered,' I told her, doing my best to hide the smile I felt inside.

As the days passed I asked the same question in round-about ways. Had she ever thought about living in England? What would she do if she went there? Would she miss her family? I began to persuade myself that her answers contained a happy subtext. She knew I would not stay in Jordan for ever – perhaps I could persuade her to follow her dream and come with me. I fantasized about the idea – about having someone by my side in the gruelling times ahead who I trusted, who I felt close to. If I could persuade Shireen to come with me, it seemed to me that all my prayers would be answered. But I refrained from asking her, because as yet I had nothing to offer.

It was some weeks after my initial meeting with Abu Firas that I was quietly going about my business at work when I got a call from the reception. 'Sarmed, courier for you.' I was perplexed. Who would be couriering packages to me here? I went to collect it and suddenly found myself having to catch my breath. It was a small package. Passport-sized. I thanked the receptionist then swiftly went to find a deserted corner of the office where I could open it in private. With trembling hands I unsealed the packaging and slid the pristine new document out of its envelope, before spending several minutes nervously examining it. My photograph was there, above the false name Adel Ahmed – it looked an odd juxtaposition, but I was going to have to teach myself to be comfortable with that.

In every way it was perfect.

In with the passport there was a brief handwritten note. 'May Allah guide your steps and may you be successful in all you set out to achieve, and *inshallah* you will arrive safely.' It was short, sentimental even, but this anonymous message from a faceless well-wisher in a far-off country meant a great deal to me. I stood there, passport and note in hand, and looked out of the window at the busy streets of Amman. I suddenly realized that whenever I had done this before, I had felt somehow inferior to everybody else down there. They were OK. They were allowed to be here. In Amman, at least, they were better than me. But today all that had changed. With the arrival of the small but powerful document in my hand, I was as good as anyone else because now, like them, I had a future.

My musings were interrupted by Bakir, shouting my name somewhere nearby. I tucked the passport safely into my pocket and went back to work.

That afternoon I went straight to the library at the British Council and applied for a membership card in my new name using my new passport. It was readily given and certainly not an official document, but I thought it might just be helpful should I run into any difficulty. Then I hurried back to Hashemite Square, where I had arranged to meet Abu Firas. He took the passport from me. 'Now you need to buy your tickets,' he told me. 'Remember you need two – one in your Iraqi name, one in your UAE name. You use the Iraqi one to leave Jordan, and the UAE one to enter Malaysia. When you have them, let me know the date you are leaving and I can forge your exit stamp for you.'

I nodded my head. How could I tell him, after everything he had done, that even now I didn't have the money for the tickets? I had racked my brains to come up with a solution. None of my acquaintances was in a financial state to help me, and I couldn't very well go to my family. There was only one thing I could think of, one path open to me that would allow me to go through with my plan. It was a long shot, and it would have to wait until the following day.

I arrived at work early the next morning, and made sure that Bakir's tea was on his desk before he had the opportunity to ask for it. He took a sip without uttering a word of thanks, then pretended not to notice me as I stood by his desk, waiting expectantly for him to realize that I wanted to speak to him. 'What is it, Sarmed?' he eventually asked, letting his corpulent body relax back in his chair and flicking his thumb from under his armpit.

I cleared my throat. 'Mr Bakir,' I began. 'I'm thinking that I might like to do some travelling.'

Bakir's face twitched, as though he could sense I was about to ask him a question he wouldn't much like.

'I was wondering if the company would advance me the money I need for my air fare.'

For a few moments Bakir did not answer. In fact he didn't even look at me, choosing instead to gaze non-committally across the room. Then he took another sip of his tea before turning to me and finally speaking. 'Unless I am mistaken, Sarmed, you do not intend to return to Amman once you have left.'

I was too shocked by his insight to reply.

His voice became sharper. 'Am I right?'

'No, Mr Bakir . . .' I started to say, but he interrupted me.

'I'm not stupid, Sarmed. I lose a secretary and my money. What's in it for me?'

That wasn't a question I could answer. I watched him carefully – his indecision was written plainly on his face. Somewhere deep inside he wanted to help me, I think, but in the end his fear of the consequences got the better of him. 'I can't authorize this,' he said with uncharacteristic quietness.

I nodded in mute acceptance, understanding that, as a Jordanian, he would not want to be seen giving money away to an Iraqi. I had no idea who I could turn to now.

Then he continued. 'I don't blame you for wanting to go, Sarmed. I've had my eye on you for quite a while now. You're a good lad, but it's been clear from the outset that you wouldn't stay here for long. Why don't you speak to Zaidoon? Maybe he will help you.'

It was a good idea. Zaidoon was Mushtaq's deputy and that rare thing, an Iraqi with an American green card. We got on well – he was a very fair person who was happy to help hardworking, decent Iraqis in the company and who always seemed to have time for my incessant questions about life in the West. I went to find him immediately. 'How much do you need?' he asked me.

I plucked a figure out of thin air – more than I would require, probably, and a seemingly huge amount to me; but to Zaidoon it was no doubt a small sum.

He considered it for a few moments. 'Very well,' he said finally. 'The company sometimes makes loans to its employees. I'm sure we can arrange something. But remember, it's a loan. If you ever find yourself in Amman again, you will be expected to pay it back.'

'And if I don't?' I held my breath.

'Then you can send it to us when you settle in the UK.' His words spoke of doing things by the book, but his eyes flashed in a friendly way that made it clear that he, at least, would not expect the money back.

I smiled at him. 'Thank you,' I said.

He nodded in acknowledgement. 'Good luck, Sarmed. If I'm honest, it sounds to me like you're going to need it. Now if I were you, I'd get back to Bakir and fetch him another cup of tea. He doesn't pay you to stand around chatting with me.'

* * *

I bought two tickets to Kuala Lumpur, one in the name on my Iraqi passport, one in the name on my UAE passport. I gave the dates to Abu Firas and two days later he returned my UAE passport, complete with perfectly forged Jordanian entry and exit stamps. I also bought an expensive suit to make myself look like a well-to-do young UAE citizen, not a desperate Iraqi refugee. It was light grey in colour, and I matched it with a pink tie: as I looked at myself in the mirror, I was reminded of my father – it was just the kind of suit he used to wear. What would he think if he saw me now? There would be a harsh word, no doubt. He would tell me that what I was doing was ridiculous, that I would never have the skill and the nerve to go through with this dangerous plan. Certainly there would be no hint of encouragement. I removed the suit and stashed it away safely for the day of my journey.

Two days before I was due to depart I went to find Shireen. She was walking to work as usual as I fell in beside her. 'I need to talk to you,' I said urgently.

She stopped, surprised, I suppose, by the tone of my voice. 'What is it, Sarmed?'

'I'm leaving.'

'What do you mean?'

'Leaving Amman. For good.'

'When?' I was pleased to note that she seemed genuinely saddened by the news.

'In two days' time. I have a flight booked to Malaysia, and from there to England. I want you to come with me.'

Shireen's eyes widened. 'Sarmed,' she said, 'I don't know what to say . . .'

Silently I urged her to say yes.

'. . . but there's just no way I can come with you to England.'

Her words were like a knife in my heart. 'Why not?' I whispered.

She looked at me with what I suppose was genuine sympathy. 'You're a sweet man, Sarmed,' she managed eventually, 'and a good friend. But not that sort of a friend. Besides, my family would never forgive me if I left them.'

'But it would be for a better life . . .'

'A better life for you, Sarmed. Not for me. The people I love are here – it's my home.'

'I thought you considered yourself a refugee.'

'I do, Sarmed. But I've lived here all my life, and home is where your family are. They wouldn't want me to leave them.'

'Maybe I could talk to your family,' I persisted. 'Persuade them . . .'

'No, Sarmed,' she said firmly, 'because I don't want to leave them either.' She lowered her eyelashes in a sorrowful way. 'Sarmed, there's something I have to tell you. I've been waiting for the right moment but it has never arrived. I'm engaged to be married.'

I was momentarily speechless, before feeling a hot flush of embarrassment creep up my neck. 'I'm sorry, Shireen,' I said finally. 'If I'd known I wouldn't have asked you. Forgive me.'

Gently she kissed me on the cheek – a particularly forward gesture for a young Arab girl. 'Of course I forgive you, Sarmed.'

We stood there in awkward silence, which was finally broken by Shireen. 'Is it safe, what you are doing?'

I shrugged, affecting more bravado than I felt. 'I'll be OK. I have good people helping me.'

'I hope so, Sarmed.' And then the words that I desperately didn't want to hear. 'I don't suppose I'll see you again, shall I?'

I shook my head.

'Goodbye then,' she said quietly but firmly. '*Allah ma'ak*, God be with you. I will miss you.'

Shireen turned and continued down the street. I watched her until she disappeared from sight.

I returned to the flat, shut the door, and kicked the wall in frustration. My emotions for the rest of that day were more confused than they had ever been. There was sorrow, certainly, tinged with shame at the embarrassment my request had caused. But as time wore on, and I was forced to come to terms with what had happened that morning, I realized how improbable it had always been that Shireen would have come with me. Not everyone was as displaced as me. Not everyone felt the need to cross over the fence to a greener field. In a strange way, I stoically told myself, it was a relief. Shireen was the only reason I had left for wanting to stay in Amman. Now she was beyond my reach for ever, and as a result I felt a renewed sense of purpose, a desperate drive to continue with my journey.

When the day arrived I rose early. My bags had been expectantly packed the night before, so I put on my suit, straightened my tie and checked my two sets of documents for the umpteenth time. Then I placed my Iraqi passport in one inside pocket, my UAE passport in the other, picked up my bags and went to catch the bus that would carry me on the thirty-minute journey to Amman airport.

It was more than seven years since I had been at an airport – when my father had brought me back to Baghdad – and I had forgotten how busy they could be. Businessmen – some in suits, others in more traditional Arab dress – marched purposefully across the concourse, paying little or no attention to the young Iraqi standing alone with his luggage and wondering where to go. Eventually I located the desk I needed, and checked in nervously but without any difficulty. I was in good time for my flight, but I decided there was nothing to be gained from going through passport control early – if they chose to question my documents, I did not want them to have too much time in which to do so – so I remained on the main concourse, pacing up and down, trying to keep out of sight of any officials as my anxiety increased with every minute that passed. At one point I killed some time at an airport café, where I ordered a Coca-Cola and sipped it slowly. If things didn't go as I hoped, I thought to myself, this might be the last time I tasted Coke for a long while, if not for ever. I had been mentally preparing myself for this moment for weeks; but now it was upon me, every instinct in my body screamed at me to leave the airport. It was too dangerous. So many things could go wrong, and if they did I would be on the first transport back to Baghdad. Every time that thought struck me, I shuddered, closed my eyes and tried to put it to the back of my mind.

Eventually, though, I couldn't put it off any longer. Taking deep breaths to calm my nerves, I approached passport control where an unsmiling border guard took my Iraqi passport. He had a computer terminal in front of him and, glancing through my documents, he typed something into the system. 'What's your father's name?' he asked.

I told him, wondering what that had to do with anything.

He tapped at the keyboard again without looking at me. 'Hmm . . .' I heard him grunt.

I tried to keep calm. 'What's wrong?' I asked.

'Wait here,' the guard said. He left his post and went to talk to another official. I watched them in huddled conversation as they examined my passport and looked back towards me. Eventually he returned to his post. 'How did you enter?'

'My entry stamps are there,' I told him curtly.

The guard shrugged. 'I think you entered illegally,' he told me. I remained silent, and as I think back on that awful moment I remember that everything around me seemed to fade into nothingness as every ounce of my concentration was directed towards what this man, on whose whim my future rested, was saying to me. 'Even if you didn't, you've overstayed. They're cracking down on people like you. It looks like you're in trouble. Come with me.' His words made my body suddenly crumple, and it took every effort just to stand up straight.

He led me to a side room which contained nothing but a desk and two chairs. 'Sit down,' he told me without ceremony. I did as I was told, watching him as he appeared to be wondering what to say next. 'We've had our eye on you,' he said finally.

My heart stopped. How could that be the case? 'What do you mean?' I breathed.

'We've had you under surveillance. You're a smuggler. You've been coming in and out illegally. You're not on the system.'

'That's not my fault.'

He stared directly into my eyes, waiting for me to say something else, and instantly I understood. He was trying to intimidate me. What he wanted I don't know – a bribe maybe, or perhaps he was genuinely suspicious of my documents and was trying to wear me down. I resolved to make sure he would do neither. 'You're mistaken,' I told him.

'You should have left the country months ago.'

'So let me leave.'

He shook his head with a nasty smile. 'I'm afraid it doesn't work like that, my friend. If you want to leave, you have to pay a fine. One dinar for every day you have overstayed.'

It amounted to a sizeable sum. The only money I had I would need in Malaysia to buy my ticket to the UK – there was no way I could hand any of it over to this guy. 'I don't have the money,' I told him firmly.

The guard shrugged and looked at his watch. 'Your flight leaves in fifteen minutes,' he said. 'I'll be back in ten to see what your decision is.' He left me alone in the room.

I sat there, sweating in my suit, while I decided what to do – though in truth the decision was made for me. I couldn't give him any money, so I had to stick to my story and pray that dealing with me would be too much of an administrative headache. If he wanted me out of the country, the easiest way was to get me on that plane.

True to his word, he returned exactly ten minutes later. 'Have you decided?'

'I told you,' I said, 'I don't have the money. I can't pay you.'

He looked me up and down, clearly taking in the fact that I was well dressed. 'You realize I have the power to deport you? All I need to do is say the word and you are on a police van back to the Iraqi border.' He must have seen the fear flicker across my face when he said that, because he nodded in understanding. 'OK, my friend,' he said in a nasty tone of voice. 'I'll do you a deal. Pay me half the money and I'll let you go.'

But even half the money he wanted would have ruined me, so I stood firm. 'I'm sorry,' I said. 'My papers are genuine, but I simply don't have the money to pay you.'

He considered that for a moment, then, 'Come with me.' He led me back to the passport control desk, and as I heard the final call for my flight I felt the eyes of everyone in the queue on me. Another official joined him and started asking me the same questions I had already answered, perhaps trying to spot an inconsistency in my story, perhaps just seeking to intimidate me more. Still I stood my ground.

Whether the official who was trying to haggle with me about my fine intended the money to go into his own pocket I can't say, but eventually it became obvious to him that I was in no position to pay it. He started huffing and puffing, like a spoiled schoolboy denied some treat, and finally took a big black stamp, opened my passport and brought it firmly down on to one of the pages. I looked at it: NO RETURN WITHIN FIVE YEARS. That meant I would be twenty-four before I could come back. 'Get out of here,' he muttered under his breath, before turning to his next passenger.

I looked at him, amazed, but he had already lost interest in me. So I turned away and sprinted to the gate, where my plane was ready to leave.

11

The Kiss

As I scrambled on to the plane, I received a host of evil looks from my fellow passengers – the flight had been delayed and it was clear to them that it was on my account. I found my seat and stared blankly out of the window waiting for take-off, my natural fear of flying overwhelmed by the excruciating need to get off the ground. Not until we were in the air would I feel as if I had put enough space between me and the passport control official who had nearly scuppered all my plans. As the air hostesses walked up and down the aisle, I avoided catching their eyes, my paranoia having convinced me that they were looking at all the passengers with suspicion, as if they were searching for someone. It was only when Jordan was far behind us that I began to relax, and then only slightly. My satisfaction at having made it on to the flight was mixed with a sense of anger at the passport official, and trepidation: I might be out of Jordan, but I was by no means safe yet.

My trip would take me first to Muscat, the capital of the kingdom of Oman, where we would wait in transit for six hours. That didn't worry me too much, as Abu Firas had thought it unlikely that they would check my papers while I was in transit, but I still felt uncomfortable with the two counterfeit passports in different pockets of my jacket as per his advice. At some stage on the flight between Muscat and Kuala Lumpur, Abu Firas had told me, I should dump my Iraqi passport: that way I couldn't be deported back to Iraq if my UAE passport was spotted as a fake. But it was too early yet – I might just need that document before I got on the flight to Malaysia.

The transit lounge in Muscat was as faceless as such places always are. Bored- and tired-looking passengers sat around, some of them reading, some of them chatting, most simply staring into space as they waited for their connecting flight. For me, though, the wait seemed to distil my panic, and I hadn't been there long before the familiar pains in my stomach started up again. I winced as I felt the stabbing in my abdomen, not because it was bad – not yet – but because I knew how debilitating it could become if I couldn't get it under control. Relaxation was the key – the pains were always exacerbated by stress – so

I made my way to the airport mosque. Perhaps a short period of prayer and contemplation would help me refocus my mind. The mosque had a comfortable carpet, so I prostrated myself in prayer and then found a quiet corner away from prying eyes where I could try to sleep. But sleep would not come, and the pains grew worse. They had never been this intense – terrible, excruciating pangs that bent me double and made walking a near impossibility. I did my best not to let the pain show in my face, but before long I was sweating, my dark skin pale and my eyes screwed up in agony. I needed help, so I went to find an air stewardess.

The woman who took me under her wing was like an angel. She sat me down, put her arm around me and cared for me as solicitously as if I were her own child. Once she had established what was wrong with me, she called a doctor in central Muscat. It took him the best part of an hour to get to me, an hour that passed as slowly as a day as the pains grew worse and worse. Once he arrived he led me to a sofa in the far corner of the transit lounge and laid me out flat before starting to question me about the pain. Where was it? Had it happened before? I tried to answer him as best I could, but I was distracted not only by my condition but also by the group of airport officials who had crowded round and were looking down at this well-dressed young man who was attracting so much attention. After listening to my responses, the doctor shook his head and turned away from me. 'I can't diagnose him here,' he told the officials. 'He needs special care, in hospital. I have to get him into Muscat.'

As one, the officials shook their heads. 'He needs a visa,' one of them said slightly apologetically. 'I'm afraid he can't leave the airport.'

The doctor shook his head in disgust at this display of red tape, but there wasn't much he could do about it. He knelt down in front of me. 'I'm going to give you a quick fix,' he said. 'Something to relieve the pain. You'll need to remove your jacket so that I can give you the injection.'

I shook my head to indicate that I was not going to remove my suit jacket. Despite the pain I was still acutely aware that I was carrying fake passports on either side of my suit, and there was no way I wanted anyone to get their hands on them; instead the doctor rolled up my sleeve and before I knew it he was approaching me with a syringe.

Almost as soon as the needle punctured my skin, I started to feel drowsy. 'What was that?' I heard myself mumbling.

'A tranquillizer,' his voice told me, sounding curiously detached from his body. The doctor's face grew blurred, as did the faces of the officials standing around him. I became overwhelmed with the desire to close my eyes and succumb to the blanket of sleep that was billowing over me, but I desperately tried to fight it. I'd had no idea I was going to be tranquillized, and although the drug had had an immediate effect on the pain in my stomach I knew I had to combat sleep. I had already attracted attention to myself, and if I was unconscious there was nothing to stop the crowd of officials from removing my jacket and discovering the secrets it contained. I forced myself to sit up. There were still people hanging around, so I folded my arms so that if I did fall asleep it would be that bit more difficult for them to remove my jacket.

Gradually the crowd of airport staff melted away, leaving just the doctor and the air stewardess beside me. Stubbornly I continued to fight off the urge to sleep, much to the surprise of the doctor. In my wooziness I heard him say to the air stewardess, 'It's not having the right effect. I need to give him a stronger dose.'

'No,' I muttered, feeling crushed by the effort of speaking.

'But you need to sleep,' he insisted.

I shook my head. 'Give it to me just before I get on the plane,' I managed to ask. 'That way I can fall asleep when we're in the air.'

The doctor and the air stewardess looked at each other nervously.

'You don't want to have to carry me on,' I muttered.

'Why won't you take my advice?' He sounded a little annoyed now.

'I just don't want to fall asleep. Not yet.'

The doctor shifted uncomfortably, aware that he couldn't force me to have an injection, but clearly worried about me nonetheless. 'OK,' he agreed finally. 'We'll do it your way. I'll stay with you until it's time for you to board; but when I say so, no arguments. Understood?'

I nodded my head, and spent the next couple of hours desperately trying to remain awake. Then, just as exhaustion threatened to overcome me, my flight was called. I rolled up my sleeve once more for the doctor, received the injection and then stumbled, accompanied by the air stewardess, towards the plane. By this time I was unaware of anyone else. I didn't know if the plane was crowded or empty, or even if there was anyone sitting next to me. I just slumped into my seat and instantly fell into a deep, dreamless sleep.

When I awoke it was dark outside. Confused by the drugs, I was momentarily surprised to be waking up somewhere other than my little apartment in Amman; even when the reality of where I was and what I was doing came rushing back to me, it took a while to shake off the chemically induced drowsiness I was feeling. Gradually I became aware of someone sitting next to me. She was perhaps a couple of years younger than me and looked to be of Asian origin. She was extremely pretty. 'Am I keeping you awake?' she asked with a smile as I yawned rather rudely next to her.

'I'm sorry,' I apologized. 'I was very tired.'

'You must have been,' the girl replied. 'You've been asleep for more than three hours.'

I looked at my watch. She was right – we were well into the flight by now. The tranquillizer had done its job well, and I was relieved that the stomach pains had subsided; I even found that I was hungry. 'Have they served any food yet?' I asked my companion.

'Not yet.' And as if summoned by our conversation, an air hostess started rattling a trolley of plastic meals down the aisle. I ate mine hungrily while the girl and I fell into easy conversation. She was travelling back to Kuala Lumpur with her family, who were elsewhere on the flight, having been to Saudi Arabia to perform the Hajj, the Muslim pilgrimage to Mecca. I told her that I was visiting friends in Malaysia.

'Where are you from?'

'The UAE,' I lied. She seemed to accept my story without question.

'And what do you do for a living?'

'I'm studying to be a doctor.' That at least was half true, and it made me feel good to be able to say it.

She told me her name was Khadija, and she started asking me about my family. In my hand luggage I had a small envelope containing some old photographs that were very precious to me. She would not know that they had actually been taken in Baghdad or Mosul, so I showed them to her, pointing out my mother, Uncle Saad, my brother and sister. She seemed genuinely interested in them, and I found the process therapeutic. I had not talked to anyone about my family for such a long time that to do so now made me feel closer to them, even if I was thousands of miles away.

After a while the overhead lights dimmed and the hubbub of conversation in the plane ebbed away. We fell silent too, and I suddenly became aware that the girl had rested her head against my shoulder. I could hear her breathing deeply. 'Are you OK?' I whispered.

She sat up again, nodded her head and smiled. There was a momentary tenseness between us, something un-spoken that made me want to break away from her wide-eyed glance, but I couldn't. And then, spontaneously, as though by some prearranged signal, our lips touched and we gently kissed.

We stayed in that embrace for several minutes. When she pulled away, she looked sheepishly at me, her cheeks faintly rosy and her big eyes blinking just a bit too much. Once more she leaned her head against me and we sat there in silence, our fingers interlocked, while everybody about us fell asleep, lulled by the calming hum of the plane's engines. It was a comfort to me to feel her warmth against my shoulder, and it allowed me to relax and collect my thoughts.

My encounter with Khadija had lightened my spirits,

but my Iraqi passport still felt like a weight in my jacket and I needed to get rid of it. That way, if I had any trouble entering on my UAE passport, they would not find it on me if I was searched, and with no Iraqi passport I could not be deported to Iraq. But hiding a passport on a crowded plane would not be easy, and in any case I wasn't entirely sure that the document wouldn't come in useful at some stage in the future. I needed to do something quickly, however. We would soon be in Malaysia, and I couldn't have the thing on me. I glanced down at the girl whose head was still on my shoulder. There was no doubt in my mind that she would help me if I asked it of her, but it would not be right to let her know the truth about what I was doing. What she didn't know about couldn't incriminate her.

But what if she could help me unwittingly? Safely? An idea started to form in my mind, and with it my justifications for what I did. Looking back, I would have to say that I am not particularly proud of my actions, but it was the only way I could think of achieving what I needed to do.

Surreptitiously I placed the envelope containing my family photos into my pocket. Then I excused myself and walked up the aisle to the lavatory. Safely locked inside, I took my Iraqi passport out of my jacket, slid it inside the envelope with the photographs, then sealed the envelope before walking back to my seat. We started talking again in hushed voices, and I waited for an appropriate moment in the conversation before making my request. 'Do you think you could do me a favour?' I asked.

'Of course,' she replied. 'What is it?'

'I'm not very familiar with the Malaysian postal service. I want to send these photos to my uncle in England as he was asking for some pictures. Would you send it for me?'

For a moment she didn't reply, and I silently cursed myself. As I had spoken the words, the plan had sounded a lot less probable than it had in my head. But I needn't have worried. 'Sure,' she said.

Thanking her, I wrote the address on the front of the envelope and handed it over. She placed it with the rest of her hand luggage, and the matter was not mentioned again. I comforted myself that, as a Malaysian coming back to her home country, it was unlikely that she would be searched; even if my Iraqi passport was found on her person, it would probably just cause her some small inconvenience, whereas for me it could spell deportation and the horrors that awaited me back in Baghdad.

And then we landed. As the wheels touched down on Malaysian soil, the familiar feeling of sick apprehension reintroduced itself in my gut, and I found myself wishing to be anywhere but where I was. 'Are you all right, Adel?' the girl asked me. I just nodded. 'Well, I guess I should say goodbye. It was nice to meet you.' She gave me her number and address in the area of Petaling Jaya, and then flashed me a coquettish little grin that I struggled to reciprocate; as the plane came to a halt, she stood up and went to join the rest of her family.

In the airport terminal I held back at passport control as I wanted to make sure that my Iraqi passport had made it safely through before I presented my documents. Queuing up, I saw the girl and her family waiting to pass through the control booth and it was with a sense of relief that I witnessed them being waved through without any difficulty. They were Malaysian, of course, but it didn't seem as if anybody was being questioned in any great detail – not that that did anything to allay the panic I was feeling at what I was about to do. I felt my stomach churning, and droplets of sweat dripping down my back; out of the blue I realized how much more crumpled my appearance was than when I had put my suit on the previous morning. It wasn't long before my turn came.

I stepped confidently up to the booth and fixed the border guard firmly in the eye as I handed him my forged documents. He leafed through the pages of the passport, stopping only briefly to glance at Abu Firas's phoney Jordanian entry and exit stamps. As he turned the page to examine my photograph I silently said a prayer of thanks to my architect friend and his dextrous skill. The border guard stared at my photograph for a moment, and then at me. I saw his eyebrows crinkle into a frown as he looked back at the photograph and I stopped breathing momentarily as he began to examine the document a little more closely. 'Where have you come from?' he asked politely.

'Jordan.'

'How long are you staying, sir?'

'A week, maybe two.'

'And where will you go to then?'

'Turkey,' I said confidently – it was another country UAE passport holders didn't need a visa for.

He continued to look through my documents as he appeared to mull over the answers I had given.

'How much money have you got, sir?'

'About a thousand dollars.'

'OK.' He continued reading for a moment then looked me up and down.

Then, suddenly, he stamped the passport, slammed it shut and handed it back to me. 'Welcome to Malaysia, Mr Ahmed,' he said with what almost passed as a smile.

I couldn't wait to leave the airport, and having collected my luggage I practically ran across the concourse to the exit doors, which slid open with a satisfying hiss. Immediately I stepped outside I hit a wall of humidity that soaked my skin – a very real and tangible reminder of how far from home I was.

I took a taxi into the centre of Kuala Lumpur. The driver made a few attempts to coax me into conversation, but I didn't speak his language and in any case my thoughts were in too much of a whirlwind for me to be able to talk sensibly to anyone. I kept pulling my UAE passport out of my pocket and looking at it: it was such a small thing, and yet it had got me so far. Fifty per cent of the way. A ticket to freedom.

I found myself a shabby hotel in a backstreet of one of the less salubrious quarters of the city – it was all my meagre budget would allow. Dirt cheap, my room was little more than a couple of metres square, with filthy bedclothes and cockroaches as roommates; sleep would be difficult, as the constant clatter of Malaysian families washing their dishes in the courtyard of the shabby tenement block opposite rang through the air seemingly twenty-four hours a day. But the squalor didn't bother me in the least. If all went according to plan I would only be there for a few nights before I managed to book my passage to London. Of far greater concern was the fact that I had to leave my precious passport behind the reception desk. I wanted to guard that little document with my life – it *was* my life – and I had tried to argue with the hotel owner, to persuade him to let me carry it with me. He was adamant: the rules were there to be obeyed, and if I wanted a room the passport would have to be stashed in the open pigeon-holes behind his beaten-up desk. Anyone could have taken it – I knew from my experiences over the past few months how active the market in stolen passports was – and this guy had no incentive to keep it safe. And so, several times a day, I would find myself wandering back to the hotel, just to glance at the pigeon-hole and check that my passage to freedom had not been stolen from me.

The following day I scoured the local travel agents and, having begged the receptionist to let me have my passport for just an hour in return for my room key, bought my ticket to London. That, at least, I could keep with me, and it didn't leave my person as I spent the next few days wandering the streets, taking in the sights and sounds of Kuala Lumpur. To me it was such an alien place – four thousand miles from home, and with a culture that could not have been more different from Baghdad or Amman. I made calls home, speaking in my roundabout way so that my family would know that I was safe without learning anything that would incriminate them. When the time came to eat, I would spend my money on cheap fast food from Western-style restaurants, as the local food was too strange for me to enjoy. And at nights I would lie on my small, uncomfortable mattress, listening to the scratching of the insects under the bed, waiting for the time to come when I could board my plane to England.

On 3 December 1995, I donned my suit once more, reclaimed my passport with an overwhelming sense of relief, and made my way to the airport. Having checked my luggage in, I strode confidently to passport control –

my previous success had invigorated me, and I knew there was nothing to be gained by a diffident approach – and handed my documents to the officer. As he began to check my papers, I looked around properly for the first time. All around me were armed policemen, thick, bullet-proof jackets protecting their torsos and evil-looking weapons slung across their chests. One of them caught me looking at him and returned my gaze with a flat, emotionless look. There was a certain swagger in his stance, as though he took a sinister pride in his authority, and I remember wondering how much different my life would have been had the same sense of pride been instilled in me when I joined the military. No doubt this man would have nothing other than contempt for a deserter like me, because although the world had branded Saddam a criminal it would no doubt condemn me too if I was caught escaping his terror in this way. The gun, and that flat stare, were a harsh reminder of how unwelcome I was.

'One moment, sir. Wait here, please.' The passport control officer broke me out of my daydream by addressing me. He went into a side room, leaving me with a queue of people behind shaking their heads in disapproval at the unwanted delay. But I was well used to this by now, so I held my head up high and did my best to bristle with confidence. A few moments later he returned, tapped the keys of his computer, then handed me the passport and nodded me on. I was through.

I waited at the gate, for some reason more nervous now than I had been at passport control, and started muttering prayers under my breath. I knew that Malaysia was a hub for people-traffickers trying to smuggle out people from the Middle East, mostly to Australia and Japan but also to Europe; so I wouldn't feel safe until I was airborne. It was with huge relief that I boarded and felt the now-familiar press of the g-force as the plane took off. This time there was no pretty girl to distract or help me – just a faceless businessman who spoke not a word for the entire flight. He did not notice, as our airline meals were cleared away, that I held back the plastic serrated knife and secreted it up my sleeve; or if he did, he didn't mention it.

I knew that I had to destroy my UAE passport to avoid any risk of deportation once I arrived in London, but in my youthful naivety I supposed that it would be better to do this once I was over European airspace in case I was somehow discovered while we were within the jurisdiction of somewhere less friendly. It was foolish of me to think, of course, that the plane would be forced to land on account of one stray Iraqi soldier, but I wanted to play it as safe as possible. The hours until we were cruising over the West ticked slowly by, but eventually, as we were flying over Germany, I excused myself and made my way to the toilets. Once safely locked inside, I took out my passport and my knife and proceeded to shred that precious document into indistinguishable ribbons. It took an age to slice my way through the laminated paper, but when I was finished I was left with an unrecognizable mass that I dropped, slightly regretfully, into the toilet bowl and flushed away. Those bits of paper and plastic that had afforded me safe passage so far disappeared in seconds. I then made my way back to my seat and did the only thing that was left for me to do: I waited.

Gradually I began to feel the familiar sensation of the plane losing altitude. It bumped and wobbled its way through the cloud cover, and my hand gripped the armrest tightly. The sudden turbulence was making me nervous, certainly; but I could not separate the anxiety I was feeling because of the juddering from the apprehension that seemed to saturate every cell in my body now that I was nearing the end of my journey. In the next hour I would find out if all the advice I had received, from Abu Firas and others, was sound; in the next hour I would know whether or not I was to be sent back to Iraq; in the next hour I would know my fate.

Suddenly the plane burst out of the clouds. I looked expectantly through the small window at the scene below. In England it was a bleak December day, misty and grey, the sort of weather I remembered with a nostalgic vagueness from my childhood, and which I would never have hoped to see in the arid heat or torrential rainy seasons of the Middle East. Fields stretched out like patchwork blankets, their shades of green and brown seeming strange to my Arabic eyes. There was the occasional town, grey and sprawling, and long lines of traffic, the car lights on full beam to brighten the way through the foggy atmosphere. It was a bland, chilly, uninviting scene; but I couldn't have welcomed that sight any more had all the golden palaces and riches of the East been spread out before my eyes. It was breathtaking. Impossible. I couldn't quite believe what I was seeing.

Twenty minutes later we were thundering down the runway. Through the drizzle I could make out the sights and sounds of the airport as the loudspeaker crackled into life and made me jump. 'Ladies and gentlemen,' said the captain, 'welcome to London.'

My eyes filled with tears and I continued to look resolutely out of the window so that my neighbour could not see that I was crying. I had made it. I had arrived.

As we passed through the gates, there were immigration officials standing by. I held my breath as I walked past them, knowing from hearsay that my life would be made a lot more difficult if I was stopped by one of them. Fortunately they were simply chatting among themselves, and so I joined the queue at the official booths of Heathrow Terminal Three passport control. I watched with amazement the ease with which my fellow passengers were ushered through – their British passports seemed to give them a genuine status that was unknown to me.

And then my turn came.

I approached the booth with a sense of expectation – excitement, almost – and a smile that was not reciprocated by the surly uniformed woman who received me; but after the aggression I had suffered in the past week, that was not going to worry me. I took a deep breath and, with a slight crack in my voice, I spoke the words that I had been practising in my head for days and days, the words that I hoped would finally mark the beginning of a new life, free from the tyrannies of my homeland.

'I want to claim political asylum,' I said.

12

A Knock at the Door

'Where's your passport?'

The woman stared at me with suspicion.

'I want to claim political asylum.'

'*Where ... is ... your ... passport?*' She repeated her question slowly, emphatically, as if talking to a child.

'I don't have one.'

She shook her head. 'I can't process you without a passport.'

I shrugged my shoulders, not knowing quite what to say. We stared at each other in silence until she finally broke the deadlock. 'What is your name?'

I told her. 'Sarmed Al-Samarrai.'

'Wait here,' she said abruptly, then left her post. A couple of minutes later she arrived back with two immigration officers, who eyed me up and down like I was a criminal before leading me to a nearby interview room. They interviewed me in a waspish, perfunctory manner, and I told them what I had done with my passport. One of them looked straight at me, eyebrow raised and a superior, authoritative look on his face. 'If we decide to, we can recover your passport, piece it back together again and deport you. You do realize that, I hope.'

His words had a crushing impact on me. I had just landed in this foreign country – I didn't know what the rules were, so it did not occur to me that they might be saying this just to make me uncomfortable. The elation I had felt before I claimed asylum was suddenly replaced by a horrible fear: what if everything I had been told was not true? What if I wasn't granted asylum after all? Everything would have been for nothing, and I would be sent back to where I came from, left to fend for myself, to fight a battle I couldn't possibly win. I could think of nothing to say to them, so I remained silent.

They continued to process me. They searched through all my luggage and took photocopies of any documentation or literature I had – my library card from the British Council in Amman with my false name on it, and a pile of tourist leaflets from Kuala Lumpur that I had stashed away to prove that I had been in Malaysia. They filled in forms and asked me questions, all without so much as a smile or a welcome. We will tolerate your presence, their behaviour seemed to imply, but don't make the mistake of thinking that you are in any way wanted here. I steeled myself against their attitude. Nobody likes to feel unwelcome, but I knew what the alternative was. 'What are the grounds of your claim for political asylum?' they asked me.

I had thought long and hard about how I would answer this question. I had been warned that if I revealed that I had been in the Iraqi military, they would take a special interest in me. I would be thrown into a holding bay and investigated, to ensure that I had not been responsible for any atrocities or war crimes. The process could take months. And so, although I was bursting to tell them my story, to persuade them that I was not the chancer they so clearly took me for, to persuade them that I was a political refugee and not an economic migrant, I held back. 'I don't want to live under a tyranny,' I told them, rather weakly to my ears. 'I don't want to serve a dictator and a criminal.'

The officers gave no reaction. They just wrote my words down.

Just as I was beginning to feel that I might never again see a friendly face, however, they released me into the care of some other officials who took me for X-rays, medical checks and blood samples. I was manhandled, prodded, poked and ordered around, but I was at least treated with a little respect, even the occasional moment of friendliness. I was asked if I had family in the UK, and I told them about my uncle Faisal in Leeds. A call was put through, he confirmed that he would receive me, and I was told to wait.

Eventually, twelve hours after we landed, I was allowed through. The sense of release brought tears to my eyes for a second time that day.

Faisal arranged for a friend of his to pick me up from the airport. I spent that night in the spare room of a flat somewhere on the outskirts of London, and the following day I was driven to Leeds, to see the man I had been looking forward to meeting for so long.

Faisal was a hero, a veteran of the Iran–Iraq war and a POW; his name was mentioned with hushed reverence back in my grandparents' house in Al-Mansour. I had not seen him since I was six years old; my grandparents hadn't seen him for twenty years. He had been a good boy, I remembered my grandmother saying. When he was a child, his brothers would spend their pocket money on bicycles whereas he would spend his on hijabs for his sisters. He was a humble, caring and religious man. 'Faisal,' she would mutter. 'He is an angel.' And as I travelled up to see him, the words my grandfather had whispered to me when I left Al-Mansour for the final time echoed in my head: 'May God be with you, and *inshallah* you will reach your uncle Faisal in England.' *Inshallah*. God willing. As I was driven to the north of England, I reflected on the fact that God had indeed been willing. I had completed my journey, and meeting Uncle Faisal was to be my reward.

To my grandmother, Faisal might have been an angel; to me he was more than that. When we first met, he gave me a somewhat horrified look. I now realize that he must have been shocked at my appearance. Gaunt and exhausted, with skin hanging from my bones, bags under my eyes and a haunted expression, I must have cut a very different figure from that of the well-fed six-year-old he remembered. He asked after his parents and siblings, but I had the impression that he might prefer not to know the true answer. 'They're fine,' I told him. 'They send their love.'

Faisal took me under his wing, and found me a place to live with two other Iraqis. He showed me around, helped me to integrate. Without him, I would have been flailing in the dark.

One day I received a call from Faisal. A letter had arrived at his house, addressed to me. I assumed that it would be from Baghdad, secretly sent by my mother or Saad, and as I clung to any small contact I could have with them I hurried over to read it. When I arrived, however, I was surprised to find something weightier than I would have expected from Baghdad. Intrigued, I opened it. A sheaf of photographs fell out, along with my Iraqi passport. And with it, in immaculate handwriting on a piece of expensive paper, was a note. 'I hope you had a safe journey. Good luck with your new life in the UK. *Inshallah* God will guide you and assist you, and keep you from danger.'

I had not told the girl on the plane anything about my plans to travel to England, for fear of incriminating her. I had not told her that I was illegal. I had not told her that I was making her an unwitting accomplice to my plans. Curiosity must have got the better of her, urging her to open up the package. Either that or I wasn't as clever as I had thought, and she had seen through it all.

In Baghdad or Amman, if you stopped someone in the street to ask them for directions, or for the time, the chances were that the conversation would lead on from there. Perhaps you would end up going for coffee; you might even be invited back to your new friend's house where they would offer to cook food for you. It is the Arabic way: hospitality is prized above almost anything. And although in Iraq you would have to be constantly on your guard for civilians who had the ear of the security forces, constantly aware of the subtext of these impromptu conversations, you nevertheless accepted this friendliness as a way of life.

How different it was in England. The last time I had been here, I was a child, unaware of such social subtleties; now I was in the thick of a cultural landscape that could scarcely have been more different from the one I had left.

I was lucky, though. At least I spoke the language, and had a genuine desire to learn everything I could about the country I had set my sights on for so long. For the first six months I was not allowed to work, but the government would fund asylum seekers to study at the local college, so I started working for my English and Business Studies A-levels – subjects that I thought would help me acclimatize. I also spent a great deal of time simply walking the streets, filling my eyes and ears with the sights and sounds of my new home, looking with wonder at how people were living. And yet I found English people somewhat colder than their Arabic counterparts – not unfriendly, just not that interested, unwilling to forge immediate relationships with a young Iraqi refugee who must have looked like any number of other foreign faces walking the streets. And so, to start with, I spent most of my time in the Middle Eastern communities. I passed large portions of my day at the local mosque, praying and socializing with people around whom I felt comfortable and, more importantly, who felt comfortable around me. Mostly these were young British Muslims of Iraqi, Egyptian, Lebanese and Syrian origin, simple, genuine, good-hearted people who had no need to ask me why I had fled Iraq or what horrors I had endured. They understood. Day by day they taught me about the way of life in the UK, how I should act, how I should talk, how I should behave. They cared for me more than anyone, and became like the family that had been denied me by my escape.

Except, of course, they *weren't* my family. My family was two and a half thousand miles away in a small compound in the shadow of the communications tower in Al-Mansour. My family was still living under the regime that would have me imprisoned, beaten or even worse if I dared to return to see them. I felt in some strange way as if my soul had been split: half of me revelled in the joy of having made it safely to England in the face of so many dangers and difficulties; half of me ached to see my nearest and dearest again. I could speak to them on the telephone, of course, but it was unsatisfactory to say the least. Calls out of Iraq were limited to ten minutes each, and even when I initiated the call we would always have to assume that the conversation was being listened to and recorded. Sometimes you could hear the heavy breathing of your silent eavesdropper. We all knew it would have proved deeply unfortunate for my family if they had let on that they knew where I was. The code we used enabled us to establish that we were all safe, but we could never speak the things that we really wanted to say or hear.

As soon as the conditions of my entry into the UK allowed, I started at college. My plan had always been to study medicine, to become a doctor and so give something back to the country that had granted me asylum. But I suppose, in my enthusiasm and naivety, I had not given proper thought to the realities of such a dream. Any qualifications I had achieved in Iraq were worthless in the UK, and the small exam I had taken when in Jordan was insufficient to get me on to a medicial course. Moreover, I would have to pursue more than a decade of study. It would be impossible, not because I wasn't keen but because I knew, now I was here, that I had to get a job. I would have to wait three years before I could be funded at university, but in any case I had no desire to live off the state, and as well as supporting myself I needed to be able to send some of my earnings – through convoluted routes – back to my family in Iraq. And I hoped that one day I would be able to help them get out. But that would take money – money that I would have to earn. Of course it could never be mentioned during my phone calls home, but every time I heard Saad's quiet, calm voice I remembered the words with which he had left me: *the genuine man never forgets his family*.

I did not neglect my studies entirely, however. In February 1996 I had enrolled on an English course, then a Business Studies course, and in my spare time I earned money painting houses. It was humble work, but I relished it; and any time I felt low I thought back to the grim realities of the Iraqi army, or the danger I had risked in working at the heart of the Hussein family's operations in Amman. As time passed I grew my hair long. I discarded the Western clothes that I had mistakenly believed to be trendy when I was living in the Middle East –

T-shirts with the insignias of heavy metal bands like Metallica and Aerosmith. I even took an English pseudonym – Louis Alsamari – in an attempt to appear more Westernized and so that I could travel back to the Middle East undetected if need be. Later I changed it to Lewis. Gradually I became more and more integrated. Although it would be another four years before I was granted a travel document to enable me to leave the country and return, I even started to have fun. After several months I found myself a more permanent job as a payroll clerk for a big company, and moved out of my shared accommodation into a small bedsit. Almost every waking hour was spent working: I had my day job as an accounts clerk, a Saturday job in a department store and a Sunday job with an estate agent. All this, on top of my studies. It was relentless, but I was determined to make the most of all the opportunities that had been afforded me.

Despite the hard work, my physical health began to improve. The stomach pains I had been suffering were diagnosed as a stress-induced ulcer and I was given treatment, but the fact that my life was now distinctly less traumatic must have played its part in the condition clearing up. But I still found myself afflicted by what I had endured: nightly I would wake from a sleep that had been troubled by dreams of Red Berets, desert wolves and flat-eyed immigration officials; I would relive my spell in the pit, as the sneering *arif* looked on; I would find myself in the cramped cell on the road from my unit to Baghdad, excrement smeared on the floor and no hope of escape. When I woke, my body would be shaking, my bedclothes damp with sweat, and I would spend the rest of the night wide awake, waiting for first light, with sleep just a distant and terrifying memory. Panic would overtake me, and I would fret about my family back in Al-Mansour. The authorities seemed to have forgotten about me and them – but how long would it be until they remembered, or their bribes ran out? Those lonely nights were filled with a series of horrifying 'what ifs'. The doctors diagnosed me with post-traumatic stress disorder: a fancy name for what amounted to an uncontrollable fear of my own past. I was referred to a therapist, who spent eight months working with me to try to conquer the PTSD. In the end he judged that it was too severe, and that I would need medication. I was prescribed maximum doses of Seroxat, and remained on the drug for the next six years.

To try to forget my troubles, I threw myself even more robustly into my work. In the small amounts of spare time that I had left, I tried to mingle with groups of young English people, and even though I gradually felt a greater sense of acceptance on their part, I never quite managed to feel comfortable, never quite shook off the feeling that I was an outsider in a strange world that had started to acknowledge me but to which I would always be an alien.

Until, that is, I met Rachel.

It was in a local bar that we met, the sort of chance encounter that you wouldn't expect to lead to anything serious – a glance across the room that led to a relationship that would change both our lives. We fell into an easy, friendly conversation that made us both feel comfortable, and from that night on we spent almost every spare hour we had with each other. I was transfixed by her beautiful long hair, by her modest smile and sparkling eyes that betrayed a vitality and fiery determination that I had never before encountered. She was older than me, ran her own business, and I was attracted by her confidence and poise. What she saw in me I can't say, but gradually, as we became closer, I opened up to her. In the time I had spent in England, I had learned to put my past into a far corner of my mind. I was embarrassed by my story, ashamed of having been in the Iraqi army and terrified that people would judge me. I kept my past to myself. But now, with the stark honesty of two people who were falling in love, we revealed all there was to tell about each other. The look of wide-eyed amazement mingled with horror and pity that I saw on Rachel's face as I told her everything I had gone through was a sudden, brutal reminder of my own past, and that I would never really be free of it.

'What about your family?' she asked me. 'Don't you miss them?'

'Of course I do,' I told her quietly. 'More than anything. But one day, maybe, I'll be able to see them again.'

'What can I do to help?'

I smiled gratefully at the offer. 'Nothing,' I told her. 'Not at the moment.'

Rachel and I moved in together, and after about six months we started talking about marriage. My uncle Faisal was a very religious man, well respected at the local mosque, and he did not like the idea of the two of us living together as man and wife without the sanctity bestowed on our relationship by a wedding ceremony, so he began to pressure us into getting married. Even if his influence on me had not been so great, however, we would have considered it. Our wedding day was not huge or lavish. It was just a small ceremony at the local register office, with two somewhat surprised-looking witnesses whom Rachel had dragged off the street. And yet, for all its simplicity, the words we spoke could not have been more poignant and meaningful. We were devoting our lives to each other, along with all that that entailed. As if to make the whole event more potent, Rachel was of Jewish extraction: her marriage to an Arab seemed to me to symbolize something particularly harmonious.

In the Hollywood movies to which I had become addicted, young couples in love promise the world to each other. They will do anything, they say. They will follow their loved one to hell and back. Little did I know that Rachel would end up doing exactly that for me.

* * *

It was not long after I moved in with Rachel that I received a call from Saad. Instantly I could tell from the sound of his voice that what he had to say was of great importance, so I restrained my usual effusiveness and listened. '*Habibi*,' he greeted me cautiously with the traditional Arabic term of affection, which served the double purpose of his not having to say my name. 'How are you? How is your health?'

'Fine,' I replied. 'And you?'

'We're *OK*.' He emphasized the word to make it clear that they were very far from OK, but he could say no more.

Soon afterwards I received a letter from Saad, sent covertly out of the country via Jordan because he knew that the authorities had teams of people reading regular mail. Its contents chilled my blood. Saad had been inter-rogated by Al-Mukhabarat, the feared intelligence service, in their Al-Haakimiya prison on 52nd Street, Karada district. The moment I read those words, a sick feeling rose in my stomach. It had been a long time since Al-Istikhbarat – specifically military intelligence – had questioned my family, and I had genuinely believed that the authorities had given up on me.

I could not have been more wrong. Saad was put into a room by himself, where his hands were cuffed behind his back. His eyes were pinned open so that he could not blink, and the light from a large projector was shone on to

304

his face. When he could stand this no more, he would be taken from the cell and either beaten or interrogated. This was repeated about every four hours, and lasted for three days, during which time he was given no food or water.

He steadfastly refused to admit that he knew my whereabouts.

When the three days were up, he was released, but it was made quite clear that he, along with the rest of my family, could expect worse than that if they did not comply with the intelligence service's demands.

When I had read the letter, I banged the wall in frustration. I knew I would have to remain calm if I was going to be of any help to them. I knew anger would get me nowhere. But anger was what I was feeling – anger and an intolerable impotence at being so far away when all this was happening on my account. When Rachel returned home, she could tell from the look on my face that something was wrong, and though she begged me to tell her what had happened, somehow I didn't have the heart. I looked around with distaste at the comfortable flat we shared: the smart furniture, the carpets, the pictures on the wall, all the trinkets of the affluent West. They seemed ridiculous to me now. How could I surround myself with such comfort while people were being beaten and threatened on my account? I felt sick to my very soul that, despite all my hard work since I had arrived in England, I was no nearer to being able to get them out. I had failed them, and they were paying the price.

From that moment on, my every waking thought was with my family. I would go into fits of panic, unable to sleep and desperate to speak to them; hours would be spent trying to get through on the phone, sometimes successfully, sometimes not. Poor Rachel, when she learned the stark and brutal truth of what was happening in Baghdad, did her best to comfort me, but it was in vain.

It was not long after I first heard the terrible news that I received another call from Saad. 'Those people I was telling you about, *habibi*,' he said before I had the chance even to enquire after his health. 'They want a bit of money.' His voice was abrupt, with an unaccustomed tinge of anxiety, and I understood what he was saying – he had to pay another bribe.

'I'll send as much as I can.'

'You must, *habibi*. Otherwise they can't do what they promised. It's too much for me.'

His meaning was clear – the amounts I had been sending home were not enough. Not now.

'I hope you're not enjoying yourself too much,' he continued. I didn't know what to say. 'You should be thinking of us now. Of your family. Remember what I told you.'

Each word he spoke was like a bullet. I knew I had to do something to help, but I didn't know what.

That night I dreamed about my mother. Curiously I did not picture her at home, or suffering in the clutches of

Al-Istikhbarat. Instead I remembered her in England, when I was a child, huddled over the phone with tears in her eyes, speaking to her family in Baghdad. There had been raised voices behind closed doors between her and my father – I had hidden in my room until they died down, but when I next saw my mother she looked like a broken woman. In my dream she gazed at me, her sad eyes seeming to pierce through me, and I awoke trembling and sweating. For a moment I wondered where I was, but was instantly grounded by the sound of Rachel breathing deeply next to me. I quietly slipped out of bed and moved to another room, where I sat and looked out of the window into the night sky. It was clear, and the crescent moon looked back down at me – the same moon, I remember thinking, that was looking down at my family in Al-Mansour, on the Bedouin desert by the Jordanian border, on the café in Amman where Abu Firas used to sit. I thought of all the people who had helped me over the years, who had got me where I was. Safe. Comfortable. Free. I would be repaying their kindness poorly if I did not now direct all my energies into helping my family, into granting them the same security that I enjoyed. What else could I do?

The next day I started making calls. I spoke to my Iraqi friends, and friends of friends, to ask whether they knew of smugglers based in the UK who would be able to arrange for my mother and siblings to disappear from

Baghdad. There were a few vague leads, rumours of people who could help, but most said the same thing: it would be difficult, and expensive. Everyone wanted to come to England, the routes were full and being watched, and the smugglers had more business than they could handle. Much better, they said, to arrange something from inside Iraq. But how could I do that? The only person I could think of who might be able to help my family was the father of my friend Hakim. He was a Kurd and, unusually, had been appointed to a governmental position as he was loyal to Saddam. Not so loyal, however, that he wasn't prepared to arrange for people to be smuggled through Kurdistan and into Turkey; but as ever there was a price tag involved. Even if I suggested to my family that they spoke to him, I knew they would need more money than they had. They had been saving everything I had sent them, but the sums involved would be far more substantial.

And so I enquired about loans. I lost count of the number of banks, building societies and loan sharks I spoke to, but they all gave me the same reply: no. I had no collateral, no equity. To borrow the sums of money I was talking about – tens of thousands of pounds – simply wasn't possible.

I grew more and more demoralized as the doors in front of me shut one by one. And then I received another call.

This time it was from my uncle Musaab, Saad's brother. His voice was breathless, concerned, but he tried to keep it level for the benefit of the third party who we suspected was listening in. '*Habibi*, you know those neighbours of ours, the ones you were trying to write to?'

'Yes,' I replied. 'I know the ones you mean.'

'They're in a bit of trouble.'

'What sort of trouble?' I asked the question with a non-chalance that I did not feel.

'They've been taken away. Locked up.'

I caught my breath. 'Locked up?' I repeated. 'Where?'

There was a pause before Musaab answered. 'Where do you think?' he asked, his voice dripping with meaning. 'On 52nd Street. And you know what will happen to them there . . .'

13

The Devil, *Iblis*

In Iraq, they tell the story of a merchant who had a servant. One day the servant went to the marketplace in Baghdad, where he bumped into what appeared to be an old man. The man turned to look at the servant, who saw that it was in fact Death himself. Death looked at him strangely, and the servant fled back to his master. 'Master,' he said, 'I just saw Death in the marketplace and he gave me a meaningful look. Please may I borrow your horse so that I may travel to Samarra and avoid what he has in store for me?' The merchant lent the servant his horse, and the servant fled.

Later that day, the merchant went to the marketplace himself, where Death was still waiting. 'Why did you scare my servant?' he asked.

'Scare him?' replied Death. 'I didn't mean to scare him. I was just surprised to see him in Baghdad. You see, I have an appointment with him in Samarra this evening.'

Al-Haakimiya. Al-Mukhabarat. The very words encapsulated everything that was evil about life in Iraq. I had been running for fear that I might end up in the intelligence service's prison, to learn all the horrific secrets its walls contained, but now my good fortune had been monstrously inverted and the ill luck meted out upon my family.

My sister had been spared. Rumours reached my ear that she had caught the eye of somebody with a certain amount of influence, an official of some description who had been stalking her, following her in his car when she left the house and taking an unwanted and unnatural interest in her affairs. By a horrible irony, this unasked-for infatuation had protected her from the journey to Al-Haakimiya, but that protection was not extended to my uncle Saad, my mother or my brother.

It is hard to find the words to describe how I felt when I heard the news. My mind was a maelstrom of powerlessness and indecision. There I was, stuck in the UK, unable to return and make amends. I had no wealth or influence, no strings I could pull or arms I could twist. There was nothing I could do. Worst of all, I had no information, no way of knowing what was being done to my family, or whether they were dead or alive. It was left to my imagination to picture what was happening to them, the desperate state they were in, and my imagination ran riot: it was not until much later that I discovered what had actually occurred.

Everyone in Baghdad knew about Al-Mukhabarat's prison. Its horrors were common currency. But few people who had experienced it first-hand would ever speak of it in detail, and even in the time that was to follow, my family were reluctant to describe it. To this day my mother will not speak of her time there, but from conversations with my brother I know something of the truth. The cells in which my family were placed were tiny – two metres by three, with five or six people in each one. All of them were accused of political crimes. The prison walls were filthy, stained in places with stubborn splashes of dried blood that attracted flies. The beds were covered with blood and semen stains. The concrete floors were similarly unpleasant, covered in bits of old food, human urine and clumps of hair; this debris attracted not only the flies but other scavengers, especially rats and cockroaches that made sinister, shuffling noises at night. Mosquitoes lurked around all the damp patches, everyone's clothes were crawling with fleas and you would find nits in your hair within hours of arriving, such was the lack of hygiene.

The smell of the cells was matched by the smell of the

prisoners: they too reeked of sweat and urine. Their clothes bore visible evidence of the squalor in which they were living: they would sweat in the heat of the day, then the sweat would dry on their clothes and the result would be thick blotches of salt on the fabric. There were prison baths but they were seldom used, and even when they were, prisoners came out barely cleaner than when they went in – the paint on the sides of the baths was peeling to reveal rusty old metal, and the sides were covered in a distinctive kind of grimy mucus.

Everyone was constantly hungry. The food only ever consisted of rice or a thin bean stew. In both cases it was clear from the taste that the raw ingredients had been putrefying somewhere, because there was always more than a hint of rot. The only time that taste was ever over-come was when salt was added to the food, but when that happened such gargantuan quantities were used as to make the food almost inedible. No matter how unpalat-able it was, however, the food was always eaten because it was so scarce.

The air was constantly thick with the fumes of cigarette smoke – almost everybody smoked, to take their minds off their desperate conditions – and it was never possible to breathe any fresh, natural air as most cells were windowless. The windows in those cells that had them were small and high up. As a result, the majority of the prisoners were ill with respiratory diseases – pneumonia and the like. All day and all night there was the sound of sneezing, vomiting and the bringing up of phlegm. The guards, of course, ignored all cases of ill health other than the most extreme: you would need to be unconscious before you were taken off for the rudimentary healthcare the prison offered.

The guards themselves treated the prisoners worse than animals, never speaking to them other than in terms of insult, referring to them as 'dogs' and 'imbeciles'. Slaps to the face were commonplace, and were among the more lenient treatments that could be expected on a daily basis. Often, and without warning or reason, prisoners were told to sit in a line on the floor, where the guards proceeded to kick them in the face and in the stomach until they were little more than a bruised and bloodied mess. On other occasions, they would be whipped all over their bodies with short pieces of blue rubber hose, about the length of a ruler.

Retaliation, of course, was unthinkable.

It took a number of weeks for them to be released, during which time they refused to speak. All the while I feared the worst; when I finally received a phone call to say they were out, I almost collapsed with relief. I was overwhelmed with the need to find out how they were, and never did the requirement to speak in our round-about, coded way seem so difficult.

Gradually, though, I became aware of the realities of

the situation. It had been made perfectly clear to my family that unless I returned, they would be recalled, and could look forward to living in the cramped cells of that stinking prison for the rest of their days – however long that might be – enduring the violent whims of whichever prison guard felt like beating them up. Their mal-treatment was not going to stop, so somehow, in whatever way we could, we had to raise the money to pay smugglers to get them out of the country. They weren't an attractive proposition for a smuggler: three of them travelling together, one a middle-aged woman who bore the weight of her difficult years heavily. It would cost tens of thousands of pounds.

Once again I tried to borrow the money, but was rejected. Rachel offered to help but her credit was in-sufficient, and Faisal was not in a position to help either. I was going out of my mind trying to think of ways to raise the cash, and all the while I knew my mother and brother could be dragged back at any moment to that stinking jail.

While all this was happening, I had been temping in the financial departments of various big companies. All day long I was in charge of transferring huge sums of money from one account to another – it was entirely straight-forward, and after a while the amounts involved, which often ran into the millions, became meaningless. Just figures. I finally found myself working in the accounts department of the bookmaker William Hill. Thousands of transactions a day passed through this department, and I fulfilled my duties unenthusiastically, always mindful of what was happening two and a half thousand miles away and constantly distracted by Saad's increasingly frequent phone calls, during which he said so little but hinted at so much. Occasionally the irony struck me that the people around me were spending all their time handling sums of money that would have smuggled a thousand families out from under the nose of Al-Mukhabarat, but never did it occur to me that I might be able to use this to help my mother, brother and sister.

Until one day, that is, when I felt the Devil, *Iblis*, tap me on the shoulder.

I was working quietly at my desk, shuffling papers around without fully taking in what I was reading. Suddenly I became aware of a conversation going on at the desk in front of me between two of my colleagues. They were working at the computer, transferring money from customers' betting accounts into the relevant bank account. Clearly one of them had his own betting account, and it came up on the screen. 'Look,' he told his friend, 'I've won a tenner.'

I watched as his friend glanced at the screen. 'Nice one,' he said. 'Shall we transfer it now?'

The winning employee nodded, tapped his password into the computer, and made the transfer. As he did so, his friend spoke. 'Hang on, you've transferred a hundred, not ten.'

The employee nodded, and with another tap of the keyboard transferred the money back. 'Nice try,' his friend noted, and they both laughed.

'What do you think would happen if I'd just left it there?'

'They'd track you down, mate, and fuck you over.'

It was as simple as that. Not only had the Devil given me a way to save my family, he had also told me what would happen if I followed the path he showed me.

I hesitated while I weighed up the pros and cons of the idea that was forming in my mind. I told nobody what I was planning to do, not even Rachel, who saw that I was increasingly distracted but put it down to the stress of the news from Iraq. The choice was a simple one: do nothing, and risk my family spending the rest of their lives rotting in prison where they would be tortured and maltreated, or illicitly transfer some of William Hill's money to my account to pay for their release. Without question, my employers and the police would catch up with me – I wasn't so naive as to believe that my actions would go undetected – but that probably wouldn't happen until there was an audit of the company, which would give me several months' grace in which to get my family out. What I was about to do would be entirely premeditated, and I felt sure that the authorities would be severe with me, no matter how extenuating my circumstances. But if I was sent to prison, so be it. At least in British prisons you didn't get tortured, brutalized or killed.

It took me several days to come to my decision, but in reality the decision had already been made for me.

The first thing I needed to do was to open a betting account. That was simple enough: ten minutes in a bright, buzzing internet café, surrounded by young people happily typing emails to loved ones, oblivious of what I was doing. Next, I had to open a number of bank accounts. The amount of money I was planning to steal was considerable, and I imagined that it would be less easy to trace several small transactions to different accounts than one big one. They would catch up with me eventually, of course, but I needed to ensure that I had enough time to do what I had to do.

The next hurdle was more difficult to overcome. The transfer of money at William Hill was not part of my jurisdiction, so I did not have access to the passwords that were necessary to effect it. The passwords themselves were guarded quite jealously: everyone who needed one had a separate password, and they were unlikely to reveal it to anybody else because they knew that it would be open to abuse. Moreover, they changed regularly. Once I had discovered a password, I would have to move quickly.

I started to fall into casual conversation with the colleague whom I had overheard transferring money in the first place. Over the period of a few days we became as friendly as the stifling office atmosphere would allow, and I would loiter by his desk, drinking coffee and chatting while he carried on with his work. He was a talkative guy, and we had no difficulty keeping the conversation going. He showed no sign of realizing the ulterior motive for my sudden camaraderie: as we spoke, I was able to glance at his fingers while he was typing. It took a few goes, but eventually I managed to work out his password. I didn't worry that this would land him in trouble: why would he use his password to transfer money to my account? In any case, I had no intention of doing anything other than telling the whole truth about my actions when the police did finally catch up with me.

I had everything I needed. The following day I waited for everyone to leave the office at lunchtime, while I stayed behind. I approached a computer terminal and, my heart in my mouth, typed in what I hoped was the correct password.

It worked.

To start with, I transferred only a small amount of money – a hundred pounds, I think – just to check that it would work. As soon as I had finished, I logged out and walked quickly away from the terminal. There had been no one watching, but I couldn't dispel the hot flush of unease that swept across my body at the thought of what I had just done. I felt sick, and continued to do so for the rest of the day.

Next morning, I checked my bank account. Nothing. The following morning I did the same. Nothing. But on the third day it was there.

Suddenly I was filled with misgivings. You can't do this, Sarmed, I told myself. It's not right. There has to be another way. That lunchtime I returned to the computer terminal and transferred the money out of my account and back to William Hill.

I didn't sleep that night, my mind awash with conflicting thoughts. It had been so easy to make the transfer; so easy to walk down the route that I knew would lead to huge trouble for me; so easy to decide, after all, not to do it. And maybe that was the right thing. Even if I sent Saad the money he needed, there was no guarantee that my family wouldn't just be thrown back into prison. Perhaps I should simply hope and pray that no harm would come to them, that when their captors realized that I was not coming back they would release them unharmed. Deep down, though, I knew it was a vain hope. It was no secret what went on in the prisons of Baghdad, indeed Saddam no doubt *wanted* his people to be aware of the evils that awaited them if they transgressed. And as I was growing up I had heard tell of enough people who had disappeared at the hands of Al-Mukhabarat, never to be seen again. The thought of that happening to my family was too much for me to bear. Even though I had a premonition that I was about to lose everything I had built in the UK, I resolved to go ahead with my plan.

The following day I hacked into the computer once more. This time, into several accounts, I transferred the very least I thought would ensure their release from prison and their subsequent escape from Iraq. It wasn't an exact calculation, but was based on my rough idea of how much I would need: a total of £37,500.

The instant the money hit my accounts, I transferred half of it, through the convoluted routes I had become used to, to Saad. Mindful of the fact that time was not on our side, I started making enquiries about how I could use the money to spirit my mother, brother and sister out of Iraq. Through acquaintances in the Iraqi community in the UK, I made contact with people-smugglers to determine the best way to get my family out, and how much it would cost. In Baghdad, Saad did the same. It became apparent, even with the William Hill money, that it would be expensive: the smugglers saw our desperation and increased the price accordingly. We soon realized that we still did not have the funds to pay someone to organize the whole thing for us, so I decided that we would have the professionals arrange their transfer to a neighbouring Middle East country; the remainder of the journey I would have to organize myself. Had I known what awaited us, I would never have made that decision.

My mother, brother and sister had a thick wad of

passport photographs taken in differing disguises that were then sent to me in England. A Kurdish smuggler met them at home and gave them cloned Iraqi passports with false Kurdish names. It would be most difficult for my brother – he was approaching the age for military service, so the penalty for leaving the country illegally would be more severe. He had the benefit, though, of looking much younger than his age, and the passport he was given stated that he was several years younger than he actually was. My mother donned her hijab, to make her less recognizable, and within a couple of days of arriving home they said goodbye to Saad and my grandparents and left, with the smuggler, in one of the familiar orange-and-white taxis that swarmed in the streets of Baghdad.

They could not simply travel west to the Jordanian border: the Iraqi border guards would quickly have seen that their passports were fake. Instead their route took them north, through my father's home town of Samarra, past Tikrit and into Mosul. From there they entered Kurdistan. Although this was still officially Iraqi territory, the Kurds had a separate administration, and so there was a heavy checkpoint at this stage. Without the help of the Kurdish smuggler their passports would never have got them through; but he had some of the border guards in his pocket. A few wads of notes from the William Hill money put the way of these corrupt officials soon bought them passage into Kurdistan. From there they continued north into Turkey, before doing an about-turn and heading south through Syria and into Jordan. The border guards in these countries had no way of telling that their passports were fake, so they passed through, if not without suspicion then at least without hindrance.

By now the British government had issued me with a document allowing me to travel abroad, and while my family were making their circuitous journey around the Middle East, I had business to attend to. I had had success travelling from Jordan to the UK via Malaysia, so I decided that this was the route I would arrange for them. However, they needed false passports, as the fake Iraqi ones they had would be no good. I had nobody like Abu Firas to help me arrange things this time round, so I would have to do it all myself.

A friend of mine, part of the Iraqi community in Leeds at the time, had been smuggled from Jordan to the UK via Romania by an Iraqi people-smuggler – an Alsamari man called Radwaan – in that country. That was a difficult route, so it seemed clear that the smuggler in question was skilled and influential. We spoke at length on the phone, not once or twice but many times as we each tried to get the measure of the other: he was persuading himself that I was serious and not simply a timewaster or, even worse, someone trying to set him up; I wanted to be sure that this faceless voice at the end of a telephone line could do what he claimed in return for the many thousands of pounds I would have to pay him. Eventually the rapport between us became more comfortable, and we reached the stage where we could talk plainly about what it was I wanted. I asked him directly if he could sort out passports for my family.

'Of course,' he replied smoothly.

'What's available? What can you give them that will get them out of Jordan and in and out of Malaysia?'

'It's limited,' he told me. 'Spanish is your best bet. Or Israeli.'

'And are they original passports? Foolproof, I mean?'

'Of course they are.' He didn't sound offended that I had asked the question. 'You can check them out before you buy, if you like. Just go to Germany, see my brother. He'll show you what you'll be getting for your money – nobody will be able to tell the difference between the passports we supply and the real thing. You won't have any trouble at all.'

Something about his manner filled me with confidence. He had the quiet, easy-going attitude that had first recommended Abu Firas to me, and he wasn't pushy, didn't try to give me the hard sell. But I only had one shot at this, and he could hear the indecision in my voice. 'Go and see my brother,' he insisted. 'He is the one you'll have to give the money to. Then decide.'

The brother was living in Mannheim with his Romanian wife and small child. My brown travel document wasn't officially recognized in Germany, but I decided that I would risk it anyway: sure enough, I got off the plane, presented my document at passport control and as soon as the officer saw the words 'Great Britain' at the top I was waved through. The contrast between the power of that slip of paper and the passports I had used in the past was almost shocking. I went to stay at the brother's house and spent hours talking to him, once more getting the measure of the man as I had done with his brother. Finally, after several hours of wary and then friendly conversation, he pulled out some sample passports. They were Spanish, and to my eye they looked perfect. The final product, I was assured, would have my family's real names marked inside, along with photographs that they had supplied me with. I smiled inwardly: these were as good, if not better, than the UAE passport Abu Firas had arranged for me. But they were going to cost thousands of pounds each – money I was still reluctant to pass on to these people, no matter how sweetly they spoke.

'How will you want the money?' I asked him.

'Cash,' he said. 'In person. Here.'

'I can't transfer it from London?'

'No.' He shook his head before smiling sympathetically at me. 'You are still worried?'

'It's a lot of money for me,' I told him honestly. 'If this does not work, my family will be stuck. I'm not rich.'

'I understand. Perhaps you should go to Bucharest,

speak to Radwaan. It's good to know exactly who you are dealing with.'

And so I did. From Germany I flew to Romania, again without the necessary visa. When I arrived at passport control, it became clear that my entry into the country would not be as simple as it was in Germany. As a stern official examined my document, though, I heard a voice above the hubbub. 'Alsamari! Where is Alsamari?'

I held up my hand, and a rather overweight woman jogged, red-faced, towards us. 'You're here to see Radwaan?' she asked.

I nodded and she spoke a few words out of earshot to the official, who immediately stamped my document and allowed me to board my connecting flight to Bucharest. Clearly Radwaan was a man of more influence than I had expected.

He picked me up from the airport, a jolly man whose friendly demeanour belied a serious, businesslike attitude to his chosen profession. We went to his house and once more he showed me some sample Spanish passports. 'These are the best,' he told me. 'Original. You can't get better than this. No one will raise an eyebrow at them. And if you don't like the finished product . . .'

I looked at him expectantly.

'You don't pay for them. It's as simple as that.'

Finally I was convinced. I had the recommendation of my friend in London, I had seen the kind of influence this man had over passport officials, and he wasn't even asking for the money up front. I went to my bag and handed him the sheaf of passport photographs my family had sent me. He smiled. 'I don't need as many as that,' he said, before selecting a few of each individual and handing the rest back to me. Then he drove me back to the airport.

Once more, as I was passing through passport control, my travel document aroused suspicion. A monster of an official, a huge man with square shoulders and a tiny square head – he looked like Frankenstein's monster – surrounded by three or four much smaller men, spoke to me in broken English with a thick Romanian accent. 'Do you have anything dangerous in your bag, like bombs, or weapons, or gases – anything like that?'

'No.'

'Where are you flying to?'

'London.'

'You're British. You have British passport.'

I handed him my travel document. 'Yes,' I said confidently.

One of his eyebrows shot up. 'This is not a British passport. Open your bags.'

Reluctantly I unzipped my hand luggage and gave it to him. It took only a few seconds for him to pull out the wad of photographs. He looked at them silently, then he glanced round at his friends. They all grinned, a nasty expression that made it perfectly clear they knew what was going on. He let me squirm for a few moments before he spoke again. 'Who have you come to see in Romania?' he asked slowly.

'I came to see my friend.'

'What is his name?'

'Radwaan.'

Immediately I saw the light of recognition in his eyes. 'Ah,' he smiled. 'Radwaan.' He turned round to look at his friends. 'He's come to see Radwaan!' he told them, and they all nodded their heads knowingly.

It was clear that they knew who Radwaan was, and what he did. It was equally clear that Radwaan had them in his pockets.

'OK,' he said finally, packing the photographs back into my bag. 'Off you go.'

As soon as I returned to England, I collected the money I needed and flew back out to Mannheim to deliver it. A week later I went back to Germany to collect the passports. They were immaculate, just as I had been told they would be. All the while, I was illegal in Germany. If I had been caught with these things in my pocket, I would have been locked up; but such thoughts were far from my mind. I can honestly say that I didn't give that danger a second thought.

By the time I had all the documents in order, my mother, brother and sister had arrived safely in Amman. I had no desire to delay things, as I was half expecting the police to knock on my door at any time on account of the William Hill money, so I booked my flight to Jordan.

But before I did anything else, I had to speak to Rachel.

She knew that I was desperate to see my family. How could she not? It had been Rachel who had comforted me in the dark days since my family had been dragged into prison; and Rachel who had put up with my prolonged absences as, unbeknown to her, I risked my liberty to obtain the Spanish passports. She had lived with my increasing distraction and panic; and at night, when my fears were increased tenfold, she had soothed me with her quiet, understanding embrace. Now I had to tell her that I was about to do the one thing that I had hoped would never be my lot: return to the Middle East, and embark upon a series of actions that could result in my family's deportation back to what awaited them in Iraq. 'I can't pretend it's not dangerous,' I told her. 'I can't pretend there's not a risk that I won't come back.'

Rachel looked into my eyes. Any intuition I had that this would be a tearful moment was instantly dispelled as she stared at me with such immeasurable determination that I was momentarily taken aback. 'What?' I asked, afraid for a minute that she was going to try to persuade me to back out of everything.

'I'm not going to let you do this by yourself.'

It took a moment before it dawned on me what she

was saying, but as it did so I shook my head. 'No way . . .'

But she was adamant. 'You don't have to do this by yourself,' she insisted. 'I'm a British citizen. I can travel wherever I like. No one can stop me from travelling with my husband, and if you're detained I'll simply refuse to leave without you.'

I continued to object – I couldn't understand why she wanted to come; but she was determined and would not be dissuaded. She gently put her finger against my lips. 'I'm coming with you, Lewis,' she told me. 'And that's an end to it.'

14

Going Back

When Rachel gave me a farewell embrace before my departure to Amman, the plan was this. She would not accompany me to Jordan, as I did not want to place her in any more danger than was necessary. Instead I would travel alone, hoping that my inability to get a Jordanian visa would not hamper my entry. After all, I had been waved through in Germany, and I knew there was a possibility that I could just pay a fee if I was stopped at the border. Once in Amman, I would meet with my family and buy them two sets of tickets to Malaysia, one in their Kurdish names on the fake Iraqi passports that would enable them to leave Amman, and one in their real names as printed on their fake Spanish passports that would allow them to enter Kuala Lumpur. I booked myself on

331

the same flight, which meant a stopover in Abu Dhabi. That was where we were to meet Rachel, who had flown from London to Abu Dhabi and was booked on the same flight to Kuala Lumpur. Although she was insistent on coming, I could not tell her the details of my plan because I did not want her to be a party to the risks I was taking. I felt sick not being fully honest with her, but it was, I calculated, the only way to keep her safe.

It was complicated and finely tuned, but I figured that I had done it once before so I could do it again.

Miraculously, I entered Jordan without any difficulty whatsoever. Again, one look at my new name and the words 'Great Britain' afforded me politeness and expedited my passage in a way that I would have thought impossible a few years previously. I paid a sum equivalent to ten pounds for my visa and was ushered into the country, all the while mindful of the treatment I had received when I had last tried to leave. As I walked through into the main arrivals area, it was buzzing with people. I scanned the crowds, trying to spot my family, and for a moment I felt a tingle of dread as I thought they were not there. But then I saw them. They were standing in a far corner of the concourse, huddled together and looking around nervously, concern etched on their faces, ignored by all around them and emanating an aura that seemed to beg everyone not to pay them any attention. Never did three people look so uncomfortable and out of place, and it was only then, I think, that the full impact of what they had been through finally sank in. Having seen them before they saw me, I almost tripped over my own feet as I hurried in their direction, but I gradually slowed down as their faces became more distinct. They looked haggard and drained. The way their clothes hung from their bodies spoke loudly of their malnourishment, and you would have been forgiven for thinking, from the black rings around their eyes, that they had been fighting. They looked like they hadn't slept in weeks. It cut me to the quick to see them in that state.

And then they saw me. As one, their faces broke into a smile that seemed only to emphasize their frailty, but I couldn't help smiling back: it was so wonderful to see them. Silently we hugged, oblivious to the crowds around us, our bodies absorbing the sensation of each other's presence as though we were thirsty and drinking deeply from a cup of cool water. There were smiles and there were tears, and I remember thinking that even if everything went wrong from then onwards it would have been worth it just for that first moment of reunion.

The smell of their clothes reminded me of Iraq, and there were other things too that somehow seemed to speak to me of a difference between us, a gulf that had arisen in the time I had been in the West. As we walked away, the three of them stayed close together, their eyes darting around nervously just as they would have done if they knew they were doing something illicit on the streets of Baghdad. I wanted to tell them to look more confident, but then I remembered how I too had felt when I first arrived in Amman, how I had run from shadows and had wanted nothing more than to blend into the background. They spoke to me humbly, almost diffidently, and of matters that seemed to me somehow simplistic. Occasionally I would catch my brother and sister looking at me with undisguised awe – a flattering yet painful experience. I suppose that in some way it made me feel superior: I had so much to teach them about the life that, *inshallah*, awaited them in the UK. But then I forced myself to remember the realities of what they had undergone in prison and since, and reminded myself that there was a strength and a depth of experience that no comfortable Westerners with their Nintendo machines and expensive Reebok trainers could ever know. So I fell in beside them, listening to the minutiae of their conversation as we left the airport.

How many times I had pictured this meeting in my head; now that it had arrived I realized I had been unprepared for how beautiful yet horrible an event it would be.

We went straight to my hotel, where I briefed them about the plan. 'As soon as you leave Jordan,' I told them, 'you are Spanish citizens. You need to be able to hold your heads up high and tell people that. Whatever you do, you can't let anyone think that you don't believe your own story. Rachel will join us in Abu Dhabi – she is so excited about meeting you.'

They nodded diffidently at me, and I secretly wondered whether they would be up to the task ahead of them. But they had come this far, through Turkey and Syria, so I had to trust them.

Four days remained until our flight. Ever since I knew I would be in Amman with my family, I had been looking forward to showing them around, taking them to my old haunts, and we did this; but somehow the city seemed shabbier to my eyes than it had last time, so far removed from the new me that I felt I was giving my family a guided tour of someone else's life. We saw the company building where I had worked, the gym, the road where I had lived, but none of those places seemed to hold much meaning for me any more. I pictured myself walking down the street with Shireen, besotted by her, and I couldn't help but smile at my own naivety. I'd come a long way since then. We ate together in restaurants I knew – more because I wanted to ensure they ate proper food than out of any misplaced sense of nostalgia – but the rest of the time was spent in preparation for our journey. I took my mum and my sister to a salon to have their hair straightened and blow-dried in a Western style, and bought Western clothes for them all, along with electronic gadgets for my brother like a personal stereo and state-of-the-art headphones. I knew that presentation would be crucial to our success: they could have the most convincing passports in the world, but if they looked like poor Iraqi refugees they wouldn't fool anyone.

We waited. We went over the plan. We didn't talk about what would happen if we failed because it didn't bear thinking about. We waited some more. And then the day for our departure arrived.

I didn't expect any problems leaving Amman, and I was right: we sailed through passport control with hardly a glance and took our seats on the flight to Abu Dhabi, which passed without incident. And, as we had arranged, Rachel was waiting for us there in the transit lounge. If ever there was a sight for sore eyes, Rachel was it: she embraced my mother as though she was her own, and instantly won over my brother and sister. I hugged her too, but we didn't say much. There wasn't much to say. In the transit lounge we showered, Rachel took my mum to have her hair done again, and we waited some more. I grew increasingly agitated, because the more I saw Rachel with my family, the more it became clear to me that you can't just put new clothes on a person and expect them to change who they are. Rachel had an aura about her, a confidence that my family lacked. Of course they did: they'd had it beaten out of them.

And then we boarded the flight to Kuala Lumpur.

The Malaysian airport had changed beyond recognition

since I had last been there nearly five years ago – now it was all marble walls and gleaming floors. It seemed more welcoming somehow. As we disembarked from the plane, I held back a little. I wanted to see my family go safely through passport control before I did – that way if there was any problem, I knew I would be around to help sort it out. From a distance I watched them present their passports. I held my breath. Moments later they were allowed through. Rachel followed – her British passport, of course, was waved though without difficulty.

My entry was more complicated. I had hoped to be able to pay for an entry visa at the airport, but it was soon made clear to me that this would not be the case. A team of task-force officers, heavily armed, arrived to take me away for interrogation. I used my mobile phone to make a desperate call to Rachel. 'They won't let me in,' I whispered urgently. 'They're saying they want to send me back to London.'

'Don't worry, Lewis.' Rachel's soothing voice belied the fact that our plan had taken an unexpected twist. 'We're through and we're safe. Leave everything to me – I'll take your family to a hotel, then come back and get you.'

I clenched my eyes shut. 'No,' I told her. It wasn't meant to be like this. I was always going to be on hand, ready to absolve Rachel of any blame should something go wrong. But again she was insistent.

Minutes later I was being interrogated again, by

unfriendly Malaysians and apologetic airline staff whose responsibility it had been to check my Malaysian visa when I had left Amman. I argued with them; I begged them; finally I accepted the inevitable – that I was to be deported to London. And it was only then that they decided they would issue me with a three-day transit visa. I felt suddenly as though all my cares had been lifted, and I hurried into a taxi to have a relieved and joyous reunion with my family at our hotel.

Stage one was complete.

Stage two was always going to be more difficult, but the fact that the fake Spanish passports had so easily fooled the official when my family entered Malaysia filled us all with confidence.

We spent the two days before our flight to London visiting Kuala Lumpur – more to fill the time than out of a genuine desire to go sightseeing. We were all too excited and nervous for that. While Rachel was not with us, I forced my family to practise the few words of Spanish that I knew, and we repeatedly went over the cover story that I had constructed for them until they could recite it with confidence. My mother had married a Spanish man living in London, which was how they had gained Spanish citizenship. She had brought Ahmed and Marwa to visit Malaysia because it was a Muslim country. They had long wanted to see Malaysia because they had heard how wonderful and modern it was, but they were looking forward to getting back home.

Every time I heard them repeat the story, I smiled. It sounded convincing; the passports were good; we were going to be OK.

On the morning of our departure the tropical rains came, like a constant waterfall purging the streets of crowds and cleansing the greyness of the city. We checked out of the hotel and piled into a taxi, the pouring rain messing my mother's neatly groomed hair as we did so, then travelled the short distance through the torrent to the airport. Once we arrived, Rachel and my family checked in separately to me, and I waited behind, watching them go through immigration. This was the last hurdle: as soon as I saw them go through, we would have succeeded.

Everything seemed to happen in slow motion. The official looked at Rachel. He looked at my family, each in turn. He examined their passports with agonizing slowness. And then he let them through.

I smiled inwardly; on the outside I did my best not to let any emotion play on my face. I walked confidently towards passport control, knowing that now my family were through I should not have any difficulty. My papers were scrutinized; they were scrutinized once more; he tapped something into his computer; and I started to feel the familiar sense of intangible dread that I remembered from my last illicit journey. Why I was kept waiting there I don't know, but kept waiting I was. I heard the final call for my flight, and looked at my watch. Five minutes and still I was being held. Eventually, without any explanation for the delay, my papers were stamped and I literally sprinted towards the gate.

The corridor that took me there twisted and turned, and I attracted a few curious glances as I tore round the corners until finally I found myself at the seating area at the entrance to the gate. And there I stood still, desperate to catch my breath but unable to do so on account of what I saw. There, before me, were three taskforce officers, bullet-proof vests on full display and US-style machine guns gripped firmly in their hands. With them was an official-looking British woman in a brown business suit. And by her side, sitting down and looking more dejected than scared, were Rachel, my mother, my brother and my sister. Apart from them, the area was deserted.

The brown-suited woman approached me. 'Can I see your passport, please?'

I handed her my travel document, and she gave it a cursory glance.

'Are these people with you?' Her face and voice were expressionless.

I felt everyone's eyes on me. What could I say? 'We're travelling together, yes,' I replied quietly.

'Are they your family?'

I nodded. 'Yes.'

She turned to the taskforce officers and gave them a nod. We've got them all, it seemed to say. One of them disappeared, and it was obvious to us all that he had gone to tell the airline staff that the flight could now depart.

There was a heavy silence, which the woman broke with her monotonous voice. 'Come with me,' she said, addressing us all. My family looked at me for guidance, but I could only nod to indicate that we should do as she said. They stood up and followed us, the armed guards walking behind with their fingers on the triggers of their guns. As we walked, I suddenly realized that in my pocket I had my family's Kurdish-Iraqi passports, documents that I on no account wanted to be discovered now that we had clearly been caught. If there were no Iraqi passports, I reasoned in my panic, there would be no deportations back to Iraq. They would have to use the Spanish passports, which I knew looked authentic. I stopped and said to the woman, 'I need to use the toilet.'

She hesitated for a moment, then shrugged and pointed at a door a little further down the corridor. 'OK,' she said. 'Toilet's over there.'

I hurried through the door. The room was empty, so I shoved one passport into each of three toilets and flushed them away, this time not bothering to shred them as I had done to my UAE passport several years before. There wasn't time for that, and as a result I watched in horror as the toilets blocked. I couldn't worry about that, though, so

I took a couple of moments to regain my composure, then headed back to my family and their armed guard. We carried on walking in silence.

My mind was churning. Surely there was something I could do, something I could say to get us out of this mess? Eventually I turned once more to the woman and said, 'Look, please, I need to talk to you alone for ten minutes.'

'All right then,' she nodded, and took me to one side.

We took a seat together by a large observation window, through which I could see planes taking off as if to taunt me. 'What's the matter?' I asked the woman. 'Why are we being held?'

She indicated the Spanish passports that she had in her hand. 'Do you speak Spanish?' she asked.

I shook my head. 'No.'

'Then why do your family have Spanish passports?'

'My mum married a Spanish man.' I recited the lie as smoothly as I could. 'She has citizenship.'

The woman acted as if she had not heard what I'd said. 'Where did you get these passports from?'

'I told you,' I insisted. 'They're naturalized Spaniards.'

'No they're not,' she almost spoke over me. 'These passports are counterfeit. They are very, very bad copies. I see them all the time – they're made mostly in Thailand. How much did you pay for them?'

She looked me straight in the eye and I saw in that

instant that I wasn't fooling her. But I couldn't bring myself to answer.

'Did you pay a lot for them?' she insisted.

I nodded.

Her face assumed an expression of something approaching pity. 'Well, let me just tell you,' she continued, 'that these things are produced in Thailand for between a hundred and two hundred dollars. They are the worst I've ever seen, and you are unbelievably lucky to have come through immigration with these.'

As I listened to her words my blood ran cold. How could I have been so foolish? Within seconds my plan to rescue my family had been revealed for the ill-conceived scheme that it really was, and I had no idea what would happen to any of us now. The woman stood up, smoothed down her suit. 'Come with me,' she said abruptly as she walked back to where the others were waiting, a look of expectation on their faces that I had to dash with a single glance and a shake of my head.

We were led to a processing area. Full of desks and computers and phones, it looked more like a call centre than anything else, and quite out of place in the environs of the airport. Each desk was covered in piles of passports and other documents, and we were given seats and told to wait. We remained there for a couple of hours, our hearts heavy, the knowledge that we had failed bearing down on us like a crushing load. Overcome by emotion, my mother started shouting at me, and I argued back but only half-heartedly because I knew that what she was saying – this was my fault, I had been too hasty, didn't I know what was at stake here? – was right. Rachel calmed us both down – how she did so I can't think, because she must have been as sick with nerves as the rest of us – but I thanked God that she was there to exert her steadying influence on us all as we fell once more into oppressive silence.

We were searched, our luggage was claimed as evidence, and then we were led round the corner from the processing area. I had noticed a few people being taken that way, and the guards who accompanied them returning alone. As the same happened to us, I realized why.

In front of us were two enormous cells, one facing the other. Fronted by thick iron bars, one of the cells contained men, the other women, and in the middle of the two, sitting down, was a fat but threatening Malaysian guard. Along the back wall of each cell were a series of doors, and in the corner was some sort of receptacle that I assumed was the toilet. Around it was a thick, dirty puddle that encroached into the main area of the cell, contaminated with something I could not quite make out, though the stench of human faeces and urine in the air gave me a good idea what it was. The part of the floor that was not wet with water and human excrement was black with dirt and covered with a ghoulish human kaleidoscope of prostrate bodies, perhaps a hundred and fifty of them in each cell. There was not enough room for them all, so they overlapped each other as they lay there, unmoving. None of them seemed perturbed by the flies that were swarming round the room. Maybe, like horses on a hot day, they were just used to them.

I couldn't bear to look at Rachel or my family. Suddenly, from behind, I heard screaming. It was my mother. '*La! La! Bidoon Sijn!* No! Not prison!' she shouted hysterically. I watched helplessly as two guards dragged her towards the prison doors; she went limp to make it more difficult for them, then continued her terrible weeping. The faces of my brother and sister were stricken, too. To have escaped the horrors of the Iraqi intelligence service's prison and undergone all the dangers they had put themselves through, only to end up in a stinking cell in a strange country: I couldn't imagine what was going through their minds. Wordlessly the women were segregated from the men.

There was nothing I could do other than try to get a message to somebody, to let people know what was happening to us. The only people I could think of were Rachel's parents: it would devastate them to think of their little girl in such a horrific situation, but they had the right to know, and maybe they could help. I had placed my mobile phone in one of my bags, but these had been checked in. Suddenly, however, I saw them reappear and they were placed a few metres away from the cell doors. Quickly I moved towards my bag to get the phone; but as I did so one of the officials, a Sikh man wearing a turban, saw me. As I lunged for my bag, he grabbed me by my arms, pulled me away, thrust me against the wall and lifted me up by my neck. He made as if to punch me with his free arm, but clearly thought better of it at the last moment. 'Who do you think you are,' he spat at me, 'doing all this hero business? You think you're Robin Hood?'

I hardly knew what to say. I had only been there a few minutes and already I had marked myself out in the officials' eyes as a troublemaker. Shocked into silence, I looked him up and down as he held me there against the wall. On his jacket he wore a badge with a grotesquely happy, yellow smiling face and the logo 'Service with a smile'.

Eventually the unsmiling official put me down, but his eyes stayed on me. I didn't try to grab my phone again.

I watched as Rachel, my mum and my sister were pushed into the cell, somehow retaining a sense of dignity – despite my mother's tears – as they stepped over the carpet of human traffic to find themselves somewhere to sit. Rachel turned and managed to force a smile at me. 'Please don't leave us here,' I mouthed at her, desperation in my face. She smiled calmly back at me. 'I'm not going anywhere,' her expression seemed to say.

My brother and I were pushed into the main cell. Silently we picked our way to the doors at the back of the cell, receiving grunts of discontent from a few of the people whose limbs we accidentally nudged but who otherwise treated us with complete indifference. Scrawled into the dirty paintwork of the doors were labels: 'The Turkish Embassy'; 'The Iranian Embassy'; 'The Iraqi Embassy'. I opened that door and put my head round the corner. The room was no cleaner or more welcoming, but it was filled with Middle Eastern faces who as one looked up to see who the new arrival was.

'*Salam*.' I nodded at them.

They greeted me in return, so I gestured to my brother and we both walked inside.

The Iraqi Embassy was no more than three metres by three metres. Instantly I could tell that its eight or nine occupants were shady characters – no doubt they thought the same of me and my brother – but they were welcoming enough, given the circumstances. We found ourselves an empty area and sat down, shocked into silence with disbelief at what had happened to us. There were single sheets of newspaper on the floor, the only protection between us and the hard, cold concrete. The strip lighting above us was intolerably bright, and the air conditioning was on full blast, no doubt to battle feebly against the disgusting stench – in reality all it did was make the place uncomfortably cold. No matter how many cells you've been in, you never quite get used to being treated no better – and often worse – than animals; but my brother and I did our best as we settled down to wait.

After a few hours, we were given food. Its arrival was announced by someone shouting outside the main cell, followed by a scrum as some of the inmates scrabbled to get their share. My brother and I were hungry, so we stood up to go and claim our food, but one of our fellow Iraqi prisoners told us to wait. 'There's always enough to go round,' he said, 'but it's filthy food. You probably won't want to eat it even when you get it.'

He was right. When our turn came an official handed each of us, through the bars, a small polystyrene box. We opened it up to find a mound of crusty, dried-out rice with a suspicious smell – the remnants, I later found out, of what they had fed the Malaysian staff at a previous meal. Laid on top were a pile of fishbones. There was no meat attached to them, just the skeleton, and it was as if we were being presented not so much with a meal as with an insult. The fish has been enjoyed, the carton seemed to say, by more important people. The bones are for you. We were also handed a nylon bag full of lukewarm water to drink.

The agonizingly slow minutes turned into hours, which turned into days. Indeed it was difficult to keep track of time in that terrible place. In the main cell, where people had been languishing for who knows how long, certain individuals had become so ill from the conditions that they were hallucinating, shouting out at shadows, laughing hysterically or causing violent fights because of an imagined slight. Back in the Iraqi Embassy we fell into conversation with our fellow Middle Eastern prisoners – Syrians, Palestinians, Iranians, a true melting pot of Arab culture – and I was astonished by the lengths to which some of them had gone to get themselves to a place of safety. A couple of them had had huge tattoos drawn on their arms and backs in an attempt to make them seem Westernized. Many of them had been trying to get to Australia, New Zealand or Japan – Japan in particular, because at the time, I soon learned, there was a large organized crime network there dedicated to the dirty business of people-smuggling. These people would ask me questions about the UK, awed that I had made it there and astonished that I had risked coming back. To kill the tedium of the passing hours I would tell them about the geography and history of Britain, drawing crude maps in the dust on the floor and even at one point telling them the story, that Rachel had told me, of how William of Orange had fought in Ireland. It was a surreal moment, seeing these rapt Middle Easterners being taught British history in a Malaysian jail by one of their number, their faces a picture of concentration like a group of children being told a fairy tale.

Occasionally I would go to the front of the main cell,

treading over the human carpet of Bengalis and Sri Lankans, and Rachel would do the same in the opposite one. The first time we did this, she smiled across the corridor that divided us and, as cheerfully as she could, called, 'You take me to the nicest places, Lewis! Oh, and by the way – when we get out, I'm going to kill you.' Then she removed something from her pocket: it was the restaurant menu from the hotel where we had been staying. 'Now then,' she called, 'what shall we have for lunch? Lobster?' And so we carried on, doing our best to crack jokes, to make light of the situation and raise each other's spirits; but we knew it was an almost impossible task. Neither Rachel nor my brother mentioned it, but we were aware that the long-term consequences for us all could be very severe indeed. And I felt responsible for everything. I had no idea at this stage what would happen to my family, but I suddenly felt a renewed sense of responsibility to my younger brother. I remembered how I felt when, not much older than him, I had been cast into that Iraqi jail on the road north from Basra; I remembered how I felt when I heard that my mother had been imprisoned. He would be going through the same feelings now, albeit with his brother by his side, and I suddenly felt the urge to give him some words of advice for the difficult times ahead.

'Hamoudi,' I said, 'I need to tell you something.'

'What is it, Sarmed?'

I searched for the words. 'I don't know what's going to happen, but you need to be strong, for your mother and your sister. Remember, this life is a test of your strength. There will be people you encounter who will try to beat the spirit out of you, but you must never let them. You can't give up. We're in prison – so what? It's just going to make you stronger. At least we aren't dying. Hold your head up high, puff out your chest, be strong and don't let anyone treat you badly.'

He looked straight into my eyes. 'I know what you're saying, Sarmed,' he replied. 'And I'll try. I really will.'

As the time ground slowly on, we became aware of how the place worked. We couldn't bring ourselves to eat the food, but thankfully I had a little money in my back pocket which I would give to one of the less ferocious guards outside the cell. He would use it to go and buy food from McDonald's in the airport – creaming a little money off the top for himself, of course – and deliver it back to us. I would have to buy enough to hand something to everybody in the Iraqi Embassy, but it felt good occasionally to have some hot food in our stomachs.

Time passed. Other prisoners arrived; a few left. After about three days, an oriental-looking man, reasonably well dressed, arrived in the cell. There was something about his demeanour that suggested to me he was a bit different to the rag-tag collection of unfortunates that he had joined, so more to pass the time than anything else I went up to talk to him. 'What are you doing here?' I asked him, after we had introduced ourselves.

'I don't know,' he said, his face a picture of innocence. 'I'm an American citizen and my girlfriend is American. I don't understand why we've been stopped.' Even then I don't think I believed him, and I was right – some time later he let his cover story drop and admitted that, even though he *was* an American citizen, he had been trying to smuggle a girl to New Zealand. More importantly to me, however, he had managed to sneak his mobile phone into the cell so that he could phone the American Consulate in Kuala Lumpur and alert them to his presence. But he didn't know the number, and had no way of finding out.

I grabbed my opportunity. 'I can help you,' I told him. 'Let me borrow your phone and I can find the number of the UK High Commission for me and the American Consulate for you.'

By now we had attracted the attention of certain others in the cell, and I became aware of them eyeing up the American's phone. No doubt everyone would be wanting to use it, and as he handed it over I noticed that the battery life was limited – we couldn't let anybody else get their hands on it and take up what precious time was left to us. I just had to hope that nobody would be so desperate as to try to wrestle the thing from me.

I used the phone to find the numbers I needed, then I called the High Commission. I explained our situation to the woman who answered, and she promised to see what she could do. 'But I doubt we'll be able to do anything for the Iraqis in your group,' she told me. 'They're out of our jurisdiction.'

I had known it was unlikely that they would be able to help my family, but hearing the words spoken so firmly made my heart sink. Still, if I could at least get myself out, perhaps I could do something for them. I was useless stuck in a cell.

Unbeknown to me, in the other cell a male guard had taken a shine to Rachel. 'What are you in here for?' he asked her.

'I don't know,' Rachel replied.

'Do you have a full UK passport?'

'Yes.'

The guard nodded and then gestured over to a female guard, as though playing some elaborate game. 'When she's out of the way, I'll let you use the phone.'

Rachel thanked him and he was as good as his word and let her out of the cell for a short while. She called her parents. They were distraught, of course, but they didn't mess around. Her dad had a government contact, and he made some calls.

Back in the cells, we waited some more.

Eventually, after we had been four days in that stinking hole, I heard my name being shouted: there was a call for me outside the cell. I was allowed out, with the eyes of all the prisoners boring into me, and taken to a telephone where someone from the British High Commission was waiting to speak to me. 'We can't guarantee to influence what the Malaysians are doing,' I was told. 'We can only try.'

'But what about my family?' I asked.

'There's nothing we can do for any of them,' the British official stated with what sounded to me like a note of boredom in his voice. 'They will have to stay here and wait for the Iraqi representative to come.'

'There must be something else we can do,' I pleaded. I knew from the Iraqis in the cell that the representative came only once a month. And when he did arrive, all he would do was take names and reprimand the inmates. 'Why did you do this?' he would demand of them. 'Don't you realize what a reputation you are creating for Iraqis in this country? They're not impressed back home with what you're doing . . .' And then he would disappear; what would happen to my family was anyone's guess.

When the call finished, I put my head in my hands and tried to fight off the furious frustration that was surging through me. Suddenly I felt a tap on my shoulder. It was the taskforce officer who had led me from the cell: he had been standing close by while I had the conversation, and clearly understood what was going on. I prepared myself to be told to get back into the cell, but I was surprised when he spoke. 'Your family,' he asked me softly in faltering English, 'did they have any documents other than the passports they were stopped with?'

I looked around nervously, unsure whether this was a trap; but I was in a corner and had no option other than to tell the truth. 'Yes,' I admitted. 'They had Iraqi passports.'

'Where are they now?'

'I shoved them down the toilet,' I said.

'OK,' he said. 'Listen to me. You *have* to get those passports back, otherwise your family will rot in a Kuala Lumpur prison. Trust me, I've seen it happen before.'

'How can I?' I asked desperately.

'Leave it to me,' the guard said. 'I'll have to take you back to the cell now, but I'll try and call you out later.'

He led me back to the cell, where I continued my wait – even more scared this time, and more frustrated at the thought that in getting rid of my family's Iraqi passports I might have ruined any chance they had of getting out of this place. In any case, the likelihood of the passports still being where I had left them was vanishingly small. What was more, my opinion of the Malaysians was at rock bottom, and I didn't expect this guard to be true to his word.

He proved me wrong. A few hours later he let me out again and led me to the toilets down which I had stuffed the passports. When we arrived there, I stepped into the first cubicle and gave thanks, first that I had caused the toilets to flood and so remain unused, and secondly that nobody had seen fit to fix them for four days. Without hesitation I plunged my arm into the water and felt inside the U-bend. There was something there. I worked away at it and finally, to my astonishment and relief, pulled out a document. It was saturated, of course, and smeared; but the photograph was intact and it was clear what it was: my mother's Iraqi passport. Quickly I retrieved the others, which were in the same condition. I shook what water I could from them, then dried them off underneath the electric hand-dryer on the wall. The task-force officer took the passports from me and placed them in little plastic bags as evidence.

And then I was led back to the cell.

It was with mixed feelings that I sat down again next to my brother. In handing the passports back to the Malaysian guard, I knew what would happen: my family would be deported. My gamble was this: as there was no direct flight back to Iraq, and as they had entered Malaysia from Jordan, I hoped that the Malaysians would deport them to Amman. At least then they would be on Middle Eastern soil, where they could speak the language and hopefully persuade – or bribe – the Jordanians to let them stay. The alternative was, as the Malaysian guard had made plain, rotting here in a putrid jail. I couldn't let that happen.

Before long, Rachel and I were released. We were informed that no charges were to be brought against us and that we were free to go back to London. 'I'm staying,' I told our captors defiantly. What else could I say? My family were still here and I couldn't desert them. We took a room at the airport hotel, where we cleaned ourselves up; but every time the water splashed on my skin or my eyes fell on the soft, fresh bedding, I would feel such anger well up in me. How could I be here while my family were in those squalid, cramped and stinking conditions? They were people too – surely it was time they were treated as such. I would visit them four or five times a day, bringing with me the hotel food that I didn't have the stomach to eat and begging the guards to give it to them.

After a couple of days, I was told they were to be interviewed. I was allowed to act as their interpreter but was forbidden from having any other conversation with them, and one by one they were taken in front of Malaysian officials and instructed to make statements. They told the truth: about their imprisonment, about their journey through Kurdistan, Turkey and Syria, about the fake Spanish passports. And then they were told what would happen to them. They had a choice: either their case would be taken before a Malaysian judge – which would take weeks, and would probably result in a further spell of imprisonment, as there was no such thing as political asylum in Malaysia – or they could pay a fine and be deported back to Jordan. The fine amounted to 2,100 Malaysian ringgits (about £365) each. Money they didn't have.

I needed to find £1,095. I was stuck in Malaysia and all I had was a cash-point card, a credit card and the ability to withdraw £200 a day. Immediately I got on the phone to my bank in England and begged them to increase my overdraft and my withdrawal limits. Rachel and I scrabbled together all the money we could – it took two days – and in the end we just about managed to get our hands on the amount we needed. We took it back to the cells and handed it over to a sneering official. He sat at his table, gave us a receipt for the money, put on a pair of latex gloves, removed the Iraqi passports from their bag, stamped them, then, having placed them in a polythene bag, held them out to us at arm's length as though they were diseased. His aloof silence spoke with an eloquence I'm sure he could not have managed with mere words. So it's come to this for you people, he seemed to say. Your lives have come to this. There was no sympathy, no indication that he knew what my family were running from or what they were being sent back to, and there was no point trying to educate him. I simply took the passports and left him to his ignorance, then went to Gulf Air to book their return trip to Amman.

And so, finally, the time came for my mother, brother and sister to be deported. Still we weren't allowed any direct contact with them. All Rachel and I could do was wait behind a glass screen at their gate so that we could see them one last time, even if we weren't allowed to talk to them. When they arrived, the sight pierced my heart. My mother, brother and sister were handcuffed, like criminals, and led by armed officials to their gate. The Western clothes that they had worn for their journey now looked like a cruel, ragged parody; my mother especially looked even more bedraggled and beaten down than when she had first arrived. As she passed us, she refused to look me in the eye, and I didn't blame her as she just shuffled past. I hung my head, and Rachel put her arm round me. My sister saw us and managed a half-smile. 'Goodbye, Sarmed,' she mouthed. 'Goodbye, my brother.' She followed her mother.

Finally I saw Hamoudi. He was walking slowly, and when he saw me his tired and worried face struggled into a broad smile. Don't worry about us, it seemed to say. We'll be OK. And then, just as I had told him to, I saw him hold his head up high and stick his chest out proudly. He nodded at me; I returned the gesture; and he walked on, disappearing from my sight as my mother and sister had done.

Walking into whatever the future held for them, without me.

15

The Genuine Man

My family arrived back in Amman, where the Jordanian officials took one look at the state of their passports. 'You can't enter our country on these documents,' they were told. No arguments. No bribes. No chances.

They were loaded, under armed guard, on to a transport and taken to the Iraqi border, where they were dumped. The Iraqi border police were unimpressed with the condition of these pitiful refugees and their messed-up documents, so they threw them straight into a holding cell to await the next military transport back to Baghdad. There they were placed in a police holding cell to await trial. They spent several days there, undergoing the brutal treatment that they surely expected, before appearing in front of a judge.

The court in Baghdad was a joke, but what happened inside wasn't funny. It looked serious enough from the outside – an imposing building with a set of scales emblazoned on the front next to the Iraqi flag and some of Saddam's wise words about justice. But there were no courtrooms or juries inside, nothing to ensure that the proper processes were observed; simply a bare office with a judge sitting at a table, there to mete out whatever justice he saw fit. What terror my family were feeling as they waited silently outside to hear their fate, I can only imagine. Perhaps, after spending so much time in prison cells across the world, they were simply looking forward to knowing how they would be dealt with. You find hidden strength at times like this: that, at least, I had learned.

My brother was called first. The room was sparsely furnished: an old desk, a flag, a fan, a picture of the leader and a radio playing Arabic music. On the desk was a pile of paperwork, and by the judge's side a secretary was scribbling notes. The judge, in his late fifties, sat there in casual clothes, smoking a cigarette. He didn't look up as my brother walked in. Why would he? This was not a person who had come in front of him; it was just another criminal to be processed. 'What's your name?' he asked.

My brother responded quietly.

The judge was handed his charge sheet, which accused him of tampering with official documents. This carried a sentence of six months to a year. He didn't ask any more questions – just glanced at it in the most cursory manner. 'One year's prison,' he announced briskly, before taking another drag on his cigarette. 'If you pay a fine, perhaps I will reduce it.' But my brother had no money, so the negotiations could not proceed. He was taken away.

The same treatment was then inflicted on my sister and finally my mother. The sentences they received were identical.

All three of them were escorted to Abu Ghraib prison.

In the years to come, the name of Abu Ghraib would become well known throughout the world; back then, for Iraqis, it was enough to inspire terror. The prison was the size of a small town, and conditions there were similar to those of Al-Haakimiya, where my family had been incarcerated previously. And now they were going to have to deal with prison all over again.

Rachel and I returned to England the same day my family was deported. To me it was a relief to breathe the damp English air, and to be treated like a real person once more. But as we returned to Leeds, I felt crushed by the weight of my failure. My family were back where they started, and I had to shoulder the responsibility. I knew I would have to try again, that I would have to raise money to bribe them out of mistreatment in Abu Ghraib and then pay smugglers to start a second attempt at escape. But money was scarce now, and all avenues seemed closed to me.

My first instinct was to get in touch with the people who had sold me the bogus passports and try to force them to give me the money back. I tried calling, but the number had been changed, of course. What did I have to lose, though? I knew where they lived, so I boarded a flight to Germany to try to track them down. Last time I had sailed through German immigration without any difficulty; this time it was not so easy. The official who looked at my travel document was more on the ball. 'We don't recognize this document,' he told me. 'You can't enter.' I wondered why the British government were issuing these brown travel documents that were not recognized by their EU counterparts.

I used all the charm I could muster to wheedle my way in. This was a legitimate travel document, I told them. It is recognized everywhere. But they went to check with high-ranking immigration people; they even checked the wording of the legislation. It wasn't recognized, they repeated. I couldn't come in.

I started to argue. I had been to Germany before, I explained, and showed them documents that proved it. The official raised an eyebrow. 'So,' he said, 'not only are you trying to enter illegally, you have already been here illegally . . .' He turned to his assistants. 'Bring him in,' he told them cryptically. 'Let him discover the hospitality of our lovely motels. I hope you enjoy your stay.' He smirked

It was only when they locked me up that I understood what they were talking about.

I was questioned, and searched more thoroughly – and intimately – than I had ever been searched before. I was left in the cell overnight, and in the morning I was hand-cuffed and escorted to a military four-by-four with a flashing light. The van took me to the stairs of a plane bound for England and I was ushered, on foot and under armed guard, to a seat. Only when I was sitting down were the handcuffs removed and, with the suspicious eyes of all the passengers on me, I was deported. There was no way I was going to get that money back.

Back in Baghdad, Saad still had some of the William Hill funds left, and he was determined to use it to get my mother, brother and sister out of Abu Ghraib. Inside that awful place, there was a religious course where inmates were instructed to memorize huge swathes of the Koran. They would be tested, and would have to speak it out loud, but if they were successful they were given a full pardon for whatever crime had sent them there, as long as their crimes were not of a horrific or political nature. Unsurprisingly, it was almost impossible for inmates to get themselves on to this incredibly popular course.

Saad was unable to use the William Hill money to bribe corrupt officials to release my family from Abu Ghraib; but he was able to buy their way on to the course. And so, after suffering the inhuman indignities of that place for longer than anyone deserved, they were set free. But as ever, we did not know how long it would be before some-one came for them once more. Their situation hadn't changed: someone still had to try again to get them out of the country.

My finances were at rock bottom. So were Rachel's. Aside from what I had sent to Saad, I still had a tiny amount of the William Hill money left, but not nearly enough to pay smugglers to get all three of them over to the UK, and I knew now that I couldn't risk trying to arrange things myself. This had to be done by the professionals, as and when I managed to earn the money; my family would have to come out one by one. With what was left of the money, and through scrimping and saving, I managed to put together enough for the first attempt, and in April 2001, about three months after my return from Germany, it was decided that my sister would try again to reach freedom.

While the secret and illicit arrangements were being made, I could concentrate on nothing else. The sense of apprehension I felt could not have been more intense had it been me who was making the escape attempt, but I had to try to keep things as normal as possible, otherwise I would have gone mad. I still had my Saturday job at a big department store in Leeds – I needed the money now more than ever, after all – and one Saturday I was going about my business in the store when, across the floor, I saw a face I recognized. It was my former boss from William Hill. He was gazing around the department as though looking for something, or someone, so I put my head down and tried to remain inconspicuous. Before long, however, I heard a voice behind me. 'Lewis!' it shouted.

I slowly turned to confront him, fully prepared for what I thought was about to happen. But when I looked at him, I was surprised. There was a big, friendly smile on his face – he seemed genuinely happy to see me. 'When you left,' he boomed, 'we had to employ an army of number-crunchers to do your work for you!' I smiled awkwardly. We chatted for a few minutes and then he left, clearly unaware of what I had been up to. For myself, I felt a surge of relief: it looked like I had some more time.

Saad made arrangements for the first leg of my sister's escape in Baghdad. He found another Kurdish smuggler and arranged a price for delivery out of Iraq. She took the same route as last time, through northern Iraq and into Kurdistan and then Turkey. From there, I arranged with somebody in the UK for her to travel on the back of a lorry to Dover, where she entered using an Austrian refugee's travel document, probably sold to smugglers by the original owner. It was a slow business – almost as painfully slow for those of us waiting to hear good news as it was for her, distracted as she was by nerves and fear. To be deported back to Iraq once was bad enough; she couldn't risk things going wrong again.

She succeeded. The thrill of excitement I felt when I took the call asking me to meet her at UK immigration was more wonderful than I can express. I rushed down there and took her in my arms, holding her for what seemed like hours in an embrace that I didn't want to end. The last time I had seen her had been in the airport in Kuala Lumpur. Then she had borne the haunted expression of a person who had had all the fight sucked out of her, who was resigned to the fact that she was going to meet an unknown and unwanted fate. Now that she had claimed asylum, however, all that fell from her. I remember thinking what a remarkable effect freedom has on people.

More to the point, we had now established that the route my sister had taken actually worked. All that remained was to raise the money to pay smugglers to get my brother and mother out, because their joy at knowing that my sister was safe was tempered by the constant fear of a knock at the door. But we were nearly there. I could almost taste the success, and in my mind I constantly replayed our imagined, joyous reunion on British soil.

Safe.

It was so close.

Not long after my sister arrived, I bumped into another familiar face: the recruitment consultant who had found me the job at William Hill. There was something about the way he looked at me that made me feel uncomfortable, but it would have been rude to turn away as I had obviously noticed him. Besides, I was probably just being paranoid. 'Lewis,' he nodded knowingly, 'how are you doing?'

'OK,' I replied, not wanting to have to explain all my troubles in the street.

'So tell me, what have you been up to?'

I shrugged. 'The usual.' Something told me to finish this conversation as quickly as possible.

'You know, it's a real coincidence,' he persisted. 'Someone came to the office yesterday asking about you.'

I held my breath.

'He said he was an investigator.'

I smiled nervously. 'Don't be silly!' I tried to laugh it off. 'What would an investigator want with me? It's not like I get up to much worth investigating.'

'Maybe not,' he said thoughtfully. 'But be careful, Lewis,' he warned. 'He looked like he meant business.'

I ran all the way home. I had expected this, of course, but that didn't lessen the shock of learning that someone was on my trail. I couldn't afford to be put away now, not with my family still stuck in Baghdad. I shut myself in a room and reformatted the hard drive of my laptop computer. I don't know what I thought anyone would find there, but it comforted me a little to feel that I was covering my tracks.

And then everything went quiet. Ostensibly Rachel and I went about our daily lives, but I felt as though a sword was hanging over me by a thread. As often as I could I would try to speak to Saad and, in our roundabout, coded way, get across to him that time was slipping away. We *had* to get them out, and soon.

It was a Saturday two or three months later that I received a phone call while on duty at the store. It was security. 'Lewis,' one of the security guards greeted me amicably, 'could you pop down to see us for a minute?'

'Sure,' I replied. I assumed I had forgotten to remove a security tag from an item of clothing – it was easily done – and someone had complained, so I sauntered down to the security offices. I arrived there to have the door opened by a large female security officer of whom I had always been rather wary. On this occasion she seemed almost over-solicitous.

'Come in, Lewis,' she said with a smile.

I walked in to find two men in suits. One of them was fairly nondescript; the other was enormous – six foot three with broad shoulders and a thick black-and-white goatee beard. Each man stood in a separate corner of the room. The big man looked at me. 'Are you Lewis Alsamari?' he asked without formality.

I nodded my head. 'Yes.'

'Please take a seat.' He gestured at a chair in front of him, and I sat down.

'Did you work at a company called William Hill, Lewis?'

As soon as he asked the question, I knew that all the horrible suspicions that had been flitting through my brain in the last thirty seconds were about to be confirmed. 'Yes,' I replied.

He nodded calmly. 'Lewis Alsamari,' he recited, 'I'm arresting you on charges of conspiracy to defraud. You do not have to say anything, but it may harm your defence if you do not mention when questioned something which you may later rely on in court. Anything you do say may be given in evidence.'

Nobody spoke. I did my best not to let the emotion show on my face as I tried to think clearly. What should I do? Admit everything? That had always been my plan, when I had assumed that my family would all be safely in the UK before I was caught. But I didn't know what they would do to me if I confessed now, and I had to make sure I was around to help my family in what I hoped would be their final attempt to leave. So should I deny everything? Or should I keep my own counsel and not say anything for the moment?

I chose to stay quiet.

The large man broke the silence. 'We're going to take you away now, Lewis,' he said firmly but not unkindly. I was led to my locker, which I opened; my wallet and keys were removed and placed into an evidence bag. 'Now then, Lewis,' I was told, 'we have a choice. I can handcuff you now and lead you out of the store. I don't want to do that, so I'm going to trust you not to run away. But the two of us will be walking very close to you on either side, so no funny business. Understood?'

I nodded, strangely humbled by the faith they had in me. If and when the authorities came knocking for my mother and brother, I knew they would not be afforded the same respect. 'Thank you,' I said.

Flanked by the two men, I was escorted to the staff entrance of the store, then out into the adjacent shopping arcade. I can't say there were no thoughts of escape in my mind, but I knew how foolish it would be to abuse the trust that had been placed in me. We walked out into the street and towards their car. I was seated in the back while the two CID officers sat in the front. 'Where's your car, Lewis?' I was asked.

I didn't answer for a moment; instead I bowed my head sheepishly. 'It's over there.' I pointed to a big building on the other side of the road.

The two men looked at each other. 'What do you mean, it's over there? That's the police station.'

I nodded. I had cheekily been parking there in order to save money – the reasons were too complicated to explain there and then, and I didn't blame them for sharing a look that displayed their incredulity. If only they knew the truth, I thought to myself. If only they knew that getting into trouble for parking my car in a West Yorkshire police car park was the least of my worries! They searched my car – an E-reg Nissan Sunny worth about £200 – thoroughly, then took me to a smaller police station for processing. Not for the first time in my life, I was placed in a cell. To my astonishment, as I was escorted in, the duty officer said, 'I'm sorry about the conditions.' For a moment I thought it was a sick joke, but one look at his face showed me that he meant it. And if he thought I would find the conditions unpleasant, he could not have been more wrong. There was a bed with a mattress, a steel water fountain and a moderately clean toilet. Compared to some of the cells in which my family and I had found ourselves, this was positively luxurious.

While I was in the cell, Rachel received a knock on the door of our house. She was having coffee with a friend, and excused herself to go and open it. It was CID. They explained what was going on, and asked to search the house. Rachel had no option: she let him in. The officers took away all my documents and my laptop computer.

Four or five hours later I was removed from the cell and taken to an interview room. 'I'm not going to charge you,' the CID officer said. 'I'm going to release you on bail. I've taken all your stuff, and you need to come and report to the police station on a regular basis so we know you're still around. But I'm going to interview you now, and you have the right to a lawyer. Do you want one?'

'Yes.'

A duty lawyer arrived. He was pleasant and friendly, and I wanted to trust him, to feel comfortable with his advice, but I found it difficult. After everything I had been through, the truth was that I trusted nobody except Rachel. I certainly didn't trust anyone in authority, no matter whether they were Iraqi, Malaysian or English. All sorts of possibilities ran through my head: that this man might be working with the police, that they might be trying to stitch me up. I didn't realize that that wasn't the way things are done in England. But I did my best to take on board what he said when he explained that I had the right to remain silent or say 'no comment' to any question, but that it could affect me in the future.

When the interview started, I was faced with a barrage of questions. I confessed to nothing.

I knew I wouldn't fool anyone, but the more I thought about it the more I realized I had to postpone the inevitable for as long as possible. I was no use to my family in jail. When the interview finished, the CID officer said, 'Right, Lewis, I'm going to be investigating this further. I'll be in touch through your lawyers.'

And I was allowed to go free. For the time being.

Suddenly, the pressure had doubled. I wasn't afraid of going to prison, but I was terrified of doing so before I could complete the job of getting my family out. I knew that it was only a matter of time before I found myself in court; when that happened I would not be able to keep up the pretence of my denial any more. But I simply didn't have the money to pay anybody to smuggle my mother and brother all the way to the UK. At the same time I couldn't risk them being in Baghdad while I was in jail. So, in conjunction with Saad, I arranged for them to flee.

They departed under cover of night, leaving the little house in Al-Mansour that had been their home for so long, and travelled north to Mosul. They remained there for a while, not safe exactly, but unknown to the authorities in that town and further away at least from the risk of being dragged back into Abu Ghraib, and I sent them what money I could to subsist on. And while the case against me was being established in England, Saad and I carried on working hard to arrange for them to be sent further north, into Kurdistan and eventually Turkey. It was far from ideal – I wouldn't be able to rest easy until they were by my side – but it was a start.

Finally the day came, as I knew it must, when I was charged. A trial date was set for October 2003 – which was about two years after my initial arrest. My solicitor told me I had two options: to plead not guilty and deny all the charges, or to plead guilty and claim mitigating circumstances. I asked what was the worst punishment I could expect to receive if I pleaded guilty. Two years, I was told. And a deportation order. The prison sentence I could endure; the deportation could have spelled death to me, but it was a risk I was going to have to run: I had never intended to deny what I had done, and it would have been pointless in any case. The evidence was all there. I just had to hope that I would receive more lenient treatment from my judge than my family had done from theirs in Iraq.

I gathered together as much evidence as I could – receipts from the fine I had had to pay in Malaysia and the like – to show where the William Hill money had gone. I wanted to prove that I had not squandered the £37,500 on parties and holidays, but rather used it to save the people I loved from imprisonment and torture. I made a statement and so did my sister; I dug out records of telephone calls to Iraq and to shady people-smugglers. I even made a plea to William Hill that I would repay the money – I didn't know how I would be able to, but perhaps I would find a way. I amassed all the mitigating evidence I could put my hands on, but in the end I knew it would come down to the sympathy of one man: the judge who was trying my case. He would decide my fate, and as my family were still relying on me, he would also decide the fate of those two faceless refugees so many miles away.

When my trial date was set it seemed a long way off, but it arrived with inexorable speed. The lawyers for the prosecution and the representative from William Hill avoided my eye as, three years after my return from Malaysia, I took my place in the dock and waited for these men to argue the rights and wrongs of what I had done. When the lawyers for the prosecution put their case, I felt like screaming at them. 'What would *you* do?' I wanted to ask them. 'Picture your own mother being beaten for no crime greater than trying to live her life quietly. What would *you* do?' But I kept quiet and hoped that my story would speak for itself.

The judge – Justice Walsh – was inscrutable as he listened to the case. I examined his face, trying to determine if there was any sign of shock or sympathy, but I could see none. He listened impassively, directing the court and asking the occasional question, but otherwise showing no emotion whatsoever. Silently I begged him to give me some sign, some indication of how he was going to deal with me, but he was aloof and professional. I would just have to wait until the verdict.

When the time came, the court fell silent. 'Stand up, Mr Alsamari,' the judge intoned.

I did as I was told. And then he started his summing-up. He recited the charges in such a way as to make them sound premeditated in the extreme: 'You stole or adapted to your own use the sum of in total £37,500 from your employers by effectively falsifying records by access to what was thought to be a secure system on the computer. You pleaded guilty when you did on a basis which is wholly exceptional, and that is set out at length by your learned counsel in mitigation, and I need not repeat it.'

I bowed my head. He did not sound remotely impressed.

'I have no doubt whatsoever,' the judge continued solemnly, 'that it is a true story by virtue of the documents I have seen, and obviously from my own general knowledge.'

There was a pause before he continued. I glanced around the courtroom. Everyone was looking at him with a rapt expression, hanging on every word he said.

'This offence for you is a tragedy. You have lost your good name, and you are an intelligent and hard-working individual who, apart from this incident, has an exemplary character.'

I held my breath.

'It is clearly an offence that justifies a custodial sentence, involving, as it does, breach of trust and the danger that others would be blamed for what you had done. I am asked to draw back from that and pass upon you a community sentence because, aside from anything else, a custodial sentence, whether suspended or actual, will affect your nationality application, and in one sense rightly so. I have listened very carefully to the mitigation on the basis of your plea, and given you credit for that plea, and I have read the many documents which have been referred to in court both from your family and from others. This is, in my experience, a unique mitigation. And I say this: that I cannot begin to imagine what it is like to have your family living within a regime which has no contemplation of human rights . . . and where the only way that you have to help the rest of your family escape is to bribe corrupt officials with money which you do not have. The knowledge that you had at that time, together with the depression you were suffering from – as I say, I cannot begin to imagine what that is like, and the dilemma that faces you.'

As I heard his words, I slowly began to realize that this man was on my side. For the first time ever, it seemed, a person in a position of real authority had understood what we had been through, and had thought of us as human beings. I wanted to smile, but the smile was pushed away by the tears that I felt welling up in my eyes. Tears of relief, and of sorrow too for my mother, who was not there to hear what was being said. Suddenly I became aware that many of the eyes in the courtroom were now on me, but it didn't matter. And it didn't stop me weeping.

The judge then announced what was to be done with me. 'In the circumstances, the sentence that I propose to pass is the maximum one that I can impose on a suspended basis. It is two years, and it will last for two years. I could, as part of my duties today, make a recommendation for deportation. I do not do so, for obvious reasons. I know my sentence will affect your nationality application and, as I have said already, it is right that it should. I cannot, given the serious nature of this matter, draw back to the point of a community penalty but, as I have indicated, I do believe that the interests of justice demand in these particular and unique circumstances that the sentence I impose be suspended.

'Understand this: that if you commit any offence punishable by imprisonment within the next two years this sentence can, in whole or in part, be activated and you will then serve it. Do you understand that?'

Through my tears I replied simply, 'Yes.'

The judge went on to say that he did not propose to make an order for me to repay the money to William Hill. That was for them to pursue in the civil courts. (They have never done so.)

For myself, I stepped down from the dock, tears still in my eyes. I wasn't pleased with what I had done – all I had ever wanted to do was work hard and make a life for myself and my family by honest means. That opportunity had been taken from me, and I had fully expected to pay the price for it.

As it was, I felt humbled by the judge's leniency: leniency that my past had shaped me not to expect.

In the months that followed my trial, the judge's warning rang in my ears: 'If you commit any offence punishable by imprisonment within the next two years this sentence can, in whole or in part, be activated and you will then serve it.' I had no doubt that he meant what he said, and I knew I had to walk the line carefully if my mother and my brother were to benefit from my help. It didn't dampen my enthusiasm to be reunited with them, however; if anything, it strengthened it.

It took a long time to spirit my mother and brother out of Turkey, which they had reached by a circuitous route, and in the months and years that followed the trial they moved about constantly, always attempting to keep one step ahead of any suspicious officials who might pay unwanted attention to their bogus Iraqi documents. I knew that, having left Iraq, they were free from torture and brutality, but they couldn't rest easy until they could claim asylum in a place of safety, as the threat of deportation was always hanging over them. To my exasperation, the route that my sister had taken became closed to me when the smuggler who had arranged it disappeared – I don't know where – and so once more I had to find a new way to enable them to complete the final leg of their journey.

My new-found trust in the British system inspired me to pursue their claim for asylum through the proper channels. But as the months of red tape turned to years, I became increasingly frustrated as gradually it grew obvious that my mother and brother would have to arrive at the UK border and claim asylum for themselves, just as my sister and I had done.

By now I had saved some money, so reluctantly but

determinedly I launched myself back into the sinister yet sadly familiar waters of people-trafficking. I had long conversations with faceless individuals in far-flung corners of Europe; I negotiated routes and prices; I directed every instinct I had into deciding who I could trust and who I couldn't. I had learned a lot about such things, after all.

In the end, I parted with a great deal of money, handing it over to a shadowy individual in another country who would arrange everything that needed to be arranged. I wasn't at all sure that I wouldn't find myself in the same situation I had with the fake Spanish passports in Malaysia, but I couldn't wait any longer. None of us could wait any longer. Families are meant to be together, and not one of us could relax until they were safely with me on British soil.

And finally, after years of trying, we met with success. My mother – frail but determined – and my brother made the fraught, risky journey. The details of how they arrived in England are another story, one that I cannot expand upon for a number of reasons; but eventually they were able, just as I had done, to speak the words I have no doubt they had been practising ever since they left Al-Mansour: 'I want to claim political asylum.'

When I heard that they had made it, it was the happiest moment of my life.

Some scenes become etched so firmly in your memory

that you know you will never forget them until your dying day. In my head there are a number of such visions: the doctor in the south of Iraq pulling a bullet from my leg; the wild wolves in the Jordanian desert; the sight of my family, bedraggled and hopeless, being deported from the Malaysian holding cell.

Now, though, I have a new scene to remember, one that puts all those others in their place. It is the memory of seeing my mother on British soil again for the first time. I will never forget it. When she made it to the UK she went immediately to join my sister, who had met and married an Iraqi man and was renting a flat in London, and I went straight there to see her. The difference in her appearance and her demeanour compared with how she had looked when I last saw her at the airport in Kuala Lumpur was astonishing. The anxiety had lifted from her face; she would always bear the scars of so many years of oppression – we all would – but there was a softness around her eyes and an ease to her smile that I did not recognize. I put my arms around her and held her tightly for fifteen minutes. We had so many things to say to each other, but sometimes words aren't enough. It didn't matter: our silence said it all. Finally she was here, along with my brother, and the happiness I felt at being reunited with them in the place I now called home was indescribable. Although there was always the nagging fear in the back of my mind that her asylum application could be turned down, my experiences had taught me to enjoy whatever moments of happiness you have, because you never know how fleeting they may be.

Of course, now my mother was here I bore a new responsibility – the responsibility of making sure that this woman who had been beaten and humiliated was able to live a life, if not of luxury, then at least of relative comfort. But that was a happy responsibility, because more than anything I was looking forward to being part of a family again, of reclaiming those years when that one simple thing that everyone in the West takes for granted was denied me. I wanted to be able to eat with them at the same table; to talk to them without the need for coded language and subterfuge; to share my happiness with my brother and sister; and to be comforted by my mother when times were bad. The night I knew that my mother and my brother were safely in the UK, I slept soundly and without interruption for the first time in years. A new chapter in my life was about to begin, and I felt almost like a new person. Sarmed had undergone all the hardships; I needed to make sure that Lewis never forgot that he was the beneficiary.

Above all, I was looking forward to having my mum live with me. When I told my friends that, they looked at me in amused disbelief. 'Are you mad?' they would say. It seemed anathema to them. Why on earth would you want to live with a parent?

I would smile and shrug my shoulders. 'I just want to know what it's like,' I would say.

But there was more to it than that. Since I had last lived in the bosom of my family, I had been abused and shot, imprisoned and hunted down. I had lived with the knowledge that my mother, brother and sister were being tortured on my account. I had put my hard-won liberty at risk, as well as that of others. I had compromised my good name in the adopted country that I loved.

Perhaps that makes me mad, or reckless. It's not for me to judge. But what I know for certain is this: I would do it all again, because if there is one thing that is worth fighting for, it is the liberty of the ones you love.

And because, ever since my uncle Saad had left me alone and frightened that night so many years ago in a small Bedouin village on the Iraqi–Jordanian border, all I had ever really wanted was to have the warmth and security of my family all around me. On that moonlit desert night, Saad spoke the words that were to shape my actions: *the genuine man never forgets his family*.

I hope I have not let him down.

I hope that, in that respect at least, it may be said that I am a genuine man.

Epilogue

One of my earliest memories is of sitting on my father's lap watching *Doctor Zhivago*. Even as a child I was transfixed by it: the awesome scenery, the grand themes, the beauty and the magnificence of it all. 'Can I be like that?' I remember asking him. 'Can I be an actor like Omar Sharif?'

'Of course you can,' he replied indulgently. 'Just so long as you don't get up to the naughty things that some actors do.'

Life, of course, has a habit of taking you in different directions to those that you had planned. In that respect, I suppose, mine was the same as anyone else's. In Iraq there was no possibility of training to be an actor. It was just an impossible dream, and one soon forgotten.

When I received my lenient sentence from the judge, however, I realized that the time had come to re-evaluate my life. In the three years leading up to my trial, I had, along with everything else, been awarded an LLB Honours law degree from studying part time – ironically learning the law while the state was practising it on me; but my conviction meant that I would never be able to practise in that field, so I cast around for other things to do with my new life. After everything I had been through it seemed almost churlish not to reawaken the dreams that I had once nurtured. What is the point of freedom, after all, if you do not use it to the best of your advantage?

A friend of mine had taken a small part on a soap opera. He couldn't go so I took his place. It fanned the spark of interest that still remained deep inside me, and I determined to do the same thing. The second I arrived on set, it all seemed to click into place. I was fascinated by everything around me – the lights and the cameras and the clipboards, the hubbub, the sense of industry and the artistic endeavour. Immediately I was on set I felt comfortable, as though finally I had found the arena in which I wanted to spend the rest of my life. Rachel and I moved to London, and I enrolled at LAMDA – the London Academy of Music and Dramatic Arts – where I studied hard. Once I had achieved a LAMDA diploma in acting, I threw myself into building a career with the same determination that I had done everything else in my life. Small parts led to bigger parts, and soon I was working regularly enough to make a living. I started my own production company, Tigris Productions, for which I am a producer.

On 11 September 2001, I had watched the events in New York unfold with the same sense of horror and disbelief as everyone else. People would ask me, as an Arab, how I felt about what had happened, but the truth was that my reaction was the same as almost everybody else's: shock and deep sorrow for the human suffering that had been caused. But it is perhaps also true that I watched the events that followed from a more rounded perspective. When the allied armies marched on Baghdad with the intention of toppling Saddam Hussein, I viewed the footage on television with mixed feelings. I remembered the last time the West invaded Iraq. I was just a boy, living in Mosul with my father. The airwaves were full of anti-American propaganda: they were a murderous invading army, we were told, and it was the duty of all loyal Iraqis to join up and fight against them.

I phoned Saad in Baghdad when my father was out. 'Is it true what they say about the American army?' I asked him.

'No,' he replied. 'They are not like the Iranians. These people have a little bit more respect for Arab life.' During the Iran–Iraq war, if the Iranian air force had been unable to approach their military targets, they would unload their bombs randomly on small Iraqi villages. If they returned with their munitions, they would probably be shot by their superiors. The Americans, Saad naively assured me, had better technology and more sophisticated weapons. They would never be so casually brutal; but it was unsettling, to say the least, to be led into a war against the most powerful country in the world.

When the US bombs started falling in 1991, I was in the car with my father, driving through the narrow streets of Mosul to buy provisions from the market. Suddenly, from above, we heard the drone of stealth fighters. Nearby there was a warehouse that stored flour, grain and other provisions, and this was the fighters' target. When the bomb hit, the impact was so great that it lifted our car into the air. As we hit the ground again, we found ourselves hurtling towards a brick wall; my father spun the steering wheel as fast as he could, and avoided a collision by a whisker. Had his reflexes not been so fast, we might have been rather less lucky that day. We jumped out of the car and took cover as best we could as the bombs continued to rain down on the store.

And so it went on.

When the second Gulf War started, therefore, I had some idea of what they were going through in Baghdad. My uncle Saad and his family were still there; friends I had known from childhood were still there; and while I thanked God that my immediate family had made it to safety, I nevertheless prayed nightly that Saad's original faith in the accuracy of the Americans' bombs would prove justified. The horror with which I watched the increasing civilian death count was excruciating: almost daily I expected to hear the news that Saad and his family were among the most recent casualties of this war that was not of their making. In the end they endured the siege of Baghdad unharmed. Many thousands of others were less fortunate.

When I saw on television the statue of Saddam being pulled down and smashed, it was a strange moment – almost as if my own past were being shattered before my eyes. Was I glad he was gone? Of course. Nobody who suffered from the brutality of his regime could think otherwise. Thanks to that man, the country I loved had been raped, and the people I loved had been tortured. When I heard that Uday was dead, crushed by the building in which he was hiding, I remembered that time in 14th Ramadan Street when he filled my friend Hakim and me with such fear, and we hadn't been exposed even to the lightest of his brutalities. It was a monstrous death, but strangely and morbidly fitting for this monstrous person.

But stories are rarely black and white, and what so many people failed to understand was that it was possible to celebrate Saddam's removal from power and yet be suspicious of the Western involvement in Iraq. I had read the history books. I knew that you didn't have to go back so very far to find a time when Saddam and the Ba'ath Party were being supported by American money and American arms. What we were seeing was just the inexorable march of politics, the arrival of George Bush Sr's 'new world order' – and, as they had been throughout recent years, the Iraqi people were merely pawns in a bigger game.

Now Saddam is dead, and I am glad he has gone to meet his maker. When I saw him being hanged I felt a mixture of emotions: revulsion, excitement, irony, the curious sense that I was reading a grisly chapter in an evil book. Saddam sold his soul to the Devil to get into power; when he tried to claim it back, the Devil got the better of him. But watching those scenes, I never once felt happy, or hopeful, for Iraq. How could I? My country seems to be the wounded widow of the world, and every other government or group or society is standing in line to rape it.

In 2006 I appeared in a major movie about the 9/11 attacks. *United 93*, directed by Paul Greengrass, told the story of the hijacked aeroplane, heading in all likelihood for Washington, that was thought to have been crashed by the hijackers in order to stop the passengers and crew gaining control of it. My role as one of the hijackers was an emotional one, but one to which I hoped I could bring some degree of empathy and realism. It was an important film, and I felt proud to be a part of it. When the film premiered in New York, however, an event occurred that in a way encapsulated so much about my life. Although the Americans had allowed me into the country to film the movie, I was refused a visa to attend the premiere. At first no reason was given; it later transpired that I was not deemed suitable to enter the USA because of my conviction.

When I learned this, I laughed; but then you often do laugh when you want to cover up more complicated emotions. They had allowed me into the country before; now they were refusing. Did they – or did someone else – have their own agenda, their own reasons for not wanting me there? I don't know. All I do know is that the invasion of Baghdad had been initiated to bring about the liberation of the Iraqi people. I had done what I had done as a direct result of oppression by the very regime they had gone to war to change. Yet now, somehow, I was the enemy. The irony was not lost on me.

But when you start from the premise that the world is not a fair place, such injustices don't affect you too much. I appealed against the US's decision – I even became something of a cause célèbre. But it was not to be. Back in England I am still denied naturalization as a citizen because of my conviction. I can't help feeling that if the British and American political authorities were totally committed to helping the Iraqi people, they would exercise a little more benevolence in my case. I'm not proud of what I did, but I do think it is worthy of a little understanding.

However, in the grand scale of things, such complaints seem trivial. My family paid the price for my freedom; I paid the price for theirs. Iraq remains a war zone. I have no doubt that it will do so for decades. As I write this, my uncle Saad lives in fear of his life. He is under daily threat of mortar attacks; his car has been burned; his business has been destroyed; he has been physically attacked. Now he lives at my grandparents' house in Al-Mansour, AK-47s at the ready. Leaflets with death threats have been posted through his door. Other men have been abducted and beheaded. He knows that if he is not careful, he could easily be one of their number.

Elsewhere in Iraq, daily civilian casualties are measured in the hundreds. Iraq, it seems to me, could be the beginning of a war across the whole Middle East. How ironic that Mesopotamia, the place where civilization is said to have begun, could very well be where it will all end. But whenever I hear the news of another bombing in a mosque or an unspeakable piece of sectarian violence, one fact is brought home to me. That despite everything – the violence, the fear and the heartbreak – that I have been through, I now have the privilege to live in a country where my safety, and that of my family, is assured. My immediate family are with me now, and the feeling that gives me is indescribable. My mother is a new woman, and to be able to see my brother and sister again is so wonderful – I still can't quite believe that they are here. As always, though, life has its ups and downs. The strain of everything that we had been through meant that Rachel and I decided to separate, but she is still a close and valued friend and I will never forget what she did for me and for my family. Which leaves my father. I would like to be reconciled with him, but at the time of writing this has not happened and I have not spoken to him for many years.

There is an old Arabic saying: 'Every day of your life is a page of your history.' I am able to look to the future with confidence, able to write those pages myself rather than have them written for me by uncaring regimes and circumstances that are unasked for but nevertheless have to be endured.

I am one of the lucky ones.

Acknowledgements

There are so many people I would like to thank. Barbara Levy, my fabulous literary agent, whose enthusiasm for my story from day one has been unwavering; Doug Young, Deborah Adams, Zoe Hood, Rebecca Jones, Emma Musgrave and all the brilliant team at Transworld, for doing what they do so well; and Adam Parfitt, without whose help this book would not have been written. Thanks also to Joanne Adamson, Tim Bevan, David Bond, Pippa Cross, Nigel Edwards, Tracey Holmes, Eric Fellner, Paul Greengrass, John Hadity, Dan Hubbard, Jan Jung, Tim Kent, Lloyd Levin, Terry Newman, Peter Nicholson, Yacine Serir, Sean Smith and Theresa Villers.

To Rachel, for being there. Also to her father.

All the unknown beacons of light who helped me along my treacherous way.

And finally, to Saad – who was a father to me when I had no father. Thank you for everything.

WAR JUNKIE
By Jon Steele

Jon Steele is a war junkie. Soon after starting work as an ITN cameraman, he began to feel at home in the kind of places ordinary people get evacuated from. Before long, he was living for the sort of rush which only comes when bullets fly around your head. Normal life just couldn't compete – bad news was big fun.

From the utter chaos of a Moscow where tooled-up Militia and Red Army fight hand-to-hand battles in the streets, to Rwanda and the horrifying aftermath of a massacre, Jon Steele has been witness to some of the most terrible events of the late twentieth century. His own personal journey takes him to Bosnia where, after seeing a small girl hit by a sniper's bullet, Jon Steele's brain finally says, 'enough' . . .

As funny as it is terrifying, as sharp as broken glass, *War Junkie* takes you on a gut-wrenching ride to hell and back, on one man's descent into the worst places on earth. You will visit places and meet people you will never forget as Jon Steel shines an unforgiving spotlight into some of the darkest recesses of modern history . . .

'The most authentic literary recreation of the hollow terror, confusion and soul-crushing cacophony of battle I have read in decades'
Evening Standard

'ACTION PACKED'
Daily Express

'BRUTALLY HONEST'
Mirror

'BURNS WITH EMOTIONAL HONESTY . . . POWERFUL AND DISTURBING'
The List

9780552149846

CORGI BOOKS

THE LEMON TREE
by Sandy Tolan

'MOVING AND PAINSTAKINGLY RESEARCHED'
Marina Lewycka, author of *A Short History of Tractors in Ukranian*

In the summer of 1967, Bashir – a young Palestinian man – knocks on
the door of his childhood home in the town of Ramla in Israel, a home
from which his family was driven some twenty years earlier. The door
is opened by a young Jewish woman, Dalia, whose family were settled
in the house after fleeing persecution in Bulgaria at the end of the
Second World War.

Thus begins an unlikely and difficult friendship, which bridges
religious divides and lasts more than four decades. *The Lemon Tree*
tells the story of this extraordinary friendship and offers a much
needed human perspective on the Israeli-Palestinian conflict.

'READS LIKE A NOVEL . . . AN INFORMED TAKE FOR
ANYONE INTERESTED IN THE HUMAN STORIES
BEHIND A CONFLICT'
New Statesman

'A FASCINATING AND HIGHLY ABSORBING ACCOUNT
FULL OF WARMTH, COMPASSION AND HOPE'
Belfast Telegraph

'EXTRAORDINARY . . . A HIGHLY READABLE AND
EVOCATIVE HISTORY'
Washington Post

'AFFECTING . . . SENSITIVELY TOLD. HUMANE AND
LITERATE – AND RATHER DARING IN SUGGESTING
THAT THE FUTURE OF THE MIDDLE EAST NEED
NOT BE VIOLENT'
Kirkus Reviews

9780552155144

BLACK SWAN